One Hundred or So Reflections from the Pastor's Desk Taken from Sixty Years of Ministry in Minnesota and Pennsylvania

Rev. Daniel W. Reid

ISBN 978-1-0980-7530-9 (paperback)
ISBN 978-1-0980-7531-6 (digital)

Christian Faith Publishing, Inc.
832 Park Avenue
Meadville, PA 16335
www.christianfaithpublishing.com

Printed in the United States of America

Contents

A Brief
Autobihistory

My First Real Plane Ride

It was December of my senior year at Princeton Theological Seminary in 1956. Ever since I started school in the year 1939–40, I had done nothing else but attend classes—through lower school (as it was called then) and high school at Germantown Academy; four years as a history major in Franklin and Marshall College, and now over two years at Princeton Theological Seminary.

Suddenly I realized after this year, no more school! I'm going to have to find a job. But where?

I had had some nibbles from vacant congregations in Ohio, but nothing resonated. Then I remembered an old friend from college days. Ernie Haddad, a veteran, who was three years ahead of me at F & M, but his wife—evidently with a degree in Christian Education—was CE director at the First Presbyterian Church in Lancaster where I had started attending (and where, the next year, I met Amy). That's how we connected.

My second year at Princeton I began working part-time at the Theological Book Agency, in the mail order department. (Many pastors wrote in for books, not having nearby bookstore facilities.) That's how I reconnected with Ernie, who periodically would write in from some far-off place called Round Lake, in Southwestern Minnesota.

Through our correspondence, I learned that he was supplying a nearby congregation in Brewster, and had been for a year. (Brewster is twelve miles due north of Round Lake, with nothing in between but farms and a stop sign at Highway 16.) I wrote to him might I explore that as a possibility for my first church? Almost by return mail, we received not only an annual report of the congregation, but also a floor plan of the parsonage! Sounded like a real possibility.

Now, it happened in those days that during the last two years of the three-year seminary experience, students were invited to take a day visiting one or the other of the national Presbyterian church boards: Foreign and National Missions. At that time, our denomination's headquarters was located at 475 Riverside Drive in New York City. I would be visiting there the last week in January 1956.

Why not do my visit, then drive out to what was then called Idlewild Airport, and fly out to Brewster?

Accordingly, plans were made. I would fly out late afternoon on a Thursday to Minneapolis, then change planes to something called Braniff out to Sioux Falls, South Dakota, where Ernie would meet me and drive me the sixty miles back to Round Lake.

Great plan. However, as I was waiting for takeoff time, it began to snow heavily. My flight was delayed, first, in order that the plane might return to the hanger to be deiced, but also because a van carrying passengers was delayed because of bad roads.

While I was waiting in the airport, the next morning's newspapers were dropped off. The unnerving headline informed us that another plane at LaGuardia Field, attempting a takeoff in the snow, had instead crashed into the East River! Great start for my first interview as a pastor.

We finally got going, and I was seated on the right side of the plane, far enough back so that I could see the engines. This was a four-engine prop-jet, which had a tendency to shoot out sparks and some flames from the exhausts. Needless to say, I couldn't sleep. Instead, I remembered that perhaps a month before, a couple of busloads of us from Princeton had attended a Billy Graham Crusade at Madison Square Garden, with its inspirational thousand-voice choir. As I sat in my seat on the plane, anxiety mounting as I watched the sparks and flames shoot out from the engine's exhaust, the final verse of one of their hymns "Guide Me, O Thou Great Jehovah" resonated over and over in my mind:

When I tread the verge of Jordan, bid my anxious fears subside.
Death of death, and hell's destruction,
land me safe on Canaan's side.
Songs of praises, songs of praises—I will ever give to Thee!

Needless to say, I made it. Ernie was there to welcome me, and we started the dreary sixty-mile drive in his big red Plymouth station wagon to Round Lake. Minnesota in midwinter can be a really

boring place. The countless empty fields were snow-covered, and of
course, traffic was at a minimum.

We arrived at Round Lake and Ernie's home and family (four
children) in time for dinner, but I couldn't eat. After the anxiety of
the trip and a sleepless night, I had a splitting headache. I just wanted
to lie down, which I did, while the family ate. The memories are a little fuzzier at this point, but I believe Ernie took me to where I was to
spend the night—in the home of the town banker (and thirty-plus-
year church treasurer) Art Kane. Art's chief claim to fame was that he
and brother Elmer (in the nearby county seat town of Worthington)
were the only two bankers not to go under in 1929. Needless to say,
Conservative was his middle name, but he was a fine gentleman.

Saturday morning, I walked the two blocks over to the church
to meet the committee. I can still see them standing there on the
landing inside the front door (like most church buildings of that
era—it was built in 1929—there were steps leading up to the second-floor sanctuary). I remember thinking they looked like a flock
of sheep in search of a shepherd. Chairman of the committee was
Henry Weaver, who ran the Skelly gas station on the edge of town
(it's still there!). I also remember Maude Halpern, the Presbyterian
wife of our resident Jewish doctor. I think there were perhaps three
or four others.

Unlike the detailed format of Philadelphia Presbytery (when
I moved back some fourteen years later), this was the ultimate in
informality. After our interview, I was to preach the next day. If they
liked it and me, they would immediately call a congregational meeting to invite me to be their pastor. If they didn't, well, all bets were
off. No Mankato Presbytery Committee on Ministry was involved.
Not knowing what else to say, I chose as my topic "I, Samuel," on
February 3, 1957. I sketched the parallel between God having to call
Samuel three times before He got through (cf. 1 Samuel 3) and God
having to do the same with me, many centuries later. Obviously, they
liked it—and I was called to my first congregation, starting August 1.
(Starting salary: $4,250 per year.)

I have no memories of an uneventful trip back home. In sub-
sequent months, there came graduation from Princeton, my ordi-

nation to the Presbyterian ministry on June 11, 1957 (in my home church, First Presbyterian in Germantown); the birth of our son, Daniel Wayne, Jr., on July 5 in Princeton Hospital; an incredible move of all our worldly goods in a rented Hertz van, with the help of a friend (who hasn't spoken to me since), Brewster and back (close to 2,500 miles) in less than a week; and our personal move towing an overloaded four-wheel U-Haul trailer behind our little '55 two-door Chevvy with its "123-horse Blue-flame 6" in order to begin work August 1. Amy and me, our nurse sister-in-law Mary Jane, a month-old son, and a cat. The Lord was indeed with us. (My dad said afterward he didn't think we'd make it.)

Thus began five years in Brewster, and over thirteen years of spiritual growth and productive ministry in the Gopher State.

The Presbynews of Lakeside Presbyterian Church, Duluth, Minnesota June 6, 1962
LAKESIDE WELCOMES REIDS ON JULY 1

Duluth—scenic city of progress and Lakeside Church—center of "Dreams Unlimited" will officially welcome the Reverend Daniel W. Reid to his new post as assistant minister on Sunday, July 1. As a part of the ten o'clock service of worship that morning, Mr. Kunkel will conduct a special recognition service for Mr. Reid. Immediately following the hour of worship, a reception in honor of Dan and Amy Reid will be held in the Fellowship Hall. Members and friends of this church are cordially invited to be present.

Mr. Reid comes to Duluth from Brewster, Minnesota, where he has served these past five years as minister of the First Presbyterian Church. During his ministry in Brewster, Mr. Reid has capably led his people both in an enlarged program and in spiritual commitment. He has served his Presbytery (Mankato) as cochairman of Youth Work, and is presently serving the Synod as chairman of the summer work camps for youth. A good example of the caliber of Mr. Reid is this quote taken from a statement of his theology: "My con-

cept of the modern pastor might be focused in his ideal: 'He should
be a prophet with a shepherd's heart.'"

Both Mr. and Mrs. Reid hail from the state of Pennsylvania,
Dan coming from Philadelphia, and Amy from Lancaster. Mr. Reid
received his BA degree from Franklin and Marshall College and his
BD degree from Princeton Theological Seminary. The Reids have
two attractive children: Wayne, who is five years old, and Deborah,
who is three and a half years old.

We welcome the Reids to Duluth and the Lakeside Church
and look forward to Sunday, July 1. Mr. Reid will be preaching that
Sunday on the topic, "The Whole Gospel for the Whole Family."

PARSON TO PERSON

Three weeks from now, our church will be rolling out its car-
pet of welcome and friendship for the Reids. Personally, Mr. Reid's
coming will mean the end of those thirty-hour days. More important than this, though, his arrival will enable us to do the following
things: develop the "Dreams Unlimited" long-range planning program, accelerate our pastoral calling, spend more time in study, and
go fishing. Note that I am careful to put fishing last.

I especially look forward to sharing in ministry with one whom
I feel is well-equipped, spiritually and in experience, to minister to
this congregation. Unfortunately, many churches this size and larger
tend to think of an assistant as primarily an assistant, not as a minister. Mr. Reid is coming to the Lakeside Church neither as an errand
boy for the senior minister nor as an apprentice waiting for his own
pastorate. In fact, he is leaving a pastorate where he has served for five
years because of the new challenges and opportunity that awaits us
here. Although Dan will be primarily responsible for our Christian
Education program, he will also be sharing in our ministry of preaching, teaching, counseling, and policy planning. It is our sincere hope
that Dan will be given every opportunity to invest his talents and
leadership into the life and work of this church.

The Presbynews of Lakeside Presbyterian Church, Duluth, Minnesota, June 21, 1963
MR. REID IS CALLED TO NEW CHARGE

Sensing a new direction in his ministry for Christ, the Rev. Daniel W. Reid, assistant minister, has submitted his resignation to the session in order to accept a call to a two-point charge in Southern Minnesota. The Reids plan to move the last week in June to the manse in Claremont, Minnesota, where Mr. Reid will serve as minister to the Presbyterian churches in Claremont and Kasson.

The Claremont-Kasson charge, which is within the Sheldon Jackson Presbytery, is located on Highway 14 between Rochester and Owatonna; Kasson, fourteen miles west of Rochester; Claremont, nine miles east of Owatonna. The Claremont church has a membership of 250 in a town of 500 people. The Kasson church has 82 members in a rapidly growing town of 1,700. Mr. Reid will spend two-thirds of his time in Claremont and one-third in Kasson.

As Dan and Amy and their three children, Wayne, Deborah, and Brenda (just born January 5), make their preparations to pull up their roots, the Lakeside Church expresses sincere appreciation for their ministry in Duluth. Mr. Reid will deliver his last sermon this Sunday, June 23, at the 10:00 a.m. service of worship. The congregation will hold a farewell party for the Reid family following the morning service.

Paul's Third Letter to Timothy
Final sermon delivered by
Rev. Daniel W. Reid
Lakeside Presbyterian Church, Duluth, Minnesota
June 23, 1963

During the last few years of his life, while he was imprisoned, awaiting almost certain execution, the Apostle Paul wrote two letters to a young man named Timothy. This Timothy seems to have been a special favorite of Paul's. In the First Letter, he refers to him

as *my true child in the faith (1:2)*. It would indeed appear that Paul
was Timothy's spiritual father, and William Barclay comments:
"Timothy's parents had given Timothy physical life; Paul had given
him eternal life."

Timothy then emerges as a young man whose family Paul knew,
whom Paul had watched and trained until he matured and entered
the ministry. And in these two letters, Paul is instructing him in the
proper administration of God's house. But more important: he is
telling him what kind of people the leaders and pastors of the church
should be. The First Letter we could call "ecclesiastical"; the Second,
"pastoral."

In the Second Letter, Paul, knowing that Timothy might be discouraged by fighting heresies within and without his charge, begins
by trying to get him fired up for work again: *"I am reminded of your
sincere faith, a faith that dwelt first in your grandmother Lois and your
mother Eunice and now, I am sure, dwells in you. Hence I remind you
to rekindle the gift of God that is within you through the laying on of my
hands; for God did not give us a spirit of timidity, but a spirit of power
and love and self-control"* (2 Timothy 1:5–7).

This morning, we are going to be a bit imaginative. We are
going to pretend that Timothy wrote back to Paul, asking him to
explain just what he meant by that last statement, and that Paul
wrote a short third letter to Timothy, in explanation of his affirmation: *for God did not give us a spirit of timidity, but a spirit of power
and love and self-control.*

I am sure that even without this fictional third letter, that verse
said much to Timothy. Certainly, it has said a lot to me as I have
attempted to discover what kind of minister God wants me to be. It
is my hope that it may also be of help to you in your understanding
and growth as a part of the ministry and witness of Christ's Church.

Here, then, is Paul's "Third Letter to Timothy."

Paul. An Apostle of Christ Jesus by the will of God, according to the promise of life which is in Christ Jesus: To Timothy, my

beloved child. Grace, mercy, and peace from God the Father and Christ Jesus our Lord.

In my former letter, I testified that God does not give us a spirit of timidity, but a spirit of power and love and self-control. And now, in your answer to me, you desire that I should make these words clear to you, because I have touched the heart of your struggle as a minister of Christ Jesus.

Timothy, my beloved child, to whom I have earlier confessed that I am the worst of sinners (1 Timothy 1:15), I can only speak of what has been given to me, borne out of my own struggle to grow in the faith which has captured me and made me its slave.

But because of what I have been given, I can testify that God has given us no spirit of timidity. He has given us courage, not cowardice; He has given us faith, not fear.

Many are the things the world fears: a physical beating, with possible loss of life; men who claim world power, who fear losing their great wealth. The world fears to take a stand, lest an enemy be made, or a job lost. The world fears loss of pride, and the shaky crutches which support it.

These are some of the things the world fears; and to escape these fears, men often tiptoe in timidity: fearful of life's meaning, and so pursuing phantoms, cultivating people or possessions in the vain hope that they may share in them: standing for nothing, offending no one, respected by no one.

As far as the east is from the west, so far has God removed this kind of spirit from those who follow Christ Jesus our Lord. The follower of Christ, especially the minister in that service, has been set free from all such fears. Boldly, I have myself faced beatings and imprisonment, shipwrecks and dangers from robbers; hunger and thirst; cold and exposure.

Never did I waver from the faith on which I stand, for Christ Jesus has *abolished death and brought life and immortality to light through the Gospel. For this Gospel I was appointed a preacher and apostle and teacher, and therefore I suffer as I do. But I am not ashamed, for I know whom I have believed, and I am sure that He is able to guard until that Day what has been entrusted to me (2 Timothy 1: 10b–12).*

Imprisoned though I am, *I have learned, in whatever state I am, to be content (Philippians 4:11b). For to me to live is Christ, and to die is gain. If it is to be life in the flesh, that means fruitful labor for me. Yet which I shall choose I cannot tell. I am hard pressed between the two. My desire is to depart and be with Christ, for that is far better. But to remain in the flesh is more necessary on your account (Philippians 1:21–24).*

Remember the words of our Lord Jesus, how He said, *Do not fear those who kill the body but cannot kill the soul; rather fear him who can destroy both soul and body in hell (Matthew 10:28).*

God has not given us a spirit of timidity, beloved Timothy. Such craven fears belong to the world, a world from which we have been set free by the precious blood of Christ.

No, God has instead given us a spirit of *power*. This is a most amazing gift of the Spirit. It is the power that drove me to my knees on the road to Damascus, blinded my sight, and revealed in an instant the truth of the triumph of the risen Lord.

And, Timothy, the most amazing part of this power is that you don't receive it until you admit that you yourself are powerless! Until you confess your weakness and your sin, until you literally become crucified, shamed with Christ, you are powerless.

This power comes not with possessions or physical strength, not with personality or intelligence: it comes with complete submission to the will of God in Christ Jesus. Every bit of strength you need, as a follower of Christ and a minister in that service, comes from this power of the Spirit of God.

Would you take a stand, amidst evils within and without; would you stand firm and erect, even though you feel completely alone in your stand? God has not given you a spirit of timidity, but a spirit of power.

Would you have stature and respect among those older and wiser than you? Among those older, and not nearly so wise? Among those who are instruments of the Devil, and oppose everything you stand for in the Name of Christ? God has not given you a spirit of timidity, but a spirit of power.

Would you, for the sake of the risen Christ, be an instrument used to change the lives of men and women? Would you, for the sake of fellowship with the risen Christ, grow *to mature manhood, to the measure of the stature of the fullness of Christ? (Ephesians 4:13b)* Would you, to preserve the faith which has become a part of you, and which you must share with all people, withstand the pressure of those who would dilute the Gospel, holding to the form of it but denying its power? Timothy, my beloved, in the face of all this, God has not given us a spirit of timidity, but a spirit of power: power to pass the breaking-point without breaking.

The moment at which you crucify yourself, with its own passions and desires, and are raised again with the Christ that is in you: you will find within you power to accomplish all this and more—power far beyond all earthly dreams of power; the power that comes from Him Who created the world, and redeemed it in Jesus Christ; to Whom be all glory and praise. Amen.

When I wrote to you before, I bore witness that God gives us a spirit, not only of power, but of love and self-control. Timothy, child of God and my son in Christ, surely I do not have to remind one such as you that it is only because of this power that God gives that we are enabled either to love or to control ourselves.

The world cannot know love; the world is under no self-discipline.

Remember when last we talked in person how I told you of the immorality and unimaginable lust and perversion in the city of Rome, men and women—yes, and even youth—entering into relations with one another at which even the beasts of the field would blush?

Remember my loving agony over our brothers and sisters in Corinth, subjected day and night to temptations to enter heathen orgies of lust and corruption in the name of "religion" and in the name of "love"?

The love in the world is self-love. It seeks only self-satisfaction. It is a thirst nothing can quench; it is a hunger no food, however tasty, can satisfy. It hates its object. It cares not whether it destroys the body or the mind. It can kill. It was of this love the world practices that the prophet Jeremiah once wrote, when he said of the children of Israel: *"They were well-fed lusty stallions, each neighing for his neighbor's wife" (Jeremiah 3:8).*

No, Timothy, it is impossible that the world can know true love, the love God has revealed in Jesus Christ. Even such a one as I, a Pharisee of the Pharisees, knowing every jot and tittle of the Law God has given, did not know love, nor even how to love, until it was revealed to me.

For it is only possible for us to love in the true sense because God has first loved us. We would also be lost and in darkness, in bondage to the lusts of the flesh, did we not know Jesus Christ, and Him crucified. For God showed His great love for us in that even while we opposed Him in sin, Christ died for us (cf. Romans 5:8).

The spirit of power God has bestowed upon us includes the power to love, for love is not something you discuss. It is something you do!

Our Lord Jesus has said that the hireling cannot truly care for the sheep. He does what he is paid to do, but has no love for the sheep and flees at the first sign of danger. He will not defend them, for he does not love them (cf. John 10:12–13).

But our Lord Jesus has also said, *I am the good shepherd; I know my own and my own know me… I lay down my life for the sheep… Greater love has no man than this, that a man lay down his life for his friends (John 10:14, 15b; 15:13).* He charged His disciples, in His last moments with them, saying *feed my lambs… Tend my sheep… Feed my sheep (John 21:15–17).*

Timothy, brother in Christ, as you serve your people, be a shepherd. Feed each lamb, each sheep, each wanderer, as each has need. Some will be healthy and strong, and need only routine care. Some will be weak and unsteady, and need much love and support. Some will not know how much help they need. Them you must win over, but you must win them over in love. Only in this way can you lead them. You cannot drive them, or they will scatter.

This kind of love, the love Christ lived as the good shepherd, can only be found in the spirit of power. For it takes power to love your flock in this way; power to make you free and open to the possibility of being hurt, if one turns against you, bites your tender, feeding hand, and wanders off in search of better food; power to overcome petty jealousies and hatreds, directed against you, and one the rest have called "unlovable," "unwanted"; power to withstand the criticisms of hirelings outside the fold who ridicule your patient efforts to feed each lamb according to its need; who think you spend too much time in this way; and who *themselves* must be objects of your love.

You will be imperfect in this work, even as the Master failed to find more than a few who would accept, return, and share His love. You will make mistakes. You will be misinterpreted. You will sometimes in weariness overlook the sickly lamb, too weak to cry out, in favor of the sheep in great distress, bleating so all the world can hear. Take care lest your ears fail to hear the cry of the aching heart amid the louder calls from noisy lips. Our failures may make you want to quit—to try some other way—to listen to the voice of the hireling.

Timothy, my child in the Lord, there is no other way, for this is Christ's way. And the power of God that enabled Him to conquer death and the grave enables you also to love as He loved.

For Him, it meant a cross. You and I, as servants, have a right to expect no better treatment from a lusty and unbridled world. But if we truly believe, there is no other way. God has not given us a spirit of timidity, but a spirit of power—the power to love.

And with the power to love, the power of *self-control.*

Ah, Timothy, how great is our Father, that He never falls short of perfection in His gifts to us. What danger there would be in commanding us to love without giving us the power to control that love!

What futility to charge us with the responsibility for changing in the eyes of the world the meaning of such a vital word without giving us the power to live a changed meaning in the eyes of the world!

When the world loves, it lusts and destroys. When the world is tempted, it gives in to temptation. When the world is angered, it strikes back and strikes out. When the world is attacked, it fights bitterly for its life.

Timothy, once you have been filled with the spirit of power for self-control, you will succumb to none of these. Self-seeking will have been removed, as you seek only to follow Christ's way. So your love will give life, not destroy it. Temptations will never end until the last day, but we are called by Him who was tempted like as we are, yet without sin (cf. Hebrews 4:15), and He has the power to prevent our yielding to temptation.

In Christ, all our pride has been removed, so that when we are angered or attacked, we are concerned not with our own words or answers, clever though they may be; we are concerned only that God may speak through us. Always stand ready to testify to the reality of the faith that it in you, in courage and love. In speech and in conduct, in what we say and do and think and feel, in what we are: God has given us a spirit of self-control. This self-discipline keeps us from being swept away; it also keeps us from running away.

It prevents our lashing out at those who attack us from without; it prevents our taking advantage of those who have given themselves to our care within: *for God has not given us a spirit of timidity, but a spirit of power and love and self-control.*

This spirit can be yours, my beloved child, even more that you have Him, as you continue to grow in grace and your desire to be like Jesus. Continue in the faith into which you have been called. Be crucified with Christ so that you can say it is no longer you who live, but Christ Who lives in you. So may the life you now live in this world be lived only by faith in the Son of God, Whose incomparable power is at work through the presence of the Spirit. Grace be with you.

Reids Moving Back East

News from the Presbyterian Churches of Claremont and Kasson, Minnesota January 1971

Dear Friends:

For the first half-dozen years we lived in Minnesota, whenever anyone would ask, "Do you ever think you'll move back East?" we responded with an unhesitating "No!" For the next half-dozen years, as we all (including our parents) kept getting older, we still answered the question tentatively, but with the hint of a silent condition: "No, unless…" (the condition, of course, being completed: "Unless the health of our parents makes it appear that the responsible thing would be to try to get closer").

I am sure you all recall that my dad (still living outside Philadelphia) suffered what had been described as a massive stroke in November of 1968. We visited that next summer as usual and returned convinced that, just as there is a time for a young pup to leave home and explore the world, there is also a time for the mature one to return home.

Now I'm not sure how much you know about how Presbyterian ministers move across the country, but it doesn't happen overnight. To begin with, we were not (and still are not) unhappy or unchallenged here; thus, it wasn't a case of "anything to get away." Besides, you folks have cared for us very well financially; thus, many opportunities to move before had lower salaries. So the field was narrow to begin with when I changed my dossier in the Columbus office to read that I would be receptive to a good offer in the Philadelphia area.

To make a long story short (and telescope the long gaps): it wasn't until April (of 1970) that anything both concrete and exciting developed, and the pulpit Nominating Committee of that church (Lenape Valley Presbyterian Church in New Britain, PA) was very careful, cautious, and selective—and in no hurry whatsoever! There were some exchanges by mail and phone, some interviews while vacationing in August, a couple of quick air trips since; until not very long ago, we were invited to preach as the candidate.

As I am sure you are aware by now, this was the purpose of our absence this past week-end. The candidacy was successful; the call was extended, and we accepted it, and our plans are to move the first week in February.

This means that a lot must be done between now and then. I hope to be able to continue to minister to those with a specific need (if someone is hospitalized, *do* call me! Don't beg off, saying, "I know you're busy." When haven't I been?); but in general, there's going to be a lot of packing and pitching going on these next three weeks.

It also means that the annual meetings this Sunday take on added significance, for in addition to the regular business of approving reports, electing elders, and the like, I will be submitting my resignation (effective January 31), and each congregation must elect a representative Pulpit Nominating Committee. The men I have asked (pending your and Presbytery's approval) to moderate the separate sessions (Stewart Robertson of Rochester First for Kasson; Stan Johnson of the Owatonna Federated Church for Claremont) will be present to moderate that portion of each congregational meeting. Each active member should plan to attend this Sunday, January 10.

Now I'd like to say a word about this congregation which turned me on, for it is far from ordinary. The Lenape Valley Presbyterian Church was organized by Philadelphia Presbytery on March 25, 1962, with 120 charter members. By the end of 1969, it had grown to 327, with 259 enrolled in the Sunday Church School. The congregation is located on busy Route 202 (which ultimately picks its way from Newark, NJ, southwest through Valley Forge, PA) midway between Doylestown and Chalfont (where the manse is located at 226 Cornwall Drive—a comfortable two miles from the church!) in historic Bucks County. There is a shopping center adjacent to one side of the property and a new elementary school on the other side, each offering countless possibilities for new forms of creative ministry. (Delaware Valley College is also only a mile or so down the road toward Doylestown.)

It is, however, the Book-of-the-Acts spirit of this congregation which really makes the prospects exciting. From the beginning, the people have sought to maintain the General Assembly ideal of $1 invested in mission for each $1 spent at home. In the course of building a first unit and purchasing the manse, this has slipped a little but has nonetheless forestalled the building of the other two units, at least for the time being.

In addition, this is a congregation much concerned with her youth and recognizes the need for an in-depth, rather than a superficial, ministry to and with young people. In fact, at every level of corporate life, it would appear that the leaders of this church are far more concerned with people as individuals than with the numbers game of recruiting more and more new members, or the edifice complex of building more and more buildings.

And—and what more can I say to show that our God answers our prayers so abundantly, if only we wait for *His* answer?—and all of this only a twenty-five-minute drive from my parents, less than two hours from Amy's mother!

Leave-takings are hard. It would be easier to sort of drop through a hole, but that would be quite unsatisfactory for all. But the way everything has worked out, from our coming here to our going, I have no doubt that this is indeed God's will; just as we have tried to love each other with His love as revealed in Jesus Christ. And I know of no better way to sum up the way I feel than in some words of Dietrich Bonhoeffer (German pastor martyred by the Nazis in World War II) from the first chapter of his great book, *Life Together.* "Our community with one another consists solely in what Christ has done to both of us... Where Christ bids me to maintain fellowship for the sake of love, I will maintain it. Where His truth enjoins me to dissolve a fellowship, for love's sake, there I will dissolve it, despite all the protests of my human love."

"The Lord gave, and the Lord hath taken away; blessed be the name of the Lord" (Job 1:21).

Sincerely and with much love always,
Daniel W. Reid

To: A & P Review Committee
September 23, 1997
Members of Session
Lenape Valley Staff
Re: Retirement of Senior Pastor

Dear Colleagues:

As a longtime student of baseball, I have on several occasions wished that professional athletes who had been onetime leaders in their field had recognized the telltale signs that they were "losing it" and retired with dignity rather than disappointment in diminishing skills. The names of Steve Carlton, Willie Mays, and Robin Roberts come to mind. I have also watched with sadness and dismay as I have seen and learned of pastors who stayed a year or so too long in the pastorate and undid much of what they spent long years accomplishing. I have always vowed that I did not want to be numbered among them. Unfortunately, events and conversations of the past months finally convinced me that, by my perception at least, it is already happening.

I came to Lenape Valley after thirteen-plus years in Minnesota, more than a dozen of those years honing preaching, pastoral, and people skills in small rural congregations. When we came here in February 1971, Lenape Valley, with a membership of 287, was not much different in its demands. In other words, the basics of ministry: inspired and inspiring preaching, a solid Christian Education program, and regular visitation, all but guaranteed spiritual and numerical growth—and with it, financial growth as well. For many years, as is apparent to all, this

approach to ministry worked, as Lenape Valley
has tripled in membership and conducted two
successful building campaigns.

Recent events here—as well as studies by those who truly care about the Church
(Presbyterian and Reformed Renewal Ministries,
the "Spirit Alive" folks, for example)—indicate
that the old approach is inadequate for a new
day. It's happening all over, but to cite some local
illustrations:

- The hemorrhaging caused by folks—
  many of whom I considered my
  friends—leaving Lenape Valley continues unabated, despite our best efforts.
- The comments made by folks who have
  remained that they have never really
  "felt a part of the family."
- The increasing difficulty in getting sufficient volunteers to share the workload
- The perception I have that my voice is
  so familiar that it isn't really heard anymore, thus eroding my ability to lead.
  (It's much like teenagers who tune their
  parents out.)

Over the years of my pastorate here, there
have been obstacles and challenges to overcome:
the possible schism during the charismatic days,
as well as the successful completion of the two
building programs. Always before, I felt I knew
what was happening and why, and that I could
lead the officers and congregation in finding
solutions and positive answers.

Currently, I am at a loss. I have reluctantly
reached the conclusion that I do not have the

creative energy, nor the ability, necessary for leading a congregation of this size in this day and age and culture. The Lord has finally gotten my attention to show clearly that, for the best interests and future ministry and mission of Lenape Valley Church, it is best that I step aside as soon as possible in order that younger leadership more in tune with today's world might lead this fine congregation into the twenty-first century. Accordingly, since I will reach my sixty-fifth birthday on February 26, 1998, I am tendering my resignation/retirement effective at the close of morning worship, Easter Sunday, April 12, 1998.

I realize that I have on many occasions publicly stated that I wanted to remain through June 1999. That was for purely materialistic purposes: getting the house paid for. It also assumed that I was capable of doing the job. The second part has been dealt with above. Regarding the first: in the back of my mind is the memory that we lost my dad to a stroke, caused by the stress of his wanting to work two more years—for purely materialistic purposes. I feel I owe it to Amy and the family not to duplicate that tragedy.

In my previous pastorates, I have always felt clearly led when it was time to leave. I have that sense as I write this. I trust you will accede to my desires, and that we can work together smoothly toward the time of transition.

In His service.
Daniel W. Reid

Retirement Announcement
Lenape Valley Presbyterian Church, New
Britain, Pennsylvania, November 1997

As a longtime fan of most sports and student of baseball, I have on several occasions wished that professional athletes who had been onetime leaders in their fields had recognized the telltale signs that they were "losing it" and had retired with dignity rather than disappointment in diminishing skills. The names of Steve Carlton, Willie Mays, and Robin Roberts come to mind. (I have sadly observed pastors with the same problem.) On the other hand, Jack Morris, who clinched a world's championship for the Minnesota Twins in 1991 with that incredible ten-inning 1-0 victory, was quoted in the April 19, 1995 Philadelphia *Inquirer* as saying that he could no longer pitch at the level he was accustomed to, so he was quitting. "I don't want to be second-best," he said tearfully.

That same spring football great Joe Montana also announced his retirement basically saying it wasn't fun anymore: "For the first time in my life, football began to feel like a job" (quoted in the April 24, 1995 *Sports Illustrated*). More recently, a few weeks ago, basketball legend Dean Smith resigned as coach of the University of North Carolina, stating at a news conference that he had observed the enthusiasm new Sixers' coach Larry Brown was infusing into his team, and since he no longer was capable of doing that, it was time to step down.

I'm sure you can see where this is heading. I can relate to all three of these gentlemen. A new year which began for me with great enthusiasm in early September had the air let out of my balloon within a surprisingly short period of time. Suddenly, I realized that the Lord had perhaps for some time been trying to get through to me His message: "That's enough." In response to that message, I announced to the personnel committee on September 30, not without a lot of emotion (and the session on October 28) that I would be retiring this spring. I will be sixty-five on February 26 and will plan to finish out the church year through Easter Sunday.

The nature of the ministry is changing dramatically. There was a time when inspired and inspiring preaching, solid Sunday School and Christian Education programs, and faithful visitation upon those in need, guaranteed a contented, supportive congregation. Those factors are no longer enough in the '90s. And while it has been kindly pointed out to me that if I were younger, I could find the creative energy and motivation to change course, investigate, and solve the challenge, I no longer have either the energy or the desire to make such radical changes as may be necessary. In the best interests of the future of Lenape Valley, it is time fresh—as in younger—leadership is brought in to search out and follow God's plan for a congregation of the '90s and into the twenty-first century.

There is another dimension as well. The originally announced plan of retiring in June of 1999 was purely financial: I thought it made good sense to get the house paid for. Finances, however, is not a good motive. It was the desire for better finances that led my dad, aged seventy-two, to seek to practice dentistry for two more years, resulting in the stress which produced the stroke which ruined the retirement. I have many of his genes; that is a set I choose not to carry. To quote Joe Montana once more: "I'm at peace with this decision. I've got a lot of new things happening in my life I'm excited about. One thing, and it sounds simple, is just not being on a schedule. To just relax—that's something I've never been able to do." Having never been unemployed for more than short periods since I was sixteen years old, that is also a lifestyle both of us covet as well.

The need for your support for Associate Pastor Steve Gribble and Lenape Valley thus becomes more important now than ever. The best thing you could do for Amy and me is to make sure that Lenape Valley continues to grow in every possible way so that at the fortieth, the fiftieth, and even seventy-fifth anniversaries, folks will still be saying, "It's a wonderful Church." Curiously, the weekend I was struggling to write this, two or three of you pressed me for my retirement plans, saying kind things about me and my ministry. I am sorry I was not at liberty to respond specifically, since the ses-

sion had not yet been told. I would be even more sorry if Dan Reid
were the only reason you were here. If that were so, then I have
failed in my ministry to you. The Church of Jesus Christ and our
service to Him is far more important than our loyalty to any of His
servants. As Paul pointed out to the Corinthians: *I planted, Apollos
watered, but God gave the growth (1 Corinthians 3:6)*. In our case:
Jack Heinsohn planted, Dan watered—but once again, God gave
the growth, and to Him and to Him alone should be our allegiance
and our service.

This will not be an easy six months. I always get choked up at
the end of the film, *Mr. Holland's Opus*. We have been privileged to
have made many good friends during our twenty-six-plus years here.
You have been most supportive during the various family crises of
deaths, divorce, and surgery; and that sense of family is something
we will never forget. You are our church at Philippi (New Testament
scholars will understand what that means). Our hope is that those
friendships will continue even though—in fairness to whomever
God has in mind as successor—I may no longer take part in pastoral
activities.

Details will be disclosed appropriately these next months. Our
denomination prohibits associates from becoming senior pastors;
that is not an option for Steve or for you. At some point, Presbytery's
Committee on Ministry will assist the session in electing a committee to recommend an interim pastor, who would then guide the congregation through the vital period of transition. As one of the elders
you elected has recently said, "I can't believe God has brought us
through these thirty-five years and is now going to abandon us!" He's
right. This will be a period of great change and challenge, with the
end result being a congregation more united and stronger than ever.
Can we count on your contribution toward that end? Thanks again
for your love and support.

From the Pastor's (empty) Desk
Lenape Valley Presbyterian Church, New
Britain, Pennsylvania, April 1998

These last weeks have been a kind of miniversion of Dr. J's last tour through the NBA: there was something special at each stop. It began with the March AA anniversary meeting, at which I am invited in order that they can thank you through me for the hospitality you have shown this important ministry for twenty years. They presented me with something very meaningful this year: the twentieth anniversary coin, symbolizing twenty years of sobriety. A couple of weeks later, at the Chalfont Fire Company banquet, I was given a beautiful "chaplain's stole" created by Debbie Bergmann, one of our Lenape Valley alumnae.

Then, between services on Palm Sunday, the Sunday School presented us with a magnificent quilt on which were the handprints of our lovable Sunday School students. In addition to the rich meaning and love behind such a gift, there is also a practical element: sometimes we have malfunctioning light fixtures, and all we need do is touch the offender with that quilt because, as everyone knows, "Many hands make light work."

Finally, there was that magnificent banquet and reception you put on for us, 365 people at Highpoint Saturday night, April 18. (Many apologized for not being able to attend—I don't know where you would have put them!) It was a perfect evening in every way, starting with the limo ride behind "Chauffeur Dave" assisted by "Footman George." To have our whole family there—brother Jack from Colorado, son Wayne from Tucson (missing Wayne's wife, Jack's wife, and Deb's husband)—was so wonderful. (We normally all get together only at weddings, and everyone's now married.) The rich variety of members and friends added to the enjoyment, including two of our neighbors, my two favorite morticians (George Wittmaier and Jim Scanlin), my old railroad buddy Greg and his wife Mary. And did you see Mary Sloan, widow of Cordell, with whom we used to have that marvelous pulpit and choir exchange with Temple Church in Philadelphia?

The program itself couldn't have been better. It was so great to have the combined First Light-Daybreak Alumni/ae Choir participating, singing my favorite of all those numbers I wrote many years ago. Thanks, Bill! And thanks to Steve for getting the Promise Keepers guys together as well, sharing a number which, during the recent Lenten series, came to have a lot of meaning for us. The alignment and selection of speakers couldn't have been better, and their comments much appreciated. I particularly enjoyed Dave and Phil's spoof on my session moderatorial idiosyncrasies! There were so many treasured gifts, some of which we didn't discover until most of you had left, or even when we got home! The First Light/Daybreak choir gave us a "pastor-sized" "boom box" on which we can now play CDs (once we buy some). The most recent Bethel class gave us a counted cross-stitch kit of the New Testament picture of Jesus kneeling. There were other individual gifts which we will acknowledge personally, and which are most appreciated as well.

Of course, we can't overlook what those of you all the way in the back may not have been able to see: the fantastic wreath with figures on it depicting all those characters who make their way to the front of the sanctuary during the Christmas pageant, and that marvelous piece of stained glass containing the Stephen Ministry symbol of brokenness and wholeness.

How can we say thanks for the dozens of cards and letters, your expressions of love and appreciation? And for the generous purse! In the background of my twisted mind, I keep hearing the voice of the announcer on *Jeopardy*, saying, "Our returning champion, whose one evening's winnings totaled over *7,400 dollars!"* It has all been overwhelming, and I for one had a lot of trouble getting to sleep that Saturday night. We do have one request. Even as after your family contains more than one child, you love that first one no less because your love has expanded: so love the next pastor and spouse as you have loved us. Do this, and any minor problems Lenape Valley may encounter will quickly fade away. Thanks again so much. We love you too.

Some Words of Inspiration

Proper Motivation for Evangelism
NEWS from the Presbyterian Churches of
Claremont and Kason, Minnesota, April 1965

Recently, there came across our desk the newsletter published by a congregation currently celebrating its seventy-fifth anniversary. It was mentioned in an offhand way that perhaps seventy-five new members could be received to assist in the celebration.

While it is a mistake to distort a casual remark such as this by tearing it from its context and blowing it out of proportion, the idea does give one pause when we consider that we will have our own centennials in Kasson next year, and in Claremont in 1967.

I couldn't help but remember, when I read this, the pastor of a personality-cult type of congregation back home, in which each year it was announced over the broadcast worship services something like: "Next Sunday is Dr. Blank's fifty-third birthday, and we are receiving fifty-three new members in honor of that occasion."

Perhaps I'm a bit overly sensitive at the point of motivation for membership, but somehow, I can't imagine Paul holding off the enraged Jews at Thessalonica by saying, "The Christian Church is twenty years old next Sunday. We'd sure like to have twenty converts to The Way" (Read Acts 17). And even though Peter tried to preserve the mountaintop experience of the Transfiguration by building three booths (read Luke 9:28–36), nowhere does he suggest: "The Master will be thirty-two next week, and we're hoping to take in thirty-two more disciples."

We are far past the point at which numbers mean anything, as far as the Church is concerned. A casual snowy-day examination of either congregation's roll book indicates a vast number of persons who have come and gone; yet, to the best of my knowledge, only one has ever listened to and responded to God's call for full-time service.

I'd love to add a hundred members to each congregation to celebrate our centennials, but of more urgency is a deeper commitment to Christ on the part of those we already have: a willingness to testify by word and deed that Jesus Christ is Lord of every part of my life!

Perhaps it wouldn't be unfair to say that what our churches need is fewer members and more dedicated Christians. Do you agree?

Kasson Services in New Church Sunday
NEWS from the Presbyterian Churches of Claremont and Kasson, Minnesota, September 1965

The hopes and dreams and prayers of many Kasson Presbyterians will become reality this Sunday, September 12, as the first services will be held in the new sanctuary, located at 6th Avenue and 1st Street, NW. This is the three-lot property purchased two and one-half years ago, at the time that the former high school athletic field became village property.

Designed by the architectural firm of Kane and Graves, Austin, the $65,000-structure will enable the congregation to escape the program claustrophobia that has hampered her witness in the community for many years. Three bright, cheery Sunday School classrooms, a spacious kitchen and fellowship hall, separate restrooms, as well as a separate office and study, will all serve to augment the preaching of the Word and the administration of the sacraments amid the reverent hush of the sanctuary. The building is designed so that the fellowship hall can be used for sanctuary overflow, and the future expansion needs for Christian Education can be handled in the area to the north of the present structure.

A great deal of gratitude is in order to all those who worked so hard to make this dream a reality: Dr. L. E. Severance and Ed Dutton, cochairmen of the Building Committee; Marjorie Johnston, Bev Livingston, Tom Ferry, Glade Chapin, and Sue Edmond, the other committee members; Bob Burdick, in charge of the financial campaign; Fletcher Gray, who headed up the painting crew. And so many others: the Burdicks, for the sod; Charles Gruhlke, for his grading; and so many other faithful like Erv Livingston Dale Johnson, Lloyd Post, and the many, many more who spent countless hours painting, laying tile, and generally finishing up.

Contractors for the building were Hagstrom and Loock, of Austin; electrical work was done by Austin Electric; and the plumbing by Wenz of Kasson. Special thanks to John Loock, for all the extras of time and concern he gave.

It will be with a great sense of gratitude that when the worship service begins at 9:30 a.m. Sunday, we will praise and give thanks to God for His goodness that has made this project possible, and to all those who, by gifts small or large, have helped bring it to fruition.

All are welcome at the worship service, and at Sunday Church School, which follows at 10:40 a.m.

Postscript

As we begin our third year together in this wide parish, it is (at least on my part) with a sense of real accomplishment. Perhaps the single, tangible monument to inspired human achievement is the fine new building in Kasson described above, the product of great faith, sacrifice, and dedicated time on the part of the membership.

Less tangible, but just as real, however, is a feeling of increasing spiritual depth I detect in various areas of endeavor. How does one go about putting into words an increased sense of real fellowship, a spirit of concern for social issues and evangelism, as well as our own local needs, a feeling that we are willing to come to grips with the great challenge of applying God's Word to ourselves and our world? It's there all right and can be contagious, as we discuss these matters with one another.

Certainly, for the Reids, this past summer was good preparation for this kind of mutual wrestling. The spiritual and social mountaintops of two work camp experiences cannot fully be described, but through opportunities to present the slides, perhaps something of what happened can be caught by those who attend.

At the same time, the vacation-at-home was every bit as good as anticipated, even though the necessary cleanup after the two storms did prevent the completion of many projects around the house. (For the benefit of nonresidents: about four inches of rain fell in an hour and one-half the evening of July 8, necessitating the church and parish hall basements in Claremont being pumped out, with no damage done. Then a severe wind, rain, and hailstorm hit Claremont July 18, ruining bean and oat crops in the immediate area, and rather effectively shredding the balance of the vegetation. It's the first time in my life I ever raked leaves in summer!) In any event, we had a good rest, got to do some things together as a family, and generally benefitted from the three weeks.

At this point, I am really waiting to see in what direction we are led in our common witness in our communities and would encourage your sharing with me in that all-important prayer for guidance, "Lord, what wilt Thou have me to do?"

September Dreaming
NEWS from the Presbyterian Churches of Claremont
and Kasson, Minnesota, September 1960

A little old church member lady in North Dakota once said to a seminary classmate from Pennsylvania, her pastor, when he left on vacation: "Don't bring back anymore o' them Eastern ideas!" Poor soul, she was married to the status quo and preferred remaining spiritually childless. Actually, one reason ministers need a month away from the job is to be able to take a good look at it and more objectively think through needed areas of emphasis, improvement, or overall creativity. It's somewhat like a coach starting the season by saying, "We still need help at shortstop" or "This year, we've got to cut down on penalties" or "This winter, we may be able to win on our foul shooting."

So then, here are some random thoughts and ideas which tumbled over one another in no particular sequence after five years on the job and 3,800 miles behind the wheel visiting the grandparents. To begin with, *I am excited* about certain things which are in prospect. Even as I planned this article, the date was set for the Claremont Adult Fellowship Retreat. Who knows what form of spiritual quickening may come from this?

In addition, it will be interesting to see what happens in Claremont with the DISC (Dimensions in Stewardship Commitment) program, particularly after the amazing response to the challenge of the Fifty Million Fund. (The church was honored at the spring Synod meeting for having the highest amount of giving among smaller congregations.) Of course, the steady growth of the Kasson Congregation is an exciting thing to share, as new vistas continue to open up. And also, for the first time in a number of summers, I have returned to a clean desk in Claremont (Yes, Virginia, there *is* a cleaning lady!), and it's kind of fun just to be able to work in there again.

At the same time, there are certain *areas of concern* I would like to share with you. Let me preface these particular remarks by suggesting that, traditionally, people inside and outside the church have taken potshots at those who attend faithfully and go through all the rituals but fail to act upon their beliefs the balance of the week. It seems to me we have developed in our parish the reverse problem: essentially good people who know how to apply the teachings of Christ during the week, but are not always able (for a multitude of reasons, good and bad) to participate in those worship and study events which provide the very foundation and motivation for Christian action!

What I am saying is that church attendance, for one thing, has been getting, should we say, a little sloppy! Part of this is probably simply "summer slump;" but I feel that a major part is simply habit: it is awfully easy to get out of the habit of sharing in corporate worship every Sunday morning!

The sessions, aware of this, are using every means (personal visits and letters) to encourage *every* able-bodied resident member to attend World Wide Communion on October 6 and, as well, to return to the worship habit as part of a normal week's routine. I might add to this that it is my personal concern that the percentage of youth attending in a given Sunday is much lower than it should be. Yet, if their parents are not there either, from whence is the example to come?

In addition, while I feel that the many opportunities for Bible Study (the circles, Men's Class, Pastor's Class, Adult Sunday School Class) are worthwhile, yet the percentage of men and women involved is distressingly low. "But I'm embarrassed because I don't know anything." Well, try it once anyway. I am quite confident you will discover your leaders don't have all the answers either!

Finally, there are *some things I'd like to see happen* this coming year. I'd like to see more children of unchurched families in *both* Sunday Schools, which would mean additional effort in visiting and chauffeuring. I'd like to see us, whether individually or corporately, make more of an impact for Christ upon our communities. I'd like to see some plans being made to hire an additional part-time staff person, perhaps a minister of visitation, to live in Kasson, starting January 1, 1970. I'd like to see the Claremont leadership get on the ball and begin to formulate some definite building plans for the next five to ten years, for both manse and sanctuary. And I'd like to see a genuine spiritual awakening in our parish.

It's nice to be back. Care to join me in the *Adventure of Faith*?

Infant Baptism in a Farce
NEWS from the Presbyterian Churches of
Claremont and Kasson, Minnesota, May 1969

Farce (fars), n. stuffing, hence farce, from *farcer*, to stuff; L. *farcire*, to stuff, fill in: so-called because early farces were used to fill in the interludes between parts of a play. 1. An exaggerated comedy based on broadly humorous situations; play intended only to be funny. 2. Broad humor of the kind found in such plays. 3. Something absurd or ridiculous, as in, his work was just a farce.

What did he say? Infant baptism is a farce, something absurd, or ridiculous? Has the man gone daft? Why, the baptism of infants in the Lord is one of the most meaningful and important things we do in the church!"

Quite true, it is, at the time. Very few parents ever approach the Sacrament of Baptism lightly. It is rather the way in which their vows, and the implied vows of the congregations, are carried out that the farcical element appears. None of this is deliberate; it just happens. But it happens so regularly in today's church (total, but including our own), that the situation is indeed not funny at all.

The implications of infant baptism are always quite apparent. The parents themselves reaffirm their own faith (thus, one at least should be an active member):

- "In presenting your child for baptism, do you confess your faith in Jesus Christ as your Lord and Saviour…"
- *And* promise so to live, through teaching and example, that the child will him/herself grow up to be a believing Christian.
- "And do you promise, in dependence on the grace of God, to bring up your child in the nurture and admonition of the Lord?"

Implied here is both a devotional life at home and the active participation of the child in the Christian Education program of the Church (Sunday School, Vacation Church School, Youth Fellowship, etc.). At the same time, the congregation as a whole is involved (thus, baptism is not a private party but a matter belonging rightfully to public worship. Occasionally, there are legitimate exceptions.) This charge is then given: "And you, the people of the congregation, in receiving this child, promise with God's help to be his/her sponsors, to the end that he/she may confess Christ as his/her Lord and Saviour, and come at last to His eternal Kingdom."

The point is simply that the congregation as a whole (through the session, of course) has an obligation to see to it that parents carry out their vows and to assist them through teaching, advising, and example. This is basically what infant baptism is all about, and what we usually think of *that day*, but the problem is that we forget. We too often fail to fully carry out the responsibility of preparing our young people for a saving knowledge of Jesus Christ.

Confirmation pretty well proves this. Confirmation ought to be a time for discussing and applying the many years of factual knowledge children have had in Sunday School, V.C.S., etc. In fact, intelligent persons in many quarters are asking, "Why this preoccupation with confirmation if Sunday School is doing its job?" Ah, but there's the rub. With all due respect to the faithful few who appear to teach week after week, regardless of weather or family plans or headaches, somehow we're missing the boat. Would you believe it is possible for a Presbyterian youth with ten years of Sunday School to reach the eighth grade *not* knowing where to find the Ten Commandments? Or never having heard the beautiful story of Hannah and Samuel? Or not knowing it was Thomas who had trouble believing in the risen Christ?

Yet, these are the facts (incidentally, which point out the irrelevance of the old practice of giving attendance pins). In addition, we have some children who are most irregular at attending anything, and occasionally one or two are not confirmed (that is, do not commit themselves to Christ) at all. So what is the answer? I see our needs as lying in three areas.

1. Parents must take seriously their responsibility for Christian Education. In the midst of lives we think are so busy, parents must take the initiative of turning off that boob tube a little earlier and reading a good old-fashioned Bible study to the children at bedtime (or selections from a modern translation such as Good News for Modern Man). For how can they follow Him Whom they do not even know? Likewise, don't send them: *bring* them to as many church activities as are available. It's ironic: we're too busy to get them to Sunday School or youth fellowship, but I've seen these same kids at every dance, ball game, and social function in town!

   Billy Graham, in the current May issue of *Decision* Magazine, tells of a spoiled teenage girl critically injured in an auto accident. On the surgeon's table, she whispered to her mother, "Mother, you have taught me how to dance, how to sip a cocktail, how to hold my cigarette, and how to dress. But one thing you have failed to teach me: how to die." Are any of you guilty of such inverted priorities? In his autobiography, former New York Yankees second baseman Bobby Richardson tells of a young boy who asked his father to describe a Christian. He said a Christian was truthful, loving, patient, and gentle. When he finished, the boy asked, "Daddy, have I ever seen a Christian?" Can your children see Christ in you? If not, then baptism was for you a farce.

2. Our congregations, and particularly our teachers, must take the *content* which we communicate more seriously. Obviously, something is missing in what is being taught. To begin with, all teachers need to recognize, regardless of the age group taught, the seriousness of their responsibility. Teachers aren't babysitters. Over the years, there is a mass of factual Biblical material, which *must* be taught. It is trite but true that the church is perpetually one generation from extinction, and the starting point for the conversion of each new generation is the Word of God.

   But some will say, "Then I won't (can't) teach! I don't know the Bible myself!" And this is doubtless true. So then, take advantage of the many opportunities to learn and study! How many teachers are regular at circle meetings? Or, for that matter, in attending worship services? And look at the interest in teacher training of *any* kind! None in Kasson, spotty in Claremont, with the usual pattern of those who need it most, able to find the least time to attend. This is not meant as a slap at anyone in particular; it is simply a statement of the trend observed over the past six years. And it isn't good. Modernists decry the teaching of the Bible without application. But isn't the trend toward seeking application with little reference to the Bible that's much worse? Our congregations must take the content of their Christian Education more seriously, or the implications of infant baptism are a rather sad joke.

3. Our Sunday Schools are suffering for want of a minister. That's right. I haven't been to Sunday School in six years (because of preaching in two churches). And that's part of the problem. We have fine superintendents, and

43

we have dedicated teachers, all of them good people who simply need a guidance they're not getting. The answer? I've said it before: let's plan now for a retired minister to serve on the parish staff as minister of visitation. He would live in Kasson and would preach once a month (among other things), thus freeing me for more work in Christian Education. He's badly needed, and a must in the next few years.

Some of this sounds sharp, and for that, I am sorry. I have attempted to speak the truth in love because I love our young people, and it hurts me to see their spiritual needs so neglected in many quarters. And after shuddering through another batch of butchered confirmation exams this year and lack of parental "push" in the really important areas, I felt compelled to speak out. Whatever else he might be, a pastor is a watchman in the image of Ezekiel 33:6: *But if the watchman sees the sword coming and does not blow the trumpet, so that the people are not warned, and the sword comes, and takes any one of them; that man is taken away in his iniquity, but his blood I will require at the watchman's hand.*

My friends, the trumpet has been sounded.

Let's Be True Fundamentalists!
NEWS from the Presbyterian Churches of Claremont and Kasson, Minnesota, September 1970

Green Bay Packers's football coach Vince Lombardi, dead now from cancer, received his final promotion last week. His mission on earth was ended. He once considered the priesthood; yet we cannot always understand our priests and pastors. So God made Vince Lombardi the (at the time) greatest football coach in history, using the basic fundamentals of Christianity; and now, I for one understand Christianity a little better. Opponents used to say of the great Green Bay Packer team of the midsixties: "You know just what they're going to do, but they execute so perfectly, there's no way you can stop them from doing it."

That was Lombardi, the premier fundamentalist of the grid-iron. Football is a game of blocking and tackling. If you block and tackle, avoid mistakes, and strive for perfection, you win games. And world championships. After the Packers won their first Super Bowl Game in January of 1967, the players spoke unashamedly of their love for each other. Lombardi himself said, "To play (football), you need discipline and self-denial."

Love, discipline, self-denial. Sound familiar? Why not, for are not these the words of Jesus Himself? *"By this all men will know that you are my disciples, if you have love for one another" (John 13:35). "If any man would come after me, let him deny himself and take up his cross daily and follow me" (Luke 9:23).* You see? No fads. No funny stuff, no razzle-dazzle on the field or in the chancel: just the basic fundamentals of love, discipline, and self-denial, executed to perfection because practiced over and over until they become a way of life.

To be sure, once the fundamentals are mastered, you are free to be fancy. It was because Green Bay had perfected the power play that Bart Starr could hit Boyd Dowler for a TD on a post pattern, on third and one at midfield. And because the early Church perfected the same basic fundamentals, it was heard when it went freewheeling into controversial areas like breaking down the barriers between the sexes and the races! The whole world knows it when a football team wins a championship as well as when it loses. It's a little harder to tell with the church (there is no Super Bowl pitting Christianity against paganism), yet there are distressing signs that we are not *more than conquerors (Romans 8:37)* in the '70s; we have not yet tasted *the victory that overcomes the world, even our faith (1 John 5:4).* We have a lot of wide-screen option plays and are quite adept at defense, but are we, as is said of some pro teams, fancy in order to hide our deficiencies?

And so, in the spirit of our former Wisconsin neighbor, Vince Lombardi, and as a tribute to the unique way in which he successfully demonstrated Christian fundamentals on the football field, I say to you: "Let's be true fundamentalists!" Let's really work on the basic fundamentals of our Christian faith so that we become more worthy of sharing the victory won for us by Jesus Christ. Among them, I would first of all list *love*. Concern. Compassion. Let's start with each other. Do you and I really love each other? Do we love our families? Our neighbors? Drop a pebble of God's love into the vast puddle of life and watch as its ripples reach out across congregation, parish, community, state, nation, and world.

Then there is the discipline of *prayer*. Not gimme-type prayer. Nor prayers written by someone else, but real Garden of Gethsemane-type prayer: *"Lord, not my will, but Thine, be done" (Luke 22:42b).* This, every day, concerning every decision. Again, the self-denial of *Bible study*. Self-denial because something else isn't going to get done: TV show watched, nap snatched, card game missed: if you are going to take the time to read God's Word, study it, listen to it, and let the Spirit who inspired it make application of it in your life. And in mine.

There are other fundamentals, of course. Worship, stewardship, fellowship, joy, peace, to name a few. But let's not make the playbook too large! Let's sincerely work on love, prayer, Bible study; then stand back to watch the incredible results!

Reflections on a Rhododendron
NEWS from the Lenape Valley Presbyterian
Church, New Britain, Pennsylvania, June 1973

Someone with foresight once kindly planted a lovely rhododendron outside my study window. There it has become practically one of the family! What fun to check each morning, to see whether a particular multiblossomed flower has opened completely, or whether another has begun. With this kind of daily observation comes another. Generally speaking, there are no beautiful lavender blossoms where there were blossoms last year. Instead, from the stems at the ends of which protrude the dried stubs of last year's blooms comes the new growth: branches and leaves. An interesting phenomenon when notices that a somewhat related specie, the azalea, sends out its new leaves almost through each bloom, the same year!

All of this, however unscientific may be the observations, leads one on to a consideration of the infinite variety of growth-patterns in an average garden. Trim a yew (or almost any shrub or tree) and new growth begins along an established branch. But accidently step on the end of a sensitive cucumber vine, and you've lost it all! On a tomato plant, the cute little blossom is but a promise of the fruit to come. On a rose, the flower is all: the fulfillment of what you've waited for! The iris doesn't seem to care too much when it's moved or divided; the firethorn is quite particular and would rather not be moved at all. Plant one tulip bulb, and you get one tulip. Plant the seed of one of the mountain pink varieties, and you should get several square feet of beauty!

Consider also the built-in clocks of growing things, triggering the blooming both of the early snow crocus, and the great autumnal chrysanthemum. Or their thermometers: corn responding enthusiastically to a summer's heat that quickly wilts tender spring flowers. And what magnificent programing in microscopic space, telling each plant not only what color and size to become, but additional instructions: "What to do in case of…" heat, drought, the coolness of the evening, some disruption such as high winds or small children or an attack of Japanese beetles. And also, to some larger varieties (wisteria, peony, hollyhock): "Don't start blooming until your stalk is strong enough to support your blossoms."

The list is endless, of course, but even these few examples should serve to remind us that our God is a God of infinite variety. But further, if He has so chosen to create so many delightfully different varieties of plant life, could He not also have made the same choice in creating people? Is it not possible that He has deliberately created each one of us to be unique? If so, should we not do with one another as we do with the flowers in our gardens—appreciate, rather than criticize, our differences? And even more: does not all this speak to us of a God of infinite caring? What a labor of love to go to so much trouble to create a gorgeous bloom that will last a few days, then be gone forever! How truthful the words of Jesus: *"If God so clothes the grass of the field, which today is alive and tomorrow is thrown into the oven, will He not much more clothe you, O men of little faith?" (Matthew 6:30)*

Of course, we see God imperfectly in nature. Christ alone is the perfect revelation. But surely, our anxieties must lessen as we look at all growing things (including people) and recognize that variety comes not through nonconformity ("Why can't you be like *him?*") but rather through design. And our faith must increase as we are reminded that our future is in the confident, creative hands of a God Who cares!

Gardens, Goals, and Patience
NEWS from the Lenape Valley Presbyterian Church, New Britain, Pennsylvania, Spring, 1974

"I planted, Apollos watered, but God gave
the growth." (Paul in 1 Corinthians 3:6)

The Lord obligingly held off the rain last Monday until evening, giving me several productive hours with Jim Brinton's roto-tiller in our community/congregational vegetable patch back of the manse. And what a delight at last to see the earth becoming granular and beginning to lose the consistency of buckshot or croquet balls!

It's been three years now since Ted Torrey came in with his little tractor and plowed up the sod, and that year we forced seeds reluctantly into the underside of the sod, with predictable results. But since then, we have been throwing in everything imaginable: leaves from Weirs and Frys, grass clippings from the church (thanks to Sam Haines' pickup), kitty litter (home-grown), the results of a compost pile that contains everything from our own and the neighbor's weeds to sandy crabgrass from Ocean City, NJ, and this spring, six bags of wood chips courtesy of Penndot and the upcoming 611 bypass, as well as peat and lime. It's a little early to predict the size of a crop, but at least we're now dealing with earth instead of a fifty-fifty mix of clay and rock!

And working out there, one has time to reflect upon certain parallels, such as our lives as individual Christians within a congregation. To start with, there very well may not be much to work with. Spiritually, we may be hardpacked clay. But, as with a garden, it does no good to wish it were otherwise ("Oh, for that good fertile black Minnesota soil!"). We and the Lord have to work with what is here. And so the Holy Spirit comes at us and in us and through us (sometimes, in spite of us) again and again and again, breaking up the clumps, softening the hardness, making us crumbly and pliable in God's hands, that is, if we are willing and receptive. Then at last, we are for Him productive soil, able to produce a fine crop for the Kingdom.

But working in the garden reminds us of the time involved. One cannot hurry the processes of decomposition or of growth. We do the planting and watering and weeding and cultivating, but it is God who still gives the growth. And so it is with people. Are we impatient with others? Wait. Are we impatient with *ourselves*? Wait! For just as one may seemingly have to throw tons of "stuff" into a garden before the results become apparent, so one may have to absorb "tons" of worship services and Bible studies and prayer meetings and mountaintop experiences before crumbling into useful discipleship of our Lord. The key to it all is a farmer's patience: stay with it. Stay with your own search, and stay with the search of others. Don't ever consider giving up! Otherwise, we could get tired and consider stopping just short of the very victory we have desired.

And we are also reminded that the point of a garden is indeed a *crop*. Likewise, the Christian. Read the first dozen verses of John 15. In verse 8, Jesus points out, *"By this my Father is glorified, that you bear much fruit."* Which raises the obvious question: are we productive plants in the garden of our Lord? Or do we just sit there enjoying the sun and the showers? No one is called to be a Christian for his own sake. The Holy Spirit is at work within us in order that we might be productive servants, sharing the love, the joy, the peace of Jesus Christ as extravagantly as a plant puts forth seed.

This spring, let us think of our lives as our Lord's gardens, that with patience and persistence we may strive toward greater productivity in His service.

One More Football Analogy
NEWS from Lenape Valley Presbyterian Church,
New Britain, Pennsylvania, September 1974

"The Vikings really don't have many plays, do they? They just execute them well." (Pat Summerall, telecasting a Minnesota Vikings preseason football game as the Juice was drained and the Bills were buffaloed.)

Summer is a great time for letting the mind wander about what might have been and what ought to be and what well should be. It's a time for observing what makes a "winner" in other fields (such as football, whether amateur or professional). And when all is said and done, we can summarize in these few words: The Pursuit of Excellence. Not being content with mediocrity nor satisfied with the status quo. Being not so concerned with the quantity of activities as with their quality. I see this as a very realistic theme for 1974–75, both for myself and for the Lenape Valley Presbyterian Church. As I look about at whence we have come and at wither we are going, I like what I see. And what seems to be needed now is not more kinds of activities, but as doing our current and projected activities better.

For example, there is the ingredient which is part of the genius of LVPC: *fellowship*. Now, as one of our friends has been quick to point out, there is fellowship, and then there is Fellowship, the capital *F* distinguishing the difference between that which is social and sometimes superficial, and that which is deeper and the gift of Christ. While there may be nothing wrong with the former, we need more of the latter to combat our loneliness and our hunger for relationships. The small-group activities and the October weekend for renewal that are planned will be fine steps in this direction. Plan to participate, to share, and find out how loved you can be!

Then there is *outreach*. A minister in a similarly growing area, when asked about his outreach into the community, replied helplessly, "It's all we can do to keep up with the ones who come to us without going out to any others." We can perhaps understand this; yet, as each "Sold" sign is replaced by people, there is an opportunity to share something very precious. It isn't that we're greedy for growth (which could in fact negate the Fellowship!). Rather, we all need to be more generously consistent in sharing with newcomers the gifts of Christ we have found here.

Next, there is *commitment*. Dedication and/or rededication of our time, our talents, our treasures. How much time, percentagewise, do you really spend on the work of God's Kingdom in the course of a week (including worship, study, service)? What are you really good at? Have you rededicated that talent to God to use in His work? And then there's that dirty five-letter word, money. What could happen to our budgetary problems if we would really become a tithing congregation? And what would happen to us individually and collectively if our commitment to Jesus Christ really permitted Him to run all our committees, projects, studies…and our lives?

Again, there is *education*. Which assumes the reality that we all have room and the need to grow, intellectually as well as spiritually. What an array of *adult* opportunities there are this fall, together with the continually strengthened youth programs, both Sunday mornings and on other occasions. Opportunities to learn more about the basis for our Christian faith, the Bible. To learn more about our Christian faith itself and how it relates to living. And to learn more about the United Presbyterian Church, USA—its emphases, its strengths, its needs, and its accomplishments. Have you signed up yet to deepen your education, your "growing up in Christ"?

Most important, there is *love*. There is ever a need for each of us to be sensitive to the loving moment when a word, a touch, a note, a thought, an act may make us living channels of God's love to men, women, and youth as revealed in Christ. Do we dare to care (with*in* as well as with*out* the church walls) more intensely, more intentionally, more completely, more sacrificially than ever before?

These are just a few areas in which doing better what we have already been doing will surely enhance the proclamation of the Good News amongst ourselves, in our community, and beyond. Making an acrostic the first letters spell FOCEL. My prayer that the pursuit of excellence may indeed be the FOCEL point of all that you and I do, individually and collectively, this coming year.

Reflections on a Screened-in Patio
NEWS from Lenape Valley Presbyterian Church,
New Britain, Pennsylvania September 1975

Someone asked me when work resumed, "Where did you go on vacation?" I had to reply, "84 Lumber, mostly," which for one week at least was true, as our long-standing dream of screening in the patio back of the manse became a reality. It's been a slow but steady progression: two years ago, the concrete floor; last year, the roof; this year, enclosed.

And as I hammered and sawed and perspired off perhaps a dozen unnecessary pounds, some basic facts about construction became increasingly apparent: the foundation must be solid and true, and the framing of the walls must be square, or no amount of moldings, caulking, or paint will ever make it right. And in the manner of preachers wandering in strange paths, all of this began to develop as a sort of parable, an illustration of one of life's great truths: that in our lives, as in a building, if the foundation isn't solid and true, and if the chief supports aren't square, paint and moldings won't help a bit. (Of course, we hate to admit this: we look in the mirror and think in terms of superficialities: "Just a little trim or a little putty, or perhaps a change in paint color, and I'll be fine," but the disappointment is predictable.)

For the Christian, that foundation must be the Lordship of Christ. Paul, in 1 Corinthians 3, speaks of himself as a skilled master builder who has laid a foundation for a congregation in Corinth upon which others were building. And he says, *"For no other foundation can anyone lay than that which is laid, which is Jesus Christ" (1 Corinthians 3:11).* If Christ is not first in our lives, the Lord of our lives, we're kidding ourselves: there's no real foundation, and the trim and paint of "churchianity" (a busyness in church-related projects) just won't replace it. The beams or chief supports include such things as daily private and regular corporate prayer and worship. At the beginning of his literary ministry, Paul wrote to the Christians at Thessalonica: *"Rejoice always, pray constantly, give thanks in all circumstances; for this is the will of God in Christ Jesus for you" (1 Thessalonians 5:16–18).* In prison, after a lifetime of testing this theory, he wrote again, this time to the Christians at Philippi: *"Have no anxiety about anything, but in everything by prayer and supplication let your requests be made known to God" (Philippians 4:6).* We can't be Christian alone: we need daily contact with God as well as regular contact with fellow-believers if we are to sustain and deepen our faith.

Another chief support is transparent honesty. We Presbyterians love to eat, but as Paul reminded the Christians in Rome: *"The Kingdom of God does not mean food and drink, but righteousness and peace and joy in the Holy Spirit" (Romans 14:1).* Somehow, we hear a lot more about the peace and the joy than we do about the righteousness, but it too is vital. The Christian is to reflect the transparent righteousness or honesty of God. We cannot play games with the truth. We must be honest with God, with ourselves, and with one another. We are to be real people, authentic in every way.

Of the many other components of a square frame, one more we should mention is love, for it was Jesus's favorite word, *"Love your enemies and pray for those who persecute you,"* He said in the sermon on the Mount (Matthew 5:44). Then the night of His betrayal: *"A new commandment I give to you, that you love one another; even as I have loved you, that you also love one another. By this all men will know that you are my disciples, if you have love for one another" (John 13:34–35).* It is this ingredient in our lives that makes us different; without love, what sets us apart?

This month, we're beginning an exciting, challenging new year in the church. September is a good month to look at the structures of our lives, individually and corporately. Are they solid? Plumb? Square? With Christ as our foundation, and a faith strengthened by prayer, honesty, and love as the frame, prospects for the future are solid indeed.

See you Sunday, as we all return to the headquarters for all your and our spiritual building needs!

Who Spiked the Dip?
NEWS from Lenape Valley Presbyterian Church,
New Britain, Pennsylvania, January 1976

My tolerance for stimulation is very low. In college, I could get "high" on two Cokes and a deviled ham sandwich! So with all the gastronomical "goodies" ingested over the holidays, it isn't too surprising that I dreamed a lot. Especially New Year's morning, after too much chip-and-dip at the party at church the night before. It was the wildest dream I've ever had. I dreamed that every man, woman, and youth at the December 14 service (when I challenged the congregation to "put Christ first in everything for six months and see what happens") actually did so!

Nothing was apparent until the annual meeting in January, when a motion was unanimously passed (by the 150 or so present) that each person in attendance would "adopt" an inactive "buddy" in the congregation and find out why that individual was inactive: sickness, hurt feelings, depression, a struggle of faith, whatever. After the adoption contact, every Sunday morning, the "adopter" and the "adoptee" would meet prior to the service and then sit together. If one or the other missed, a telephone call that afternoon would seek the reason why.

Telephones in the homes of committee chairpersons and the pastor rang incessantly as members pestered: "Where can I serve? Where and how can I help out?" The original eighteen members of the Sunday morning adult class grumbled, "We've lost our closeness" since 150 parents began attending faithfully to augment their knowledge of the Christian faith and better fulfill their baptismal promise to "bring up their children in the nurture and admonition of the Lord."

Members of the stewardship committee wore glazed expressions on their faces as the sudden increase in tithing tripled each Sunday's offerings. Chairpersons of the mission, Christian Education, worship, property, and long-range planning committees especially could be heard babbling something about "prioritizing the excess." Space on a Sunday morning became a real problem because each member took seriously the mission-field dictum, "To pray for at least one non-Christian friend and talk to him/her about Christ." With everyone bringing a friend, even the front rows were filled!

Space was also at a premium at the Tuesday evening prayer and praise gatherings. Folks were actually passing up hockey games and bridge clubs and other fun things in order to come share what the Lord had been doing in their lives and to receive the blessing of the Spirit! When in my dream I got to Pentecost Sunday, June 6, it was too much. Who would ever believe Presbyterians sitting for over two hours listening to the witness of dozens of men and woman and young people who had put Christ first in every area of their lives the previous six months? When the deacon on duty slipped into the office to order pizza-to-go for three hundred people, I woke up! Crazy dream. These are the kinds of things that happened in the New Testament, not in America in a Bi-Centennial year! Guess I'd better stay away from the dip in the future. You just never know what impossibly wild ideas it can give you.

Happy New Year anyway.

New Testament Want-ad
NEWS from the Lenape Valley Presbyterian
Church, New Britain, Pennsylvania, June 1978

Wanted: a perfect Christian. Answers to Andrew, Thomas, Barnabas, Paul, Bar-Zacchaeus. Can be either gender, Any color or nationality. Call 345-1099 any morning.

Strange ad? Not really. In one person or five (or multiples thereof), the qualities exemplified by these New Testament personalities are the qualities we will need increasingly to emphasize next fall and in all the weeks and months following.

Andrew, because whenever we meet him, he is bringing someone to meet Jesus. In the First Chapter of John's Gospel, we read of John the Baptist pointing some of his followers toward Jesus. Andrew was one of them, *but he first found his brother Simon (John 1:41)*. It was to Andrew that the boy with the five loaves and two fish came, offering them to feed the five thousand (John 6:8–9). And it was Andrew who, along with Philip, brought to Jesus the Greeks whose curiosity was the sign for which Jesus had been waiting (John 12:20–23). What a vital member of any congregation is Andrew, bringing others to meet Jesus.

Thomas, because he asks hard questions, prompting answers we might not otherwise hear. Of all the disciples, he would feel most at home in a suburban congregation. It was he who asked Jesus where He was going, bringing about that marvelous answer, *"I am the way, and the truth, and the life; no one comes to the Father, but by me (John 14:6).* His conditions for a post-resurrection faith, and the enthusiastic conviction which followed once they were met, inspired Jesus to say, *"Have you believed because you have seen me? Blessed are those who have not seen, and yet believe" (John 20:20).* We need a Thomas to ask hard questions and help bring our plans and purpose to a more inspired focus.

Barnabas, because he is in the encourager, and neither pastor nor congregation could long survive without him. The world (and the church!) is filled to the brim with people who see only gloom and darkness, who see only the stray cloud in an azure sky, who love to say things like "It won't work!" or "We never did it that way before." It was Barnabas who brought the newly converted Saul/Paul to the disciples (who *were afraid of him, for they did not believe he was a disciple [Acts 9:26–27]*), who went to Tarsus years later to look for Paul, as the first missionary journey was being planned (Acts 11:25), and who took under his wing the discredited John Mark (Acts 15:39), who had earlier abandoned Paul during the first journey. How indispensable is the encouragement of a Barnabas!

Paul, because he has the theological maturity to see to the heart of an issue, and the compassion to know that the way of Christ is the way of love. How easy for Paul to have become bitter because of his trials as a Christian. How easy for him to become cynical because of the constant challenge to his authority! Yet, he told the feuding factions at Corinth, *"Make love your aim" (1 Corinthians 14:1),* and his friends at Philippi, from a prison cell: *"Rejoice in the Lord always…*

I can do all things in Him who strengthens me" (Philippians 4:4, 13).
What faith! What perspective! What an example of what being totally
committed to Christ can mean.

Zacchaeus, because in a world of theory and abstraction, his very
real stewardship offers a stinging challenge: *"Behold, Lord, the half of
my goods I give to the poor…" (Luke 19:8).* The effect of Christ upon
him was to trigger the signing of a 50 percent pledge! Regrettably,
the size of our pledges too often reflects not the size of our income
but the size of our faith! Zacchaeus stands as a reminder that for one
whose life has been turned around by Jesus Christ, nothing given in
return can be too great.

That's who we need: Andrew the evangelist, Thomas the realist,
Barnabas the encourager, Paul the joyous and mature lover, Zacchaeus
the exemplary steward. Any applicants?

On the Lighter Side
NEWS from Lenape Valley Presbyterian Church,
New Britain, Pennsylvania, Summer, 1978

At our May session meeting to receive new members, Sam
Haines shared this "devotional" found in the St. James Lutheran
Church newsletter and doubtless borrowed there from someone else.

"Now, hear this parable: A certain board of elders was examin-
ing a candidate for church membership. One of the elders asked the
candidate, 'What part of the Bible do you like best?' 'I like the New
Testament best.' 'What book in the New Testament?' 'The Book of
Parables.' 'Would you kindly share a parable with us?' So the uncer-
tain candidate bluffed his way as follows:

> "'A certain man went down from Jerusalem
> to Jericho and fell among thieves; and the thorns
> grew up and choked that man. And he went on
> and met the Queen of Sheba, and she gave that
> man a thousand talents of gold and silver and a
> hundred changes of raiment. And he got into his

chariot and drove furiously. And when he was driving along under a large tree, his hair caught in a limb and left him hanging there. And he hung there many days and nights, and the ravens brought him food to eat and water to drink.

"'One night while he was hanging there asleep, his wife Delilah came along and cut off his hair, and it dropped and fell on stony ground; and it began to rain, and it rained forty days and forty nights. And he hid himself in a cave. And he went out and met a man who said, 'Come and take supper with me.' But he said, 'I cannot come, for I have married a wife.'

"'And the man went out into the highways and byways and compelled him to come in. He went on and came into Jerusalem, and he saw Queen Jezebel sitting up in a window, and when she saw him, she laughed, and he said, 'Throw her down.' And he said, 'Throw her down out of there again.' And they threw her down seventy times seven; and of the fragments, they picked up twelve baskets full. Now, whose wife will she be in the Day of Judgment?'

"There was no one on the board who felt qualified to answer or question the candidate further, for each had a deep suspicion his own Bible knowledge was as sketchy as that of the candidate. The board voted the applicant into church membership and then recommended that the Christian Education Committee initiate plans for a program of Bible study in the congregation."

[Note: that is precisely what the LVPC Christian Education Committee has done!]

The Feeling of Being Rejected
NEWS from Lenape Valley Presbyterian Church,
New Britain, Pennsylvania, Winter, 1979

[Note: This was written after I had spent two weeks toward the end of a snowy January at the Yahara Center, outside Milwaukee, Wisconsin, being trained to teach the two-year (twenty lessons each in Old and New Testaments) Bethel Bible Study series. I went on to teach it perhaps a dozen times in Lenape, as well as at Pine Run and Roslyn.]

Something funny happened when I joined the Yahara Tabernacle Choir (made up of those attending the conference): I wasn't discovered. I hadn't planned to respond to the call for volunteers in the first place, but a couple of folks sitting near me said, "You can sing, better join." So I joined, mentally carrying with me my repertoire of Faure, Mendelssohn, Mozart, and Bible School. The leader, the dynamic Betty Mansfield, didn't know one of us from the other, so when she needed folks to do short solos (we sang at each morning's worship services and practiced during coffee breaks), she sort of pointed toward folks who looked like perhaps they could sing. The black Methodist pastor was asked. The Presbyterian pastor from Hawaii was asked. Naturally, the priest was asked. Others with distinguishing features in one way or another were asked, but not me.

Now, I have always said that I believed I had the kind of face that looked like it had already been waited on, so at first, I didn't think too much about it. But as the first week wore on, it began to bother a little. I would stand where I could be seen and not get called on. I would sort of hide, acting like I didn't want to be called on, and I didn't get called on. I tried to exercise my personality and cultivate some kind of relationship with Ms. Mansfield, but I still didn't get called on. The last straw came when she asked for a show of hands of who would like to do solo parts, and even with my hand raised, I still didn't get called on. And I was hurt and disappointed. After all, how many sermons have I preached on "You only get to keep what you give away"? I was trying to make a contribution, and not only did no one want it: no one seemed to know I was trying to make it!

In time, I found I really didn't care whether I sang with the chorus or not. I lost my enthusiasm in general and in particular (for the worship experiences). I lost my sense of humor, and joy turned to self-pity. "If they don't need my talent, they really don't need me," was the thought going through my head.

And then, Hosea-like, it suddenly hit me that I had been involved in a living parable of what churches often do to and with their members. And my mood quickly changed as I realized that the Lord was trying to teach me something through this experience (which He may or may not have set up in the first place). You see: the Christian is in a quandary. He is taught not to volunteer. He is taught not to march up to the head table, but to sit at the foot and then be *invited* up front (Luke 14:1–11). That way, we retain our humility and take positions of prominence only in response to some form of "call."

But what if the call doesn't come? What if those in charge see that the head table is full and leave it at that, ignoring the possibility that perhaps extra chairs could be added? What if those in charge of committees see that they have the proper number of warm bodies serving and don't check out the possibility that someone is sitting at the back of the room, waiting…waiting…waiting to be invited up front? This was a powerful lesson for me. I have now fully experienced the pain of being ignored and would hate to see anyone else put through this experience! For we do lose people who want to help, who need to help, who have the talent with which to help, when we don't take the time to find that out, or (and I've seen this happen) when we say in effect, "That's okay. Joe and I have done this for fifteen years. We don't want anyone else to intrude on our private domain."

Think about it, all who are in charge of things. Is there someone in the back row of your chorus waiting to do a solo for the Lord and silent because unasked?

What is a Prayer Vigil?
NEWS from Lenape Valley Presbyterian Church, New Britain, Pennsylvania, September 1980

Generally, a prayer vigil is a time of spiritual feeding, either during occasions of crisis (national or personal) or before undertaking some great endeavor. Luke tells us that Jesus spent all night in prayer before selecting His disciples (6:12).

Ours is the latter. Specifically, it is the opportunity for Reaffirmation, Recommitment, and Renewal, as we plan how deeply we want to invest ourselves in mission within and without the church walls in 1980. The concept is not new: my first exposure to it came several decades ago from the Rev. Cliff Channer, at that time pastor of the First Presbyterian Church, Windom, Minnesota. (They called it "R" Day.)

The idea is this: after you have attended one of the neighborhood coffees and the received the *information* you need prior to pledging for 1980, we invite you to come to the sanctuary for *inspiration* at any time from noon to noon, Friday–Saturday, October 26 and 27. A host or hostess will be there at all times. In the privacy of your own walk with the Lord, you will have opportunity for Reaffirmation, Recommitment, Renewal. Literature will be available to assist you. Remain as long as you need to, then place whatever response to the "Rs" you feel led to make (including your pledge card) on the communion table as you exit.

Consider what this might mean. To become a member of a Presbyterian Church (and, presumably, any other Christian Church), each of us at some time had to profess publicly Jesus Christ as Lord and Savior of our lives. But for some, that was a long time ago. For others, it was done in early adolescence. Perhaps peer pressure or an emotional experience played a part. Thus, we need opportunities for *Reaffirmation of Faith*: to pledge ourselves anew to follow Jesus Christ wherever He leads. In Gordon Cosby's Church of the Savior in Washington, DC, that pledge has taken (in part) this form:

> "I recognize that the function of the Church
> is to glorify God in adoration and sacrificial ser-

vice, and to be God's missionary to the world, bearing witness to God's redeeming grace in Jesus Christ.

I believe as did Peter that Jesus is the Christ, the Son of the living God.

I unreservedly and with abandon commit my life and destiny to Christ, promising to give Him a practical priority in all the affairs of life. I will seek first the Kingdom of God and His righteousness.

I commit myself, regardless of the expenditures of time, energy, and money, to becoming an informed, mature Christian.

I believe that God is the total owner of my life and resources. I give God the throne in relation to the material aspect of my life. God is the owner. I am the sower. Because God is a lavish giver, I too shall be lavish and cheerful in my regular gifts.

I will seek to be Christian in all relations with my fellow man, with other nations, groups, classes, and races, (and) will seek to bring every phase of my life under the Lordship of Christ..."

Once recommitment is made to Christ, some flow of service must occur as a result. We are judged, not on our words, but on our service (see John 15, especially verses 4–6). No congregation ever has enough fruit-bearing members, making *Recommitment of Service* a vital part of this time of renewal.

In the Church of South India, these are the minimum standards of Christian fruit-bearing:

1. Attend all services of worship
2. Daily private worship
3. Attend a class of doctrine
4. Must learn to read the Bible for himself

5. Must tithe
6. Must eat a meal with someone of another caste, and thus lose caste with one's own and prove he is a Christian
7. Must win someone else to be a Christian

We, of course, are far more sophisticated and advanced than all that. Each of us is already doing numbers 1–5 (we are, aren't we?); number 6 doesn't entirely apply, and only when we get to number 7 do we begin to see the relevance. The things we most need fruit-bearers for in Lenape Valley are the things most basic to our lives as Christians: extending ourselves to visit neighbors or visitors to our congregation, to share our faith and invite them to have fellowship with us. Committing ourselves for more occasions of gathering as the Body of Christ through coffees and family nights. Making it a point of personal responsibility to help keep our buildings and grounds looking the best, remembering that only our best should be offered to Him who sent us the Very Best.

Then, as a part of the response that you will surely be led to make when you strengthen the walk you have with the Lord, you will have opportunity to make a *Renewal of your financial pledge* for 1981. These pledges guide us in our budget-making. They tell us how far you want to move Christ's mission forward into 1981. If you have never pledged before, we urge you to do so (just as you already do to a bank or department store). Understandably, if your financial situation changes, you may adjust accordingly.

Of course, if you are not a member, or are convinced that pledging is not for you, we still invite you to participate in the prayer vigil. There is a Presence in our sanctuary when darkness has shrouded the simple appointments that is truly inspirational. Even if you do no more than come, sit, meditate, and experience, you will be moved. (Incidentally, transportation will be provided for those who need it.) Then, on Reformation Sunday, we will celebrate the cumulative results of your commitment, and offer them to the Lord for His use. Plan now to be a part of this time of Reaffirmation, Recommitment, and Renewal in the life of Lenape Valley Church, and over these next weeks, pray that God's Spirit may touch each heart and life in our church family.

An Attempt to Prioritize Time
NEWS from Lenape Valley Presbyterian Church,
New Britain, Pennsylvania, October 1980

Perhaps you remember an old commercial from Ma Bell detailing the effort made by the salesman who arises early, catches a plane, and journeys hundreds of miles to see a potential customer, only to be interrupted by the allegedly "smarter" salesman who sleeps in but uses the phone.

With all due apologies to our several families for whom Ma Bell provides an income, I'm with the guy who cared enough to make a personal call. For all its good and time-saving benefits, the telephone basically is an intrusion. When we call someone, we have absolutely no idea what is happening at the other end: a meal, a nap, sickness, a private conference. Few of us remember to ask prior to a prolonged conversation, "Am I interrupting anything?" (And how embarrassing it is to be interrupted, like that salesman, in the middle of someone else's appointment, by someone who never gives you a chance to say "I'm busy now. Can I call you back?") Of course, to cut someone off is to hurt feelings, and that's embarrassing and regrettable also. The reason for this little chat on telephone courtesy is the fact that by the time you read this, I should be more or less established in my new office at the church and, thus, more readily accessible both to phone calls and to drop-ins. This is by design; I want it that way.

My first year in seminary, I was assigned a brief biography of the great Scottish preacher-writer James S. Stewart. Providentially, down the hall from us in dear old Hodge Hall was a graduate student from Scotland who had studied under Stewart (Duncan McLaughlin, appropriately, was his name). When asked to describe his former teacher, Duncan said, "Immanently accessible." In other words, always available. I have always felt that this was the ideal for a parish preacher. Accordingly, I have never been "unavailable" during hours of sermon preparation or other study. (Some large-church pastors are, you know. The secretary will say something like "Rev. Whindie is working his sermon now and cannot be reached. Can he call you back at eleven?") A gentle plea periodically to stay away from Mondays has been my only real attempt at restricting calls.

But increasingly, we have a problem I feel I should share. The genius of Lenape Valley is the conscientious effort to give individualized attention to all its members, friends, and families. Needless to say, this is far more difficult to do now that we have more than five hundred members than it was when we had one-half or even one-quarter as many. But we still try. The only way this individualized attention can continue (even with the projection of added staff sometime the next few years) is to put some on hold while a previous commitment is honored and sometimes gently to remind folks: "Remember, there are others also." It's sort of like catching your family doctor in the hospital as he's rushing from an auto accident to a heart attack. He really doesn't want to hear about your child's cold right then, but when he's free, he'll give you all the time you need.

Someone gave me a picture a while ago of a baby with lipstick kisses covering his face, and the caption: "Some days there isn't enough of me to go around." How true that can be sometimes. With the many burdens so many of you are carrying, and our intent to help you if at all possible, frequently there are time conflicts. Yet, with your understanding, patience, and Christian courtesy, and the realization that if a phone call or a chance visit is cut short, it's only because there is another lamb somewhere in need; there will eventually be enough love to go around, and each of you should receive the attention you deserve.

An Overheard Conversation

NEWS from Lenape Valley Presbyterian Church, New Britain, Pennsylvania, November 1980

One of the wonders of our modern world is the electronic "bug," which enables people to snoop on conversations of others without their knowing it. Trouble is we always bug the wrong people and situations. It would be so much simpler to "bug" the enemy, Satan, thereby discovering what he has planned and how to recognize his evil hand at work in seemingly innocent situations. Fortunately, through my many contacts with Friends in High Places, I was recently given access to a recorded conversation taken from just such a bug, planted in the office of the Archdemon Churchwrecker, New Church Regression Division. With apologies to the late C. S. Lewis (*Screwtape Letters* author), the conversation with Junior Demon Insidious was reported to me as follows:

A.C.: "Well, Insidious, what do you have to say for yourself? Ten years ago, after your predecessor Implausible failed utterly to stop that trapeze artist (what was his name? Heinsohn?) from establishing a new congregation where formerly there had been a cow pasture, I gave you the opportunity to thwart that hick from the farm, Reid, who obviously knew nothing at all about the suburbs. And now, just look at the new building, growing attendance and membership, and what seems to be growth in the lives of many. *Our* enemy is claiming victories all over the place. What do you have to say for yourself?"

Insidious: "What can I say? How can I do anything, when for the dedication of the new sanctuary they bring in their Synod Executive, one of their (I hate to say it) most inspirational preachers, who takes as his text one of the most unfortunate things Jesus (excuse my language) ever said: *Upon this rock I will build my church; and the gates of hell* (that's us!) *shall not prevail against it (Matthew 16:18).* How can we fight an enemy like that?

A.C.: You sniveling moron. Didn't you learn anything in Demon School? The first thing we try to teach you idiots is that you

can't hope to defeat a congregation from the outside! Any prim-
itive fiend knows that, you repulsive clod!

Insidious: Begging your pardon, Your Dishonor, but how can we ever
hope to win?

A.C.: Well, in all honesty, some give us no hope at all. But if we can
implement my Four Steps to Disaster in that Church (and others like it), the victory will be ours indeed. Listen carefully, and
take good notes:

1. Build a personality cult around the preacher. Give him a
    swelled head so that he and his "fans" think every idea he
    gets and utters is (pardon the expression) 'inspired.' Flatter
    him with invitations to serve on important committees, to
    make guest appearances everywhere, and to get involved
    with radio and television. If handled properly, the congre-
    gation will gladly divert benevolence money instead for
    staff to 'free' their beloved pastor to serve in this way, which
    diffuses his talents so that no one is deeply touched and
    feeds their own collective egos.

2. Unfortunately for our purposes, there is an increasing
    number of those who have a close relationship with *our*
    enemy. Plant within their minds seeds of spiritual snobbery
    so that they become more concerned with judging others
    than of loving others not yet as spiritually mature, or who
    perceive their relationship in a different way.

3. There are also many of great talent and intellect in that con-
    gregation. Increase in them frustration at the typical ineffi-
    ciency of the church and get them so wrapped up in meet-
    ings and organization that nothing is ever accomplished.

4. Regrettably, I keep hearing those words which pain me:
    'evangelism" and 'outreach.' All right: let them have their
    blasted outreach committee. But keep them so busy plan-
    ning and disagreeing on strategy that no one ever gets
    visited!

Follow these tried and true steps, my young fiend, and we shall triumph indeed!

Insidious: Thank you, Your Dishonor. I shall immediately get back to my task of ruining that congregation from the inside, using the enemy's own people.

A fantasy? Yes, but unfortunately containing far too many grains of truth. *"Pray that you may not enter into temptation" (Luke 22:40).*

How to Keep Your Head
NEWS from Lenape Valley Presbyterian Church, New Britain Pennsylvania, October 1981

"If you can keep your head when all around you others are losing theirs, then obviously you don't understand the situation" (Origin unknown). But for Christians, it isn't that way at all. At least, it shouldn't be. More and more of late, it seems that we are being assaulted by anxieties and tensions of all kinds. Now, it goes without saying that these come from myriad sources, including physical. And I really don't want to seem to belittle or oversimplify the stress anyone may be battling.

Yet, I do write as one who, in my first years of ministry, fought a tension-induced facial skin rash for an entire church year, and followed that soon after with a bout of duodenitis and a near-ulcer. So for what help it may be to you who are fighting the same kind of battle, and in answer to the many concerned folk who ask, from time to time "how do you stand the pace?" let me suggest some disciplines I've found helpful.

1. *The Discipline of Devotions.* We liberals chuckled to ourselves in seminary when pious professors told of getting up at 5:00 a.m. to pray for the world. I don't know how

many of my fellow-cynics learned the hard way, as I did, that such a prayer life is not a pleasant option: it's a vital necessity After all, if Jesus did, shouldn't we? If I don't have my half to three-quarters of an hour each morning of some kind of inspirational reading a Bible passage, the Mission Yearbook, and our parish prayer booklet, I feel it all day. And so, probably, do those I touch.

2. *The Discipline of Diversion.* There is nothing wrong with finding some kind of activity that completely diverts the mind from a stressful situation. Curiously, many find their involvement with LVPC provides that kind of diversion for them from their jobs. Since LVPC *is* my job, I have other interests that can completely occupy my mind during free time and let me return fresh to the demands of the day.

3. *The Discipline of Digging*, or some other physical activity. Paul, one of the great thinkers of Scripture (or anywhere), said in 1 Corinthians 9:27: *"I pommel my body and subdue it."* In other words, he kept himself in shape physically so that his mind would be in shape also. Too many of us at middle age lose what in earlier years was not a discipline but a joy! Now it's work. Yet, I find that, in season, I must dig in the garden or play softball or racquetball (or even take hospital stairs two at a time) in order to rest well and keep the mind fresh.

4. *The Discipline of Devotedness.* Love would be a better word, but then it wouldn't be alliterative, would it? The idea is that each of us needs a cozy nest where we can lick our wounds, be ourselves, and find a healing touch. I am richly blessed, not only to have this at home, with wife and family, but here in our fellowship as well, surrounded by so many caring people. Yet, to receive that kind of love, one must be loving. That's how it works. *We love because He first loved us (1 John 4:19).* We must be lovers in order to be loved. And when we are devoted to others and their needs, in the spirit of Christ, it comes back to us daily in so many affirming ways.

This certainly *is* oversimplified. It's a good outline for a book, with each discipline a chapter. Yet, in a nutshell, as from time to time I try to analyze why I continue to have an energy and enthusiasm that many at my age (forty-eight) lose, I think these are the reasons. At base, it's a spiritual thing. Jesus keeps me/you young. But as well, it's a common-sense thing. I don't have to try to save the world all by myself: Jesus already did that. And in finding the rhythm of life God has for us (as He ordained it from the beginning: Six days on, one day off), we are able generally to relax and be restored in order to be able to deal with the pressures of the day.

Starting Point for Faith
NEWS from Lenape Valley Presbyterian Church, New Britain, Pennsylvania, October 1983

"[A]nd (Jesus) went to the synagogue, as His custom was, on the Sabbath day." (Luke 4:16b)

Uncle Bill Edmond (neighbor in Claremont, Minnesota; local realtor, Presbyterian elder) had a standard question for each newcomer to our small country town in southeastern Minnesota: "Where do you go to church?" And if there was no answer or denomination we could provide (all we had to offer was Roman Catholic, Missouri Synod Lutheran, and us), he'd ask him/her/them, especially if it appeared they might be experiencing some problems: "Why don't you come to church?" Not very sophisticated. Bill (an older man) just instinctively knew that something happened to those who worshiped regularly, as opposed to those that didn't.

It's different in the suburbs. We don't have milk cows keeping us home. We're farther from the land, therefore (as studies have shown) farther from the Lord. We also work under more pressure than the farmers I knew (both corporate and temporal pressure), thus the extremes of either needing to get away on the weekend or staying 'neath the sheets. And, yes, perhaps the lawn is too long, or the car is dirty. But perhaps there is something we're missing. Do you remember falling in love? I still do: three phone calls a day (from only two miles away), eventually every Thursday through Sunday nights together. Time stood still: there was never enough. And suddenly, it was 3:00 a.m. Saturday morning and a cross-country meet to be run that afternoon. But who cared? When you're in love, you can't ever find or spend enough time with the beloved, and the time between encounters goes about as slowly as time is capable of moving.

How much do you love the Lord? It really seems as if that's the real question relevant to the regularity of worship attendance. Any of the other reasons/excuses folks give for sporadic, irregular attendance pale to insignificance next to the concept: Why wouldn't you want to be in the house of the Lord, in the Presence of the Lord, in company with others who also love Him? How many starry-eyed young girls would accept a proposal like this: "Honey, I love you and want to marry you. But once we're married, I'll be home only when it doesn't interfere with my schedule. I can love you just as much on the golf course, the tennis (racquetball) court, or playing poker with the boys, as I can holding you tenderly in my arms. And oh yes, don't be bugging me for money all the time. I'll let you have whatever is left over after I've satisfied my own insatiable desires." Would any girl accept a proposal like that? And yet, how often have we in effect said this to the God who loved each of us so much, He gave, fully and willingly, His only Son to die on the cross as the once-for-all sacrifice for our sins? And the incredible thing is He keeps on loving us any way, even when we persist in loving other things more.

The text points up Jesus's personal need to worship on a regular basis, even though He didn't agree with the stance of the "denomination," even though He recognized the hypocrisy of the leadership, even though He wasn't always welcomed warmly by the other worshipers! (Read Luke 4:16–30) He worshipped because He wanted to be with the One He loved, His Father. Should we be any different than the One we call Lord? Should not the God, Who put us first, claim first place in our lives, in our stewardship of the time, the talent, the treasure He gave? Don't you generally try to spend as much time as possible with the one(s) you love? How much do you love the Lord?

See you in Church Sunday.

When Life Tumbles In, What Then?
NEWS from Lenape Valley Presbyterian Church,
New Britain, Pennsylvania, November 1984

We have been playing around with the concept these fall months of what it could mean to have Jesus Lord of *every* area of our lives. We hinted, for example, at the budget implications, as summer drew to a close, should He be truly Lord of our wallets and purses? My, it would be fun watching the session having to wrestle with what to do with all the money!

Then last month, we talked about what it means, or could mean, to have Christ Lord of worship, using some insights from our vacation visitation in which I realized that there was something wrong in my attitude in approaching three of these four services (I never intended to imply there was anything wrong with the services themselves, because there wasn't): an attitude of "let's get this over with so we can get on to a more important part of the day" rather than "Lord, what neat thing do You want me to hear in this service of worship?" I suspect that some of you might have identified with me in this.

Now, as we approach Thanksgiving, I want to broaden this a bit and raise the question: What does it mean to believe that Jesus Christ is Lord of *all* of life? What does that say to us when things are not going so well, when it seems as if something or someone has a foot out to trip us up every time we get some momentum going, or shoots a hole in our balloon just when it begins to soar?

I'd like to take a personal illustration and look at it through the eyes with which I would have dealt with it at different stages of my spiritual pilgrimage. Last Saturday, we drove up to Franklin and Marshall College in Lancaster for my thirtieth class reunion, and just as we entered the city limits, Amy's relatively new (to us) Lynx just stopped. At this writing, it is being repaired, and we are awaiting word on when we can exchange the rental car for our car.

At one point early in my life, I would have been in the *temper stage*. I would have vented a lot of undirected anger, probably with some decidedly unministerial and colorful language and railed against whatever fates decree that things happen to autos after the warranty runs out, and what kind of agency sells you a car that breaks down inside of two months? There was a time early on when I would have reacted in that way, and probably some of you at least can identify with those feelings.

Then there was a period when I might have been at the *self-accusation stage*. Like some Old Testament prophet, I would have (verbally, at least) rent my garments out there on Route 222, put on sackcloth and ashes, and lamented my fate. Why did I forget the warning of the local mechanic who, when I asked what he thought of the Lynx, said to be sure to get the timing belt changed soon, otherwise much evil could befall me. I forgot, and it did. Furthermore, why didn't I take out the insurance recommended by the dealer, which seemed expensive at the time but in retrospect would have been cheaper than the probable total bill for repairs will be. Yes, sometimes we do a marvellous job of flagellating ourselves over our errors, whatever they might be.

Later, there was a time when I was at the *demonic stage*, when I was acutely sensitive to the possibility that the devil was out to get me, to hold me back, to shoot me down, and discourage me. This is helpful in the sense that it at least reminds us of Who the enemy is, but it tends toward a spiritual paranoia that is counterproductive. If one concentrates all the time on what the enemy has done, is doing, or apparently plans to do, one develops a kind of losers' mentality: "How are we going to fail this time?"

Fortunately, I believe I have progressed to the stage at which I cannot only verbalize, but truly believe that *God is in control*. The good news was that the belt didn't break during the 915 miles of the previous weekend (a night in the mountains or out in Route 80), but late morning on a clear day, around the corner from the only garage open in all of Lancaster! Yes, it was annoying, but we weren't delayed more than an hour, and life has gone on as usual. You see, when we believe that God is in control (which is what Easter means), we can greet setbacks with Joyce Landorf's great line: "Gee, Lord: what neat thing are you going to do with this problem?" And what a difference that makes, not only in our attitudes, but in our relationships with others.

On Lowering Our Expectations
NEWS from Lenape Valley Presbyterian Church, New Britain, Pennsylvania, February 1985

If you like high-scoring games, you'd have *loved* this one. It was the last of the eighth, and *seven* home runs had already been hit. However, since three were by San Francisco, the Phils were trailing 7-6 that Saturday night, July 7, 1979.

Mike Schmidt led off. He had already hit three home runs in three times at bat, numbers 25, 26, and 27 in a season not halfway finished. The Phils' pitching was in shambles, so good old Tug McGraw volunteered to start. He gave up a run on two hits and a walk in the first, but Schmitty tied it leading off the second, and Maddox followed with his fourth of the year to put the Phils ahead. Then Mike Ivie hit number ten with Jeff Strain on base for San Francisco, so the Phils trailed again when Schmidt came up in the third, with two out, and Bowa and Rose on base via walks.

The first pitch disappeared into the left-center stands, and the Phils led once more, 5-3. The Giants scored one in the fifth, but Mike led off the sixth with his third of the evening, and reliever Ron Reed took a 6-4 lead into the seventh. But then his fastball started hitting bats, and back-to-back homers by Clark and Ivie netted three runs, and the 7-6 lead. So now Number 20 was back up again. The large crowd came alive. Could he do what few had ever done before and hit *four* home runs in a regulation game? The answer came quickly: on a 1-1 count, a soft fly ball to Larry Herndon in left. Final score, 8-6. And someone booed. "Say what?" you ask. Yes, someone booed the man who had hit three home runs in three times at bat and driven in five of the six runs the Phils had scored. But then, should anyone have expected this? You see, the problem wasn't Schmidt's inadequacies as a hitter. The problem was the overadequacies of our expectations. It's a problem that gets in the way of many of our relationships.

A young singer does a beautiful job of communicating in song God's Good News of Jesus but gets nervous and sings half the wrong verse (which nobody else notices). And he/she feels the whole work has been spoiled. Inadequate performance? No. Overadequate expectations.

77

A bitter foster mother watches as the despised boyfriend (last year's king) places the crown on this year's homecoming queen, her adopted daughter. There were tears. Of joy? No. Anger: "He couldn't even put the crown on right." Inadequate performance? No. Overadequate expectations.

Some Sundays I go home after two marvelous services, thinking not of the mystery of the foolishness of preaching but of some dumb thing I said in passing to someone at the door. Inadequate performance? No. Overadequate expectations.

You call your office (or any office) at your leisure and convenience and feel cut off when the conversation seems short and curt because you can't know what has been going on in that situation, or what the immediate situation might have been. Inadequate performance? No. Overadequate expectations.

As we have been discussing Lordship, it struck me one day that we also need to make Christ the Lord of our expectations. How much more patient and gentle and kind we would all be if we could dispose of our overadequate expectations! And we should. You see, we all have this problem. It's called in Greek *hamartia*. It means "a falling short," or simply "sin." We are all born with this disease, and what's more, it's contagious. Paul wrote to the Romans, *"All have sinned and fall short of the glory of God" (Romans 3:23).* That means that on any given day, at any time, any of us can fall short of our or someone else's expectations.

Along with our other burdens and problems, let's turn our expectations for ourselves and others over to the Lord and see how much more patient and kind we will be.

Keeping Your Head Above Water
NEWS from Lenape Valley Presbyterian Church,
New Britain, Pennsylvania, April 1987

"How are the mighty fallen in the midst of the battle" (2 Samuel 1:25a). These words comprise part of David's lament after the death of King Saul, and Saul's son, David's close friend, Jonathan. The

words were used in the Hollywood version of *King David*. A film which appeared on Showtime some time ago.

I thought of this when, some time ago, I heard and read about the "fall" of Jim (and Tammy) Bakker from the leadership of the well-known television ministry, the PTL Club. While I rarely, if ever, watched the program, and certainly would not consider myself a "fan" of the Bakker's, my heart goes out to them in what must be for them a very humbling time. Every pastor should not only be able to empathize but should also murmur, "There, but for the grace of God, go I." The story is a familiar one. The Rev. Mr. Bakker came out of Michigan to become a national figure on television, speaking perhaps to more with a single sermon than most of us address in a career. What a target for the Enemy! And finally, a combination of the pressure of the job and the revelation of one unfortunate indiscretion combined to force Mr. Bakker not only to resign from the PTL Club but from his Assemblies of God denomination as well.

I sympathize with him because the year I was moderator of Presbytery (1985). I was all too aware of how many were looking up to me, trusting me, affirming me, and making me feel terribly important. I felt the power of the position, especially, for example, when I arrived at a large fifteenth anniversary banquet just as it was beginning, and as I entered the hall, everything came to a dead stop, no one spoke or did anything until Mr. Moderator was seated and comfortable. That sort of ego-trip can get to you, if you let t!

My point is this: all of us have certain weaknesses or habits (perhaps a choice vocabulary) we left behind when we accepted Christ's invitation to "Follow me." Mine was the choice vocabulary. Now, had I slipped when I was in the pulpit of my first small congregation, had one of those nasty four-letter words or perhaps a double-entendre adlib slipped in, I'd have heard about it, but I'm sure it would not have cost me my job, nor would it have been the end of the world.

But: had something like that happened when I was ordaining or installing a pastor, or when I was bringing "greetings from Presbytery" and was expected to be funny in the midst of being adored, well, it would have been a far greater problem. Why? Because my stature was so much higher; so many more were looking up to me, and so many more would have been touched by my indiscretion. I felt far more a target for Satan when I was moderator than when I was an unknown country pastor in rural Minnesota.

The well-known TV pastors, the pastors of "tall steeple congregations" are much bigger targets for the enemy than those who may be working even harder but in the comparative anonymity of smaller parishes because the wider the audience, the more potentially who can fall and be lost to the Kingdom when the leader, because of his or her humanity, slips.

So please pray for all leaders daily, that we may be given strength to withstand the temptation that is there (whether we realize it or not). One message of Easter is that God in Christ has the power to overcome all things, sin and death, and our own weaknesses. Paul wrote, *"I will all the more gladly boast of my weaknesses, that the power of Christ may rest upon me...for when I am weak, then I am strong"* *(2 Corinthians 12:9–10).* Let us admit that we are all weak, that the triumphant resurrection power of Jesus Christ may be ours!

What Do You Believe?
NEWS from Lenape Valley Presbyterian Church,
New Britain, Pennsylvania, November 1988

Mike Sanford, Christian pastor with a burden in his heart to share Christ, killed by a truck before his fifty-eighth birthday. Al Holbert, premier race-car driver whose Christian witness was respected by all, killed in a plane crash at age forty-one. It doesn't seem fair, does it? At least, that is the kind of question many raise, including some of you, when someone close—family member, neighbor, close friend— is struck down at a time or in a manner which doesn't seem fair. At least, if we were writing the rule book, we wouldn't have scripted it that way. As it is, we are tempted to throw our heads back and cry "Foul!" (Or as Carol Burnett did so graphically in the old movie *Pete and Tillie,* go out into the backyard and scream out our anger at a God who seems to let this happen.)

Joyce Landorf, as she discusses the unfairness of being saddled in her own family with an "irregular person" who never understands, affirms, or even hears her, says that at last she is reduced to the basic questions: "What do I believe? As I wrestle with the hurts and the anger and how God fits into all this, What do I believe?"

I'd like to share what I believe, as I reflect on the loss of my old friend Mike, as well as others over whose youthful remains I have attempted to conduct comforting services and have tried to communicate a word of Christian hope to those who are grieving.

First of all, I believe strongly that there is a war going on: a war between the powers of light and the powers of darkness; a war between the forces of good and the forces of evil; a war between God the Father, God the Son, and God the Holy Spirit and His eternal archenemy, the devil, Satan. To be sure, our Easter conviction is that the war has been won, that God through Christ will ultimately triumph, just as (to use Oscar Cullman's illustration) once the beaches of Normandy had been taken on D-Day, we knew that victory in Europe over the Axis powers (in World War II) was assured. But in between, there were casualties. That's where we are now: between the D-Day of Easter and the VE Day of Christ's return and God's ultimate triumph. And because of that situation, and the furious anger of a defeated enemy, some innocent warriors for the Lord become casualties (Why should Satan pick off evil folk? That would only strengthen God's hand!) Remember that we are engaged in spiritual warfare (read the last verses of Ephesians 6 for a Scriptural perspective on this.

Secondly, I believe strongly the promise of Christ "*I am with you always*" *(Matthew 28:20)*. I believe the promises of God through the prophets, such as in Isaiah: "*Fear not, for I am with you; be not dismayed, for I am your God; I will strengthen you, I will help you, I will uphold you with my victorious right hand*" *(Isaiah 41:10)*. I believe them because I have experienced their fulfillment in my own life and have seen them fulfilled in the lives of the many who are going through far more than I have ever endured. Trust those promises.

Finally, I believe strongly that God has the power to bring good out of evil. Read the story of the man born blind in John 9.

Remember how the disciples wanted Jesus to determine where the guilt lay. Who sinned? Who is being punished by this blindness? (They didn't know their own Scriptures. Read Psalm 103:8–14 for an example.) But Jesus replied, "You're asking the wrong questions. The real issue is: Does God have the power to bring good out of evil, light out of darkness?" And to prove that He did, Jesus healed the man. Look with the eyes of faith for the good that God has power to bring out of even the worst of situations.

Want proof? Read on. Two years ago, our dear Minnesota friend Karen became a widow when her husband of fifteen years died of cancer, leaving her with two young sons. Recently, she wrote this to me: "In our discussion Friday, I told (my friend) what you'd said about it being OK to be angry with God for losing John. I went through a lot of things, but never angry at God. Now I realize if my faith is as strong as it should be and my beliefs as a Christian are firm, how can I be angry at God for taking the ones we love to Paradise? Death deserves celebration; grieving is for the survivors. And we need to know that God will keep the bereaved under the shelter of His wings."

Wow! May such faith be yours and be cause for great celebration this coming Thanksgiving season.

A Message from the Flu
NEWS from Lenape Valley Presbyterian Church,
New Britain, Pennsylvania, February 1992

These are not the easiest times in which to be walking one's Christian pilgrimage, whether as clergy or laity. In one way or another, what happens in Washington (or, as the case might be, doesn't happen) touches each of us eventually. The (current) economic slump touches families and individuals, which in turn touches the congregation's resources, which touches the spirit of those planning to use those resources. In addition, one is upset by the hurtful things husbands and wives too often are doing or saying to each other (and, indirectly, also to their children). One hears by the grapevine teachings and attitudes being promulgated in the public school system, which are alarming (has there ever been a grandparent who didn't say "I'm sure glad my children are out!"). Sometimes friends disappoint us (although perhaps our expectations were too high to begin with). Sickness and death are our constant companions. And of (in my case when writing this) battling a touch of the flu doesn't contribute to a particularly jolly mood.

These feelings are not new. Christians throughout the ages have had to cope with similar (or far worse) problems. It is significant that the Apostle Paul, after listing all those persecutions he had endured in his service to Christ, concludes, *"And, apart from these others things, there is the daily pressure upon me of my anxiety for all the churches"* (2 Corinthians 11:28). (But read also 2 Corinthians 12:8–10.) In recent times, Christian speaker Joyce Landorf, grappling with discouragement and uncertainty, finally asked herself? "What do I believe?" These words came back to me in recent days as I was battling what surely was a flu-inspired time of mild depression and discouragement. I, too, had to ask, "What do I believe?" as a professing Christian. Four verses came to me as almost an immediate answer to my question, and I'd like to share them with you.

What do I believe? I believe the *Motivation* for the Christian is found in Romans 5:8: *"God shows His great love for us in that while we were yet sinners Christ died for us."* How long can we remain discouraged when we remember that while we were still stubbornly resisting Him, while we were still claiming lord of our own lives, while there were still many areas of our lives we had not surrendered to Him, in His unconditional love, God sent His Son to pay the price for *sins* we didn't even want to admit we had committed! It is when we finally come to grips with that personal, unconditional love that we are motivated to live for Him and forget all else. That motivation changes our priorities (particularly our use of time and treasure), as well as our attitudes. What a difference in our congregation if each of the (current) 833 members listed on the roll accepted personally that gift of unconditional love? For how can we long remain discouraged, how can we say No to a God who loves like that?

The second thing I realized I believed was that the *Conviction* of the Christian is found in Paul's great definition of faith in Romans 4:21: *"being fully convinced that God (is) able to do what He (has) promised."* Paul is here referring to Abraham, specifically with regard to the promise of a son and heir, even though Abraham and Sarah were well past childbearing years. What has God promised that relates to our time? There are dozens upon dozens in Scripture; reflect upon this one: *"Fear not, for I am with you; be not dismayed, for I am your God; I will strengthen you, I will help you, I will uphold you with my victorious right hand" (Isaiah 41:10).* This is an Old Testament version of the theme that runs through not only Paul's words in 2 Corinthians 12, but as well in the modern parable, "Footprints": it is when we are weakest and most in need that He fills us with His strength. He literally picks us up and carries us over the rough spots. The ultimate conviction is God's plan *will not be thwarted!* His is the victory, a victory confirmed in Christ's resurrection.

The third verse and reminder that came to me was that the *Promise* for the Christian is found in Jesus's words to the disciples in the UPPER ROOM, in John 16:33b: *"In the world you have tribulation; but be of good cheer, I have overcome the world."* Of course, there are still problems and difficulties: Jesus promised there would be! Where did we ever get the notion that when we chose to follow Him, we'd have lawns without crabgrass? But the promise is that the world is not going to win. In truth, it has already lost. Christ is the victor; and regardless of whether or not circumstances make us happy, our *joy* ("good cheer") comes from sharing in His victory.

The final reminder was that the *Strength* of the Christian is found in these words, tucked away I John 4:4b: *"He who is in you is greater than He who is in the world."* How long can we remain discouraged, depressed, hopeless when the victorious Christ is within us. If that is *not* so for you, you do have a problem! Better invite Him in at once! But for the many in whom He dwells, we should have a supreme confidence that nothing the Enemy does in our nation, our families, our schools, even our churches, will endure. He Who is in us is greater than he (the devil) who is in the world. And don't ever forget it! I've seen the end of the story: the good guys win! Believers

don't lament "Look what the world has come to." They proclaim,
"Look what has come to the world!" and share Jesus Christ. Let's
make a priority of reminding each other of His strength, His victory,
in 1992!

Vision in a Park
NEWS from Lenape Valley Presbyterian Church, New Britain, Pennsylvania, April 1992

(Before reading this, please review the Sixth Chapter of John's
Gospel and Matthew 25:31–46)

There are occasions when, in the midst of my morning devotional time, I slip into a kind of a trancelike state. I'm never sure
whether this is the result of a heightened spiritual state, not enough
sleep, or the fact that the caffeine hasn't kicked in yet. In any event,
from time to time it happens, and I receive visions and insights I've
never had before.

Recently, as I was praying for guidance as to how to attempt
to meet the needs of a growing congregation—financial, spiritual,
emotional, timewise, and so on—I seemed to be transported to a
park, call it Peace Valley Park, if you like. The location really doesn't
matter. And as I walked along in this park, I came upon a man sitting
alone on a bench, his head down, his shoulders slumped. As I drew
nearer, I could see that he was sobbing. So I stopped to see if I could
be of help. "Sir," I began tentatively, "I don't mean to intrude on your
privacy; but it is apparent that you are distraught. Would you care to
talk about it? Then perhaps I could be of some help, or at least direct
you to someone who can."

"Thank you," he replied then paused to collect himself. "I'm not
sure that you can be of any assistance, but perhaps it would be helpful if I can just share my feelings, my hurts, my loneliness." At this
point, I imagined all kinds of things. Was he a recent widower? Had
he suddenly become unemployed? Had unfeeling children rejected
him and sent him out to fend for himself? I waited patiently for him
to resume. "I have a large family," he began. "They are good people,

every one of them. They are honest, they work hard, they are motivated and goal-oriented. Yet it is those same good qualities in them that makes me sad because sometimes these attributes get in the way of our relationship." His voice broke, and I waited for him to collect himself once more.

"How does that happen?" I asked, trying to be helpful.

"Well, for one example, being an organized person, I set regular times to meet with and have fellowship with my family. It is a time in which we can share experiences, inspire one another, and reaffirm our love for one another. But there are increasing numbers of my family that do not come at the appointed time. I wait for them, praying nothing has happened to them, but they do not arrive. Afterward, I discover that there was a lawn to be mowed, a game to be played, a car to be washed, or extra sleep to be coveted. I guess I can't set their priorities for them, but it hurts when they just don't show up. I miss them so…" He was silent a minute, then he went on, "Sometimes, and I really hate to say this, I feel used. When some of my grandchildren were small, I used to see them all the time. Their parents would demand extra time of me, asking me to share the wisdom of my years, my experiences so that these precious little ones would be raised correctly. I gave of myself many times over. But now…" and his voice cracked once more "some of these who almost achieved adulthood, and with whom I could now rejoice in sharing fellowship and plans for the future, I never see anymore. I hate to think this way, but it's almost as if they have gotten from me what they wanted and now they have no more use for me." At this point, tears came to my eyes also, as I saw how much this hurt him. "There is one more thing, but I hesitate to say anything to anyone about it. It's so petty, and yet it bothers me." I waited silently. "Well, you seem like a caring sort, so I guess I can trust you, It's…about money. A long time ago, when I was extremely rich, I took all my possessions and gave them to my family, putting them in a trust for them, under the condition that each take a percentage of that income and send it to me regularly so that I would be taken care of as well. Many of them have fulfilled the terms of the agreement. Some have far exceeded anything I could have hoped for. But you know…" his eyes filled once more, "almost half my family sends me little or nothing after I gave everything I had to them. That hurts as much as anything."

I had closed my eyes in sadness and grief as he concluded his lament. When I realized he had stopped talking and I opened my eyes once more, he had vanished. And suddenly, from the sweetness pervading the atmosphere by that park bench, I knew. The man was Jesus, and his family was Lenape Valley. "Truly, I say to you, as you did it/did not do it to one of the least of these, you did it/did not do it to me."

Quantity or Quality
NEWS from Lenape Valley Presbyterian Church, New Britain, Pennsylvania, Winter 1994

I've been talking a lot lately to my good neighbor, George Coulton (since deceased), once an engineer on the Doylestown railroad line and a New Britain resident, still (with his wife Kathy) a faithful member of the New Britain Baptist Church. We've had many occasions for conversation because we have been scraping ice and shovelling snow together a lot: our parking places (all five of them) occupy a chunk of our adjoining properties. Back when this all began, a couple of weeks ago (as that all it is?), I had mentioned I had been out the night before to a memorial service here, and we were fortunate in that the snow didn't begin until almost all of us were home.

Then I added: "We have really lost a couple of grand saints lately: one of them ninety-seven (Esther Loos); then, only two weeks later, another, who was ninety-five (Arthur Wilkinson). Think of it! That's nearly two hundred years of Christian pilgrimage between them." And George replied, "Isn't that something? I wonder how they lasted that long." There followed one of those rare moments when you hear yourself saying, by way of inspiration or in answer to a prayer you don't remember praying, something you didn't know you knew! I said, "Perhaps it was because they were such kind people."

Now, on the face of it, that's not an entirely accurate statement. If being a kind person were the only key to long life, only the unkind would die young. And we know that is not true. My first ever funeral, a few months out of seminary, was a stillborn baby. As a green assistant in Duluth, I had to deal with a crib death while the senior pastor was on vacation (and didn't do so very well). In Claremont, Minnesota, a really great just-graduated high school senior drowned, and a fine young man accepted at law school, elder son of our organist in Claremont, was killed in Vietnam. Many of us here in Lenape still remember the tragic deaths of Mike Torrey and Andy Raab. We cannot say that kindness is a guarantee of long life.

But it can sure guarantee a *quality* life, which may perhaps result in a *quantity* of life as well. Both Esther and Arthur are remembered as kind and giving people. Until a month before her death, Esther daily made rounds of the medical center at Pine Run. One of our members there said she could almost set her clock by Esther's regular visits. Arthur, on the other hand, is remembered for his kindness to his family. His greatest happiness came when his family was happy. He died quietly, surrounded in the mountain home he loved by all the members of that family. Giving to others, friends and family alike. Is it not possible that that could be the key to quality, if not quantity, life? Let's dig into Scripture a little bit to see what answers we might find there. One of the first things we discover is in the Beatitudes (or as Robert Schuller puts it, "The Be-Happy Attitudes"). After stating that the poor in spirit, the mourners, the meek, those who hunger and thirst for righteousness, the merciful, the pure in heart, shall be blessed and have special rewards, Jesus adds, *"Blessed are the peacemakers, for they shall be called sons* (and, presumably, daughters) *of God" (Matthew 5:9).*

Then, over in that great Eighth Chapter of Paul's Letter to the Christians at Rome, in the fourteenth verse, Paul adds to our equation: *All who are led by the Spirit are (children) of God.* But then in Galatians 5:22–23, he writes: *"The fruit of the Spirit is love, joy, peace, patience, kindness, goodness, faithfulness, gentleness, self-control."* You see what we've done here? If we are Christ's, we are Spirit-filled. We are children of God (*heirs of God, fellow-heirs with Christ, Paul promises in Romans 8:17);* but more than that, we take on a quality of life that includes being a peacemaker as well as being kind and gentle (among other neat things). How's that for a quality of life?

Not being a medical person, I can't relate that sort of quality of life to quantity of life with any laboratory studies or statistical evidence. By observation of many years, however, I would suggest two things: anger, bitterness, selfishness, prejudice, hatred are self-destructive. They are a poison as deadly as any bottle marked with skull and crossbones. With even one of these ingredients, even a long life is but an existence. There is no quality to it. On the other hand, I believe that prayer impacts healing in an individual's life by changing the person's attitude, by opening him or her to the fruits (which may even include physical healing) of the Spirit. When that happens, regardless of the length of days, there is quality of life—the abundant life Christ promised in John 10:10.

Because this is new to me, I share it not completely thought through. I apologize for gaps or inconsistencies in thought. But I leave you with Jesus's words in Luke 6:38: *"Give and it will be given to you: good measure, pressed down, shaken together, running over, will be put into your lap."*

What Do We Get Excited About?
NEWS from Lenape Valley Presbyterian Church,
New Britain, Pennsylvania, April 1996

Had a wonderful evening recently at the Confirmation Banquet, as longtime friend Jim DiRaddo challenged the confirmands, their parents, and a number of their sponsors with the change that was to take place in the old admonitions when they were growing up. He reminded all that when we were young, fidgeting our way through interminable worship services, we were told three things: "Be quiet!" "Sit still!" and "It's almost over." He went on to say that following their March 24, 1996 confirmation, if they truly believed, they could neither keep quiet nor keep still, and it wasn't almost over: it was just beginning!

I recently reflected upon the first of his points with reference to the accounts of the first Easter Sunday. Both Mark and Luke tell of some of the faithful women who had gone first to the tomb to finish anointing Jesus's body, only to find the stone rolled away and the tomb empty and who then returned to the disciples. Mark, who wrote first, adds *"And they said nothing to anyone, for they were afraid"* *(Mark 16:8)*. Luke records that they did indeed tell their story to the disciples but received no response: *"[T]hese words seemed to them an idle tale, and they did not* believe *them" (Luke 24:11)*.

Interesting. Sort of reminiscent of that question which has in recent years been making the rounds: "What do you get when you cross a Presbyterian with a Jehovah's Witness? Someone who knocks at your door and doesn't say anything." Really strange when you consider that sometimes Jesus instructed those who came to faith to be witnesses: to share with others what had happened to them.

There was the cleansed demoniac (Luke 8:26–39) who wanted to tag along with Jesus and the disciples, but Jesus said, *"Return to your home and declare how much God has done for you."* And he went away, proclaiming throughout the whole city how much Jesus had done for him. Then there was the healing of the man born blind (John 9) who confronted the authorities (who subsequently excommunicated him) with these words: *"Whether (Jesus) is a sinner, I do not know; one thing I know, that though I was blind, now I see."* Sometimes, early in His ministry, Jesus, for reasons we can only conjecture, instructed folks to say nothing about what He had done for them, and they could not keep still. Witness the deaf mute who was healed (Mark 7:31–37): *"And Jesus charged him to tell no one; but the more He charged him, the more seriously he proclaimed it."*

What do we get excited about to the point at which we can't keep quiet? Well, *being loved* comes to mind first. Remember, guys, when she first said "Yes"? Could you keep quiet about that? Or, gals, when you actually got that diamond on your fourth finger, left hand? Well, friends, God loves you and proved it by sending Jesus

Christ into your life. Isn't God's loving you personally (to quote St. Augustine) "as if there were nobody else to love" something to talk about?

Then there are *unexpected gifts* or awards. Some years ago, at the annual Chalfont Fire Company banquet (I had been chaplain for twenty years since 1984), I was called forward to receive a beautiful plaque (on display at home) proclaiming that I had been elected Honorary Life Member (of which only four such awards, at that time, had ever been given). This was totally unexpected, and not something I felt I had earned or deserved. Just like God's grace. He has given us an unexpected gift, Jesus Christ, because He loves us and wants to cleanse us of our imperfections so that we are equipped to spend eternity with Him. In our gratitude and excitement, how can we keep silent about that? And doesn't that give us motivation for deeper commitment and service?

Among other things we tend to talk about constantly, there are the *victories* of the teams we root for or play on. If anyone would ever ask (don't!), I could give you an almost pitch-by-pitch description of a championship church league softball game several decades back in which I played a significant role in helping an overmatched, underdog team earn a championship trophy. It was so great! And so is Easter. That's what we celebrate: the victory of an underdog. Love seemed beaten down by hate, truth by falsehood, Christ by the secular and religious authorities. Yet, on Easter Sunday, who won the crown, the trophy, the victory? Jesus, our Saviour, our Lord, our friend! With such a fantastic come-from-behind victory over the guilt and shame and dirt of our past, and over the power of death itself, how can we keep quiet? How can we keep from singing? What else is worth shouting about?

It has been well-said that evangelism is nothing more than one starving beggar telling another where he has found bread. You and I are the privileged: we have found bread, as well as love, grace, joy, and a family. Why not tell your starving friends and neighbors about it?

Inspiration through an Old Quarterback
NEWS from Lenape Valley Presbyterian Church,
New Britain, Pennsylvania, September 1996

Inspiration comes to me from a variety of quarters: a powerful anthem or a moving solo, a sunset, a personal testimony or story of great faith, apropos of nothing in the midst of morning devotions, just to name a few examples. And sometimes while reading of how someone became a champion in professional sports. And so it happened that I found something I wanted to share with you while reading at odd moments in the Scheie Eye Institute lobby and on the beach, *Tarkenton*, coauthored by former Vikings-Giants-Vikings quarterback Fran Tarkenton, along with *Minneapolis Star* and *Tribune* columnist Jim Klobuchar (who is a kind of Art Buchwald/Erma Bombeck of the sports pages.) (Published by Harper and Row at $8.95).

In the course of the book, Fran had some observations on Coach Bud Grant which struck me as applicable to all of you men who are in charge of other men (and women, of course), but also which had wider application to the Christian faith. (Note: some of you will probably look at the Vikings's four Super Bowl losses and scoff at thinking Grant was a winner, but the Vikes had the fourth best record in pro football over the previous ten years, including the four bowls, while the Rams, with a better record, never got there, and Oakland, with the best record of all, never got there until last year.) Trouble is most modern writers are too young to remember the old (formerly) Brooklyn Dodgers of the '40s and '50s, who got to the World Series almost every year only to lose to the Yankees. (There! Now I feel better.)

Tarkenton first suggests: "If Grant has anything else close to a professional beatitude, it is this: The consistent shall inherit the titles. The team with the emotional and technical ups and downs are the losers. The ones who play at an even plane, again assuming a certain level of competence, the ones who play under control, are the ones who win." That makes sense, doesn't it? The consistent boss, the consistent parents, the consistent teachers, are the winners: people come to know what to expect, and are not kept on edge by decisions that vary from one day to the next, by a mind that keeps changing, or anger inconsistent with the deed. Christian bosses, parents, teachers attain this consistency through the consistency of their own spiritual nourishment: daily prayer and Bible study, regular worship, regular times of spiritual renewal. To do things only when one "feels like it" is to prepare to be a loser in life.

The author continues: "Because he is in command of himself, he can evaluate a football player honestly and incisively; and that means he can build football teams of stability." Good conclusion although poor theology. The simple truth is I am incapable of being in command of myself unless I am under the command of Christ. William Barclay paraphrases the oft-misunderstood third Beatitude (Matthew 5:5) with comparable words: "O the bliss of the man who is always angry at the right time, and is never angry at the wrong time, *who has every instinct, and impulse, and passion under control because he himself is God-controlled,* who has the humility to realize his own ignorance and his own weakness, for such a man is a king among men."

Fran goes on: "Grant is a football man, all right, second to being a family man... He told me he once walked into his office on a Sunday in the off-season to pick up something he forgot, and ran into one of the executives. The executive was up to his eyeballs in work. Grant said he admired the man personally and respected his work, but he simply could not understand a person being so consumed by his occupation that he had to be down there seven days a work, feeding on it, letting some very precious time drain away from him that he might better use, to let his life be more balanced. A time for work, a time for relaxing, a time for family, and a time just to breathe and walk among the high reeds at sunset. Grant can do that. He is a compartmentalized man. I think the greatest strength Grant has with his players is their knowledge that he sees those things, has his values in order, that he is a moral and ethical man who happens also to be one tough rock to beat." Are we listening, all of us fathers whose children wonder where we're off to now; all mothers who are winners in the community but losers in the home?

Finally, Tark concludes: "(Grant) parts with some of his colleagues, who maintain rigid codes that give them no space to maneuver. Some coaches make a spectacle of that. They force a confrontation. The management has to support either the coach or the star player. One way or other, the team is going to lose. Grant avoids confrontation whenever he can... He knows that if it came to a showdown he would have the support of management. But why bring it to that? (He) is one of those leaders with the sense to know when a stand has to be made, and when it can be sensibly postponed or avoided. He doesn't believe in making decisions until he absolutely has to."

Sound wishy-washy? In this age of "telling it like it is" and "letting it all hang out," yes. And yet, one wonders how many relatives, friends, and church members you and I have driven away under the cloak of "being honest" and calling "confrontational" what was in reality a venting of spleen. I have maintained many relationships over the years by mentally tearing up those angry letters written (with justification, of course) in my mind at 1:00 a.m. Had I said what I was thinking before I cooled down and gotten the situation into perspective, I would have lost in friendship far more than I would have gained in satisfaction. Remember the words of the forgiven Apostle Peter: *"Christ, who suffered for you, is your example. Follow in His steps: He never sinned, never told a lie, never answered back when insulted; when He suffered He did not threaten to get even; He left his case in the hands of God who always judges fairly"* (1 Peter 2:21–23, LNT).

So, parents, if you want a home that is a winner; bosses, if you want a job that is a winner; members of LVPC, if you want a congregation that is a winner, consider this interpretation of the facets of personality of a respected winning coach of a professional football team: (1) Let God be in control of your life so that you are always in control of any situation; (2) Be consistent, as our God is consistent, so that others will always know what to expect of you and can rely on you; (3) Get your priorities straight. You can't be a winner in life if earning a living is your top priority; and (4) Develop the mind of Christ: the patience that seeks every possible means of reconciliation before confrontation is reached.

See you in the winners' circle, for we have the promise, *"in all these things we are more than conquerors through Him who loves us" (Romans 8:37).*

Is Your Baby Ready for Confirmation?
NEWS from Lenape Valley Presbyterian Church, New Britain, Pennsylvania, February 1998

Got one of those familiar phone calls the other day. You know how it goes: "We're new to the area...had a new baby...haven't found a church yet...do we have to become members to have the baby baptized?" Yes, you do, and you're in luck: we're just beginning a new series of membership classes. "Well, we're not quite ready for that yet. You see, I was raised Catholic, but we had a bad experience, and soon..." And so it goes. There is something about becoming a new parent which, somewhat like Pavlov's famous dog (you remember: "Ring bell, salivate!"), produces a frequent knee-jerk reaction: "Oh, we need to find a church in which to have the baby baptized!" Now don't get me wrong. Many times, that desire is sincere. Some of our most faithful families came to us with that in mind, and I would have to guess, without actually taking a census that the majority of parents offer their children in baptism for the right reasons.

But there are those who evidently feel that baptism is sort of the last of the "shots" a newborn must have to protect it against the germs of spiritual warfare. That done, they can relax and not have to worry about anything until it's confirmation time! But wait a minute: what's wrong with this picture? What's baptism all about, anyway, and why take it so seriously? Let's start at the beginning. Our friends in those traditions which accept only "believers' baptism" are correct when they say that we cannot point to a single text in Scripture that states, "And so the baby was baptized." One reason for that is that the early Church was composed almost entirely of adults, new to the faith. However, we have texts such as that involving the conversion of the Macedonian jailer: *"And he was baptized at once,* with all his family *(Acts 16:33).* Peter said in that great sermon on Pentecost: *"The promise is to you* and to your children…" *(Acts 2:39)*. And of course, there is Jesus's famous invitation: *"Let the children come to me, and do not hinder them, for of such is the kingdom of heaven" (Matthew 18:14)*.

When Martin Luther was eliminating all those elements in Roman Catholic theology he did not find in Scripture (including five of their seven sacraments), he retained the tradition that (as stated in our own baptismal formula) "the children *of believers* are to be numbered with the holy people of God" (italics mine). Therein lies the rub. In our culture, we tend to equate "believer" with "church member" even though in reality, there are many church members who are sort of borderline believers. (Case in point: if you were confirmed at age thirteen and became a church member, then dropped out, went to college, got married, perhaps only attended the 11:00 P.M. Christmas Eve Service for about ten years, then came back with a child as a candidate for baptism, if you were still listed as a member, you were entitled to it although the depth of your faith could well be questioned. Yet, a born-again Christian new to the community should first have to commit to membership. What's wrong with this all-too-common picture? If you have an easy answer to that question, please let me know.)

Moving on: all obstacles having been cleared away, what actually takes place in infant baptism? In our tradition, the parents (or parent, singular, if only one is a member) makes two affirmations: first, the renewal of his/her/their commitment to Jesus Christ as Lord and Savior. Now you see why someone can't just come in off the streets and have the kid "done." There is a spiritual commitment involved, which ordinarily implies membership in a congregation.

The second affirmation is agreeing to the quaint phrase, "to bring up your child in the nurture and admonition of the Lord." It's at this point that, despite the mandatory conference with the couple and one of the pastors prior to the baptism, the train sometimes jumps the tracks. Think of what is implied here: nurture means teaching and example. It means taking seriously the words of Moses to the Israelites: *"These words which I command you this day shall be upon your heart; and you shall teach them diligently to your children, and shall talk of them when you sit in your house, and when you walk*

by the way, and when you lie down, and when you rise" (Deuteronomy
6:6–7).

And you say, "You've got to be kidding!" Knowing today's society, I hear you. But who determines the way in which we spend our time? What is the point of all that goes into paying the mortgage for the big house if it is not a home? What is the point of a child investing countless hours in knowing how to be a good athlete if an auto accident or rare disease takes that child before he or she knows the Lord? Affirming the baptismal questions implies taking a hard look at time priorities in the family in order that time each night be given over for a Bible story, prayer, and questions about God. And since they are hard to answer, it then becomes necessary to make Sunday School (for parents as well as for children) and worship a priority each week as well.

Then there's that part about "the admonition of the Lord." That simply reminds us of Who is ultimately in charge. We pray in the baptismal prayer of consecration: "As in humble faith we present this child to Thee, we beseech Thee to receive him/her, to endue him/her with the Holy Spirit, and to keep him/her ever as Thine own." Do you see what is happening here? In baptism, the child is being given back to the God Who first breathed life into that child, and who in response to your commitment is breathing the Holy Spirit into the child! So it is no longer our child, but God's, and it becomes our responsibility as parents to let the child know that in every possible way.

Then suddenly, the child is almost grown up, a young teenager. Ideally, he or she at this point has learned of God through the parents' teaching and example has learned of Christ's love through them, the Bible stories, and Sunday School teachers, and perhaps has even begun to have some concept of what it means to be Spirit-filled. Confirmation then should simply be a review of all that, an opportunity to put it all together and a chance for the youth to declare publicly what was confessed for him/her long before: "Jesus Christ is my Lord and Savior." Thankfully, there are many youth who attend these classes having already made that commitment.

Would that it happened more often that way. Unfortunately, confirmation all too often becomes a twenty-week crash course in what the student should have been learning in the first fourteen years of life. But at least, they are there. More of a problem for me are those situations in which the promises were made fourteen years ago and then forgotten. The child never grows, never develops spiritually; and when all of the sudden the opportunity for confirmation comes, the response can be "Are you kidding? I'm not interested in that church stuff. I've got too much to do." Thus, the original question "Is your baby ready for confirmation?" Because when he or she is baptized, that's your spiritual responsibility. Please take it seriously!

A Christian Acronym
NEWS from Lenape Valley Presbyterian Church,
New Britain, Pennsylvania, March 1998

Since when I attended both Germantown Academy and Franklin and Marshall College, both were boys-only, I grew up accustomed to male cheerleaders. The Hassold twins (actually, there were triplets: the sister attended Stevens School) at GA; the vertically challenged Al Shpeen (a dwarf) at F & M, leading us in cheers for victory are memories I shall always recall fondly. So it is not unusual to think of myself as, along with many other roles, a cheerleader. "Vict'ry, Vict'ry is our cry: V-I-C-T-O-R-Y!" That's the message that needs to be heard in the church, as well as the arena of the athletic field. So permit me the privilege of leading you in a relevant cheer for Victory!

Gimme an *S*—S: as in *Share* your love. Oh yes, in most cases, you already do this quite well. We have experienced it here for over a quarter-century! But the love of God in Christ for all needs to be shared with all, including those who may be more difficult to love: the quiet, fringe members who never seem to want to participate, those who have drifted away unnoticed, those in the community who may be unlovable because they have never experienced the unconditional love of Jesus Christ. Share your love with them all!

Gimme an *A*—A: as in *Adore* God in regular worship. The key to a strong congregation is faithful attendance at worship. There will be strangers in the pulpit the next couple of years (I retired from Lenape Valley a month after writing this, on Easter Sunday, April 1998), but that shouldn't matter. What should matter is that God will be there each and every Sunday, and our object in worship is to praise Him, glorify Him, and give Him thanks for all He has given us. We come to worship to give, not to get; the getting comes only as we give.

Gimme a *C*—C: as in *Commit* to Jesus Christ. The first question asked at the reception of new members at baptisms, as well as at ordinations and installations, is "Do you accept Jesus Christ as your Lord and Savior?" When that is a reality for you, all of life falls into place, the difficult times as well as the good times. When those are just words to which you give assent in order to accomplish a short-term goal, you will fall short in every area of life. Commit to Jesus Christ, and the rest will take care of itself.

Gimme an *R*—R: as in *Review and Renew* your promises. How many times have you stood at the front of a sanctuary and made solemn promises to be faithful to your commitments at confirmation? Marriage? When a child was baptized? When you were ordained an elder or deacon? What's your track record of promise-keeping? Our God has never made a promise He didn't keep. Are you a promise-keeper?

Gimme an *I*—I: as in *Invest* your time, your talent, and your treasure. Suddenly, there will be lots of things that won't get done unless *you* do them. Did you turn off the lights when you left the room? Did you catch the name of the visitor(s) and introduce him/her/them to the pastor? Did you jot down the prayer concern about someone you know, so as to send a card or make a phone all or visit? Did you sign up for that task for which volunteers were requested? Are you keeping your pledge current so that the ministry and mission of Lenape Valley may continue? The future of the congregation is entirely dependent upon the willingness of the membership to make this kind of investment.

Gimme an *F*—F: as in *Fly* in the face of tradition! Attempt new things for God and His church! Look at what's working and see how perhaps it can be done better. Look at what isn't working and bag it! The worst possible thing that anyone can say over these next couple of years is "Dan never did it that way." Maybe Dan should have.

Gimme another *I*—I: as in *Inspire* others with your faith and manner of life. Times of transition are times when the ministry of the laity is subjected to greater scrutiny than ever. No matter who you are, where you are, or what you are doing, someone (besides God, of course) will always be watching. Are the officers faithful in worship and in their duties? Does the lifestyle of the members outside the sanctuary reflect the teachings and professions inside? Especially remember, you may be the only Bible many others may ever read.

Gimme another *C*—C: as in *Continue* to grow spiritually and *demand* of your leaders' programs and services that help you to grow. Don't settle for second-best. In receiving you into membership, a dual covenant was made—you to Christ and His Church; His Church also to you to assist you in becoming more spiritually mature. Make sure this happens.

Gimme an *E*—E: as in *Expect* great things of God and His appointed leaders. The Bible is filled with stories of God accomplishing the impossible, using not just faithful people, but even those who didn't know they were being used. Peter walked on water only as long as his eyes were on Jesus. Keep *your* eyes on Him and prepare to be amazed at the results.

So put 'em all together and whaddya got? S-A-C-R-I-F-I-C-E: Sacrifice! That's the name of the game. It's what brought us this far and what will guarantee continued growth in every area in the days, months, and years to come. Or as Paul wrote to the Corinthian Christians at the conclusion of that great chapter on the resurrection: *Thanks be to God, Who gives us the victory through our Lord Jesus Christ (15:57).*

That same ministry can and will be yours, but it's not automatic. But if each of you commits yourself to Sacrifice as a lifestyle as well as an acronym for spiritual growth, you will experience a victory beyond your wildest dreams. God guarantees it; and He never made a promise He didn't keep.

Some Thoughts
on Christmas
From the Hearth

NEWS from the Presbyterian Churches of Claremont
and Kasson, Minnesota, Christmas 1964

In the short, action-packed time we have been privileged to serve this parish, we have been rewarded in so many ways that it would be impossible to enumerate all our blessings. Would that we could repay the many kindnesses individually, but unfortunately, the size of the parish prohibits this degree of personal attention.

However, there are some gifts of a spiritual rather than material nature we would like each of you to accept from us this Christmas. To each person, baptized, confirmed, or simply interested in the work of our congregations, we would like to give:

- A sense of the reality of God's continuing Presence in all that we do, good acts as well as bad, as well as each time we pray, together with a knowledge of the great freedom that comes with commitment to Him.
- An appreciation of the transforming power of the love of Christ, not only upon the individual, but upon all with whom you share this love (including many it would be easier to ignore or even hate!). No more wonderful and amazing power is available to us anywhere. Isaac Watts wrote, "Love so amazing, so divine, demands my soul, my life, my all," and in 1 John 4:18, we are assured that *"Perfect love casts out fear."*
- A sensitivity to the strengthening power of the Holy Spirit, giving courage amid depression, vision amid life's fog, energy amid weariness, hope in the midst of grief and pain. How reassuring are the words of the prophet: *"They who wait upon the Lord shall renew their strength, they shall mount up with wings like eagles, they shall run and not be weary, they shall walk and not faint" (Isaiah 40:31).*
- A realization that the Word of God we call the Bible is a living Word: the words we hear in answer to prayer not only complement but refer us to this Word. Further, there is an interrelationship between God's revelation on paper and

His revelation within our own hearts so that it is impossible for us truly to live until we begin to obey.

- And overall, a confident knowledge in the validity and sincerity of all God's promises which, if we believe them, will not only bring us ultimately to Paradise but introduce us to that state here on earth.

These are some of the unmerited gifts the Reids have received, sometimes reluctantly, over the years. We'd like to share them with each of you if you will accept them. And may yours be a blessed Christmas!

Our Christmas Wish
NEWS from the Presbyterian Churches of Claremont and Kasson, Minnesota, December 1967

As Thanksgiving melts into Advent, the preparation for Christmas, the thoughts of the manse inhabitants turn more than usual to the things we have been given. We have a task to do, a task that needs doing, and the God-given strength and enthusiasm for it. We have been given love and a sense of belonging. We have received much support, prayer, vocal, financial, from the many and the whole. And in gratitude, we have tried to respond in kind.

Actually, when you think about it, all that you and I attempt to do for one another is but a response to what God has already done for all of us in Christ. *We love because He first loved us,* the First Letter of John has it. This means that the very best we of the manse can wish for you to receive is that which God wants you to have! If you want to get specific, Scripture suggests at least these three gifts God wills for all:

1. *"I have no silver or gold, but I give you what I have; in the name of Jesus Christ of Nazareth, walk,"* Peter said to the man born lame in Acts 3:6. God would have us be physically and mentally whole. There are those, of course, who

104

are sick or handicapped through no fault of their own. But in our day, many more have literally worried themselves sick. To you, God wants to give a strong body and a sound mind, but even more, the faith that creates a life in which God does the worrying, and you and I do the obeying.

2. *"Peace I leave with you, my peace I give to you... Let not your hearts be troubled; neither let them be afraid" (John 14:27).* Jesus offered this, His only legacy to His disciples, the night of His betrayal. He means here, of course, an inner calm, an inner tranquility, freed from anxieties and tensions and worries. It is the state of mind that only becomes aroused when another is attacked or maligned, not self; it produces a Christlike person more concerned about hurts to the helpless than hurts (real or imagined) to oneself.

Obviously, this condition of the heart can only come about through peace made with God; therefore, it is a peace which comes with the forgiveness and cleansing made available through Jesus Christ. *"Be not afraid: for behold, I being you good news of a great joy..."* This was the message of the angels when Christ was born (as recorded in Luke 2:10). This gift of joy is in fact a unique feature of Christmas. Amid all that was wrong with the world then (as now)—joy! Even Jesus, on the eve of His crucifixion, could say to His disciples, *"These things I have spoken to you, that my joy may be in you, and that your joy may be full" (John 15:11).* It is this joy which produces smiles and laughs, friendship and warmth. More, joy (rather than cosmetics) produces the real beauty in a person, for it is the radiance that comes from Christ within.

3. *"A new commandment I give to you, that you love one another: even as I have loved you..."* Jesus again, that same fateful night, recorded in John 13:34.

The commandment to love covers everyone: family, friends, neighbors, relatives, enemies, people who are different or demented, people who are unappealing or obnoxious. Everyone. The command is to make every contact with them an expression of love (concern) for them. *"Perfect love casts out fear" (1 John 4:18)*. It is this attitude toward all persons which most fully reflects our obedience to Christ. Our Christmas wish, then, is that each of you may open his/her hand and heart to receive what God in Scripture says He wants to give: the faith that produces wholeness of personality; the forgiveness that produces peace, joy, and loving compassion for every individual.

Is There Life on Earth?
NEWS from the Presbyterian Church of Claremont and Kasson, Minnesota, December 1969

"I came that they may have life, and have it abundantly" (John 10:10b). About this time last year (1968), Apollo 10 took men farther away from the earth than they had ever been before. And the astronauts marveled at the sight: the smallness of our planet against a backdrop of the universe, the first "earthrise" ever witnessed by man. And they reflected that, from that distance, the question could legitimately be raised, "Is there life on earth?"

From our distance, the same question could be raised. For example, the question could legitimately been raised on August 13 of this year if you had access (as we did) to the Philadelphia papers. Here are some of the gems recorded (and noted down) on that date:

- The twenty-ninth gang murder of a teenager so far in 1969, the third in the last twenty-four hours.
- The nurse raped in her bedroom near the corner of Chew and Mt. Pleasant Avenues. (We pass that corner en route to my parents' home: it's only a half-mile away).
- Two teenage boys attacked by gangs (presumably because they wouldn't join), one at the corner of Germantown Avenue and School House Lane (a block from my high school: I frequently waited for a trolley on that corner),

the other at the major intersection of Germantown and
Chelten Avenues, a half-block from my home church.

• Bill Lennon, father of the lovely Lennon sisters of Lawrence
Welk fame, shot to death by an unknown assailant.

And so the question posed hypothetically by the astronauts
sounds strangely real: "Is there life on earth?" For surely, existing in
the kind of society described above could hardly be called "living."
Yet, centuries ago, a man named Jesus of Nazareth, about to be dis-
posed of by the same kind of society, said to His friends: *"I came that
they may have life, and have it abundantly."*

"I came," and that coming was what we usually refer to as the
first Christmas. So then, Christmas is for the express purpose of
bringing life to earth, and not in short measure, but abundantly,
pressed down, running over. But what has happened? Nothing that
didn't happen twenty centuries ago. Those who rejected Him (God-
in-human-flesh) showed it by clinging to their pride, building up
barriers between themselves and God, and between themselves and
each other. And has this really changed? Of course not.

Whenever today pride rejects God's way, there remains a separation from God reflected in a separation between all humans. Now,
if you like, you can point to the economic differences between the
haves and the have-nots; you can talk about laziness and alcohol and
drugs and "easy welfare payments" and all the rest of it. But basically,
there is only one problem: Sin, which Calvin defined as "man's inde-
pendence from God."

In concrete terms, Sin occurs whenever any of us says, "Look,
God, if I need you, I'll holler (i.e., phone for the minister and have
him say a prayer), but as long as things are going well, I'll spend my
money and my time and my life any way I please." And then we
wonder why it is we seem to have everything yet have nothing! Life is
empty, boring, shallow; and we can't get along either with ourselves
or our neighbors.

My good friends, if there were only one gift that were mine to
give each of you reading this this Christmas Season, it would be that
gift of Life Abundant the first Christmas was planned to provide!

Few of you have experienced big-city tensions, yet tensions you have. How often this past year have you resisted what is plainly God's will for your life and ended up feeling depressed or arguing with a neighbor, or snapping at a clerk, or losing sleep over how you will meet the payments of the latest necessity (perhaps spelled T-O-Y) you were conned into buying? Is that what you call living? Or is it simply existing?

Yet, both the New Testament and the historical records (as well as many personal testimonies) show clearly that anyone who sincerely makes a "Declaration of Dependence" upon God by receiving Jesus Christ personally as Lord (boss!) and Savior (rescuer from the mess caused by Sin) suddenly undergoes a transformation and begins to Live!

Such lives reflect the cleansing forgiveness made possible by Christ's death upon the cross; hence, a freedom from feelings of guilt. Thus, there is also an inner peace, a calm, an absence of tensions and anxieties. In addition, such lives, reflecting accurately the personality of the Christ Who dwells within, radiate joy and love (neither possessive nor permissive but concerned), as well as the power to meet difficulties and overcome them, not try to ignore or escape them.

Do these words *peace, joy, love, power* describe your life? If not, why not? Why not begin to live, rather than merely to exist? Even if I could afford to give each of you something material this Christmas, I wouldn't do it. Few of you really need anything added to your lifestyles. That which I most fervently want you to have is that which too many of you with equal fervor have resisted, namely Jesus Christ in your hearts, ruling the ways in which you spend your money and your time, the way in which you talk and act and think, the way in which you plan for the future and list your personal priorities.

I want you to have Life this Christmas because Christmas means God wants you to have life in abundance. Won't you receive His gift, permit Christ to rule in your heart; and really begin to live? My constant prayer is that you will.

Three Original Christmas Gifts
NEWS from the Presbyterian Churches of Claremont
and Kasson, Minnesota, December 1970

Each year the thrilling Advent Season, that time of year when we prepare our hearts for the coming of the Christchild, gives us occasion to express our thanks to all of you for all the good things (tangible and intangible) received throughout the year gone by and to share as well those good things we have so undeservedly received from the merciful hand of Him Whom we all seek to serve.

In particular, as one rereads the too-familiar Christmas story (in the Gospels of Luke and of Matthew), he is struck by three great gifts to all those initial participants in the miracle of the Incarnation seemed to receive. These are gifts you and I may still receive from our God, even today. I am referring first of all to The gift of *awe*. Of wonder. Amazement. As we read the story carefully, we see that this gift was received by Zechariah (Luke 1:12), Mary (Luke 1:29), the neighbors of Zechariah (Luke 1:65), the shepherds (Luke 2:9), those who heard the shepherds' story (Luke 2:19), and the wise men (Matthew 2:11). All were thunderstruck with the idea that our great God, Creator of all that is, would condescend to become one of us in order to demonstrate His way of living. May we in humility be privileged to recapture this gift of awe this Christmas.

Then there was the gift of *joy*. How difficult to be joyous while being an oppressed, captive people. Yet, this incomparable gift was received by all the recipients! It was given to Zechariah (Luke 1:14), Elizabeth (Luke 1:41–44), Mary (Luke 1:47), Elizabeth's neighbors (Luke 1:58), the angels (Luke 2:10), the shepherds (Luke 2:20), the prophetess Anna (Luke 2:38), and the wise men (Matthew 2:10). Many of you who are reading this may be terribly unhappy, or at least unjoyful. You have great difficulty in being (or appearing) cheerful. Will you not, this Christmas, receive the Lord Christ into your heart, and with Him, His gift of joy?

Finally, there was the gift of *renewal of faith*. For how could God break into history in this marvelous way without inspiring those touched by His Gift, those who received His several gifts, to a renewal of trust and confidence in Him? As we look at the familiar story, we suddenly realize that first Mary then (Luke 1:38, 45), Zechariah (Luke 1:64), the shepherds (Luke 2:17), Mary and Joseph together (Luke 2:22–23), and Simeon (Luke 2:27–32) had occasion to renew their faith in the power and salvation of their God. Amid all the busyness of this season, will you not take time for renewal and accept that great gift of faith which you and I cannot manufacture but which we can only receive as a gift from God?

There seems to be a gift missing, doesn't there? That's because, oddly enough, we find it used not in the Christmas stories themselves but in John's reflection upon them. And that is the gift of *love*. For what more can be said than our desire that all share fully in this, the greatest of God's gifts? *"For God so loved the world that He gave His only Son, that whoever believes in him should not perish, but have eternal life" (John 3:16).*

At the Start of a New Year...
NEWS from Lenape Valley Presbyterian Church,
New Britain, Pennsylvania, January 1974

It is a time for retrospect and prospect: to think back over the "Four more weeks until..." He did *indeed* appear; to think ahead to the fifty-two weeks that, please God, we will all be granted in 1974, and to speculate upon the new blessings our generous Lord wants to give to all who are open and receptive.

In retrospect, this past Advent-Christmas season was one of the most beautiful and meaningful that the Reids have ever experienced; we trust you found it to be the same. The many expressions of love, appreciation, generosity, and encouragement that were given in so many ways are deeply appreciated and are an inspiration for the days and weeks to come. Onetime charter member Helen Yorke, in reflecting upon her gifts of friendship and goods, likes to say of you, "There never was a church like this one." Our personal reaction is to whisper a grateful "Right on" and "Amen" for there is indeed a

Spirit present Who constantly reminds one that the New Testament is more a modern diary than an ancient history book.

David Augsburger, in his oft-referred-to book *The Love-Fight*, calls the kind of inspiring, affirming love we have all sought and shared "warm fuzzies." Well, the kind of "warm fuzzies" that have been floating around recently found expression in a lot of wonderful ways of late: that beautiful pageant whipped into shape by our favorite director "Ms. Liz" (Westcott) (or is it Cecily B. deMille?), whose attention to detail undoubtedly included the snow outside! The wifty, wildly wonderful "Carols and Pudding" bash so many of you attended and enjoyed Christmas Eve, at which we finally tossed off our Presby-bitions and decided to applaud those great kids with a spontaneous song fest around the piano, giving it all a living-room atmosphere (and who but lovely Mel would know off the top of her head *all* the words to the "Twelve Days of Christmas"?). And it was kind that none of you mentioned the subtle significance of a preacher singing about a wild boar...

And then the Candlelight Communion. And what can really be said except that the "warm fuzzies" so in evidence during and after that service brought all the fun, the frivolity, the work and planning, the worry, to the kind of destination right there next to the manger, toward which all our Christmas scrambling ought always to lead. And let's not forget *you*, the worshipper, the helper, the pray-er, whose support is vital to it all. I like to think it's been more than just an energy crisis that has maintained your consistent support Sunday mornings for both church school and worship; your willingness to let us try almost any reasonable medium for expressing the really Good News of Jesus the Christ, and your encouragement toward that end, are deeply appreciated.

So then, what of the New Year? Well, prognostication really isn't my thing (after all, I only picked the Vikings over Dallas by 3!), one reason being that God always wants to give us far more of the right things than we can ever possibly desire *or* deserve. But it strikes me that our "warm fuzzies," our ever-increasing openness and honesty with one another, the momentum that grows with our enthusiasm, the deepening relationships we are less afraid of having with one another, are a solid and firm foundation for whatever the future holds.

A wise man I once thought of as my "pastor" used to like to say, with reference to occasions when the Spirit might move: "Let's get together and see what happens." Right on, Ron! Let us Lenape Vallians continue to get together as often as we can for worship and prayer and praise and thanksgiving, for seeking guidance toward new and better ways to serve within and without our church family, for the sheer joy of being together; for a study of God's Word and a listening for it. And let's just see what happens! Let's plan, yes. We're experts at that! But let's continue to be open, always, to receive all those good things our generous and loving God has planned for us in the year(s) to come.

A Modern Christmas Story
NEWS from Lenape Valley Presbyterian Church,
New Britain, Pennsylvania, December 1976

Now it came to pass, in the fullness of time, that God's Word again became flesh and dwelt among us, born of a virgin, coming according to prophesy to bring to a close this present age. And the virgin's name again was Mary. And when the time came for her to be delivered, Mary was driven by her compassionate, steady boyfriend Joseph to the new Suburban Community Hospital (her own parents were at a party at the time). But when it was determined that Mary had no Blue Cross and no Blue Shield, neither hospitalization nor parental signature: the smiling nurse apologetically stated that there was no room in the maternity ward. And so it was that with Mary's pains coming closer and closer together, Joseph found a clean warm barn adjoining a nearby veterinarian's office. And so it happened that the Christchild was born, with Joseph gently but apprehensively assisting, and a Shetland pony, a half-dozen three-month old Collie pups, two Jersey heifers, and a full-grown Saint Bernard looking on. They wrapped the baby in a sterile sheet taken as they left from a table in ER.

Now there were in that same county far too many churches, each claiming to proclaim the Truth, each demanding that its minister spend too much time oiling ecclesiastical machinery, settling squabbles between the loving members, and doing the kinds of things the brothers and sisters in the congregations might better be doing themselves. And so it came to pass that Joseph took his six dimes to the nearest pay phone to try to inform at least one pastor that the days were fulfilled, the prophecy had come to pass, and Christ had indeed returned.

He let his fingers walk down the yellow pages (under "Clergy"), dialed five pastors and a priest, and talked to one janitor who reported that the pastor was attending a prophecy conference; a secretary who reported that Father was hearing confessions and couldn't be reached; a cute three-year old who didn't know where Daddy was, but baby brother wanted to say "Hi!"; a recorded response, telling Joseph to leave name, number, and message at the sound of the *beep*; an answering service; and a tired-sounding minister on his way to a meeting who hadn't time to talk.

Joseph returned to Mary, made sure that she was warm and comfortable, and that the child was nursing properly and set out to tell anyone who would listen that God had indeed kept His Word! He visited a Presbyterian Church first and stumbled onto a session meeting, but since he hadn't given notice ten days prior to the printing of the docket, he was told to return next month after giving proper notice. Next, he saw a lot of lights on in the Blessed Mother Awaiting the Parousia Catholic Church, but upon entering couldn't get past the hard-voiced lady selling Bingo cards. Finally, he found a Baptist Church holding a prayer meeting, but because of the length of his hair, he was asked to leave.

Joseph, tired, frustrated, filled with a mixture of anger (for himself) and anxiety (for Mary), stopped at a diner for a cup of coffee. As he sat dejectedly, slumped over the table, eyes downcast, a perceptive teenage waitress, instead of asking his order, sat opposite him and offered a listening ear. Touched by her concern, Joseph poured out the grandeur and misery of Mary's experience and his. Quickly taking off her apron, the waitress told her boss she had to leave early and went with Joseph to his old car. She directed him a few blocks away to her small but comfortable home where within about a half-dozen cordial people had gathered informally for Bible study, songs of praise, prayer, and a deeper discernment of the real Presence of Christ.

Joseph shared his story with them, and the waitress' parents immediately left the group to accompany her and Joseph back to Mary's side. As they hurried to his car, they almost knocked over a lonely old man from the nursing home up the street, out for his nightly walk. Abandoned long ago by his family, this old man had for years taught an adult Bible class and knew his Scriptures, Old and New, backward and forward. He asked what the excitement was, and when they told him, his eyes lit up with the enthusiasm of a score of years long gone, and he insisted upon joining them!

And so it came to pass that they all drew near to the veterinarian's barn and went in and found Mary and the sleeping Christchild and silently they fell to their knees in adoration and worship: Joseph, the long-haired adolescent steady boyfriend; the compassionate teenaged waitress and her Spirit-filled parents; as well as the wise old man; not to forget the Shetland pony, the six Collie pups, the two Jersey heifers, and the full-grown Saint Bernard.

No physician was there, nor any nurse (hospitals can't afford nonpaying guests). No clergyman was there, nor elder, nor deacon: all were so deeply committeed, they couldn't afford the time.

But… When you least expect Him, He'll be there;

Long ago He caught us unaware.
Who would have thought, who could have predicted that
God would have acted in quite such a way?
Strange as it was, He sent us a Savior.
He was there—in a baby boy.
When you least expect Him, He'll be there;
Read the morning headlines with a prayer.
You'll be surprised what events He uses, what
People He chooses to show us His way.
That's how it is, thru all time and hist'ry.
He is there: and He's here today.

(Avery and Marsh)

How about you? Will you have time for Him this Christmas? Or when He returns? May your celebration of Christ's birthday this year be the most meaningful ever!

Some Gifts for the Congregation
NEWS from Lenape Valley Presbyterian Church, New Britain, Pennsylvania, Christmas 1977

I am sitting here trying to visualize each of you and what you might need this Christmas and reflecting back on the joys and the sorrows of the year we have just shared. Permit a kind of stream-of-consciousness offering of gifts: please select those you need most or which you know you can share with someone else, remembering that all gifts really come from God, whose greatest Gift, but not Whose only gift, was the One Whose coming taught us what real giving is all about.

Perhaps the most important gift I could give you is the *assurance that God is with you*. That's one of the titles of Jesus: "Im-manu-el" or "God-with-us-(you)." So many of you are fighting battles of loneliness and alienation: family, church, society, one of those or in combination. There is nothing emptier and more depressing than feeling alone. But you're not. God is with you and wants to talk with you. He is with you and wants you to let Him love you! Remember that Jesus promised, *"I am with you always" (Matthew 28:20)*. He wasn't kidding! Accept the gift of God-with-you this Christmas.

Another gift that many of you need is the *gift of self-worth*, self-confidence, even self-love, if you will. How often do we hear plaintive cries such as "I'm not needed... I have nothing to offer... I am unworthy... I'm just no good!" Hey, friend, Jesus Himself said that the second most important commandment was to love *yourself* (after loving God, and prior to loving your neighbor as much as...). Christmas reminds us that "God so loved the world..." which makes us feel sort of swallowed up. But it was St. Augustine who reminded us that "God loves *each* of us as if there were no one else to love," and that's the gift I want you to accept and use this Christmas.

Remind yourself each morning: Christ died for *me*! I have worth. I am someone.

A gift many have difficulty in receiving is the *gift of understanding and application*. Why is it that congregations often have been charged with hypocrisy and have been scolded for sub-Christian performances? It is because all of *us* (clergy included!) have difficulty, first, in *understanding* what it means to be completely committed to Jesus Christ, and second, because when we do come to understand it, it takes even longer to learn to apply that knowledge to everyday situations. Thus, on Sunday, we proclaim "Jesus Christ is Lord!" But we don't know how to let go and let that be a reality, and our actions and words from 12:05 p.m. Sunday on may still proclaim, "*I* am still lord." Please, for your own growth, your own inner peace, and for the good of the congregation, take His gift of understanding and application. Let Christ really *be* Lord of your everyday life!

There is also a gift which needs constantly to be renewed because the lack of it comes back to haunt us again and again, and that is the *gift of the ability to prioritize*. To arrange the elements of life in proper order. To take Christ's command, *"Seek first the Kingdom of God and His righteousness, and all these things* (food, clothing shelter, life's necessities) *shall be yours as well" (Matthew 6:33)* and apply it every day to the ways in which we use our time, our talents, our treasure. We would never need to ask for money, to campaign for volunteers, to scold because too few attended a service, a class, or a program "everyone wanted" because of busy-ness, if we could all prioritize as Christians, if we would simply write "Jesus Christ" at the top of our lists of how we plan to spend the hours, the skills, the funds God has bestowed so generously upon us. Accept this Christmas gift of the ability to prioritize: to arrange your life according to God's ordering.

My, I could go on suggesting things it seems to me that you and I need so desperately in order to function as Christians. We need *patience* with God and with each other. We need more *joy*, more *freedom* to let God do His thing in our lives, more *inner peace*, more *love*, especially for those who differ with us, and more *faith* that God really *does* know what He is doing, and we should cooperate with Him rather than fighting Him.

Surely you must see a gift there you can use. Take it and make it yours, remembering that every good and perfect gift comes from God. May you receive this Christmas the gift(s) you need most!

A Christmas Acronym
NEWS from Lenape Valley Presbyterian Church,
New Britain, Pennsylvania, January 1985

"What can I Give Him, poor as I am?
If I were a shepherd, I would bring a lamb.
If I were a wise man, I would do my part.
Yet what I can I give Him: give my heart."

Those words have been a part of our Christmas pageant since its inception, and I think of them as this day after Christmas 1984, I try to imagine what I could possibly give you, the good people of Lenape Valley Church. This has been an outstanding year in many ways: financially, numerically, spiritually. Your desire for growth is evident in many areas. What could you possibly need?

Well, since none of us has as yet "arrived," there came to me this acronym, containing in easily remembered form some gifts you already have, but which I would, if I could, increase in each of you in the year to come.

C is for increased *commitment* to Jesus Christ as Lord of every area of life. The constant struggle for us all is between what *we* want and what *He* wants in terms of our use of time, talent, and treasure. Is there still some area of your life that needs to be committed to Him?

H is for *happiness*, or better, *joy* (I suppose we could have used *J* and added a footnote for Spanish pronunciation) that comes with the inner conviction (not just head knowledge) that in Christ, God really is in charge of every situation.

R stands for *responsiveness*, especially in subtle ways. Is there a "What do you think?" or "Would you like?" question in the newsletter? Respond without being asked or phoned. It saves everyone a lot of time and increases communication.

117

I is for the *insight* that comes with increased Bible study, as more and more we learn how to apply God's truth to our everyday decisions and problems.

S represents the *sacrifice* we are sometimes called upon to make when God's plans come first. Is a birthday party on *the* day really more important than youth group or confirmation class? Is the lawn really more important than Sunday worship? Is the ball game really more important than Communion? These are the kinds of things I think of.

T stands for the *trust* we never seem to have enough of in any congregation. My experience of committees, sessions, and the complex administration of Presbyteries, Synods, and the General Assembly has been that they are peopled by sinful people trying to do their best, just like you and me. When we disagree (a stance to which we are, of course, entitled), let it always be because we may see a situation differently, and not because we mistrust anyone's motives or commitment.

M is for the *memories* we ought to have as Christians: memories of what God has done victoriously in our lives in days and years gone by. Too often, our faith is crippled by a sense of "What have you done for me lately?" The Israelites over and over again were strengthened by the memory, *"I am the Lord your God, who brought you out of the land of Egypt, out of the house of bondage" (e.g., Exodus 20:2).* May we be strengthened by the memory of a similar deliverance from our own personal kind of slavery.

A is the *alertness* that comes with really caring: the alertness that senses someone is new to our worship service and needs to be shown to a seat, introduced to the pastors, and invited to return; the alertness that remembers that some of our older folks need rides after dark and would come to an evening service or event if only they were invited and transported; the alertness that misses people and seeks to learn why they are absent.

S, the second time, means we must be *spirit-filled*. That's not quite right: the Spirit comes into our lives in baptism. Remember that we *are* Spirit-filled is more like it, for then we will develop more and more those fruits of the Spirit that make all of the above possible, beginning with love, joy, and peace. In other words, Be what you are, for you are a Spirit-filled child of the living God.

I don't need to tell you what that acronym spells. I just want to remind you that these are the kinds of gifts our loving God is ever more ready to give than we are too often willing to receive, and the gift of Christ is the proof. Believe, and receive, and live abundantly!

The Twelve Days of a Lenape Valley Christmas
NEWS from Lenape Valley Presbyterian Church,
New Britain, Pennsylvania, January 1981

(A reflection to the tune of you-know-what...)
On the First Day of Christmas, Lenape Valley gave to me
A Wolff gorgeous Christmas tree.
On the Second Day of Christmas, Lenape Valley gave to me
Lizzie recruitin', and a Wolff gorgeous Christmas tree.
On the Third Day of Christmas, Lenape Valley gave to me
Craft Group a-hangin',
Lizzie recruitin', and a Wolff gorgeous Christmas tree.
On the Fourth Day of Christmas, Lenape Valley gave to me
Advent Candle-lighting, Craft Group a-hangin'
Lizzie recruitin', and a Wolff gorgeous Christmas tree.
On the Fifth Day of Christmas, Lenape Valley gave to me
Sermons that run too long,
Advent Candle-lighting, Craft Group a-hangin'
Lizzie recruitin', and a Wolff gorgeous Christmas tree.
On the Sixth Day of Christmas, Lenape Valley gave to me
Choirs rehearsin', sermons that run too long,
Advent Candle lighting, Craft Group a-hangin'
Lizzie recruitin', and a Wolff gorgeous Christmas tree.
On the Seventh Day of Christmas, Lenape Valley gave to me
Congregation's love-notes, Choirs rehearsin',
Sermons that run too long!
Advent Candle lighting, Craft Group a-hangin',
Lizzie recruitin', and a Wolff gorgeous Christmas tree.
On the Eighth Day of Christmas, Lenape Valley gave to me
Youth going carolling,

Congregation's love-notes, Choirs rehearsin',
Sermons that run too long!
Advent candle lighting, Craft Group a-hangin',
Lizzie recruitin', and a Wolff gorgeous Christmas tree.
On the Ninth Day of Christmas, Lenape Valley gave to me
Angels with dead batt'ries, Youth going carolling,
Congregation's love-notes, Choirs rehearsin',
Sermons that run too long!
Advent candle lighting, Craft Group a-hangin',
Lizzie recruitin', and a Wolff gorgeous Christmas tree.
On the Tenth Day of Christmas, Lenape Valley gave to me
Sunday School with cookies,
Angels with dead batt'ries, Youth going carolling,
Congregation's love-notes, Choirs rehearsin',
Sermons that run too long!
Advent Candle lighting, Craft Group a-hangin',
Lizzie recruitin', and a Wolff gorgeous Christmas tree.
On the Eleventh Day of Christmas, Lenape Valley gave to me
Candlelight Communion, Sunday School with cookies,
Angels with dead batt'ries, Youth going carolling,
Congregation's love-notes, Choirs rehearsin',
Sermons that run too long!
Advent Candle lighting, Craft Group a-hangin',
Lizzie recruitin', and a Wolff gorgeous Christmas tree.
On the Twelfth Day of Christmas, Lenape Valley gave to me
Praise to God for Jesus!
Candlelight Communion, Sunday School with cookies,
Angels with dead batt'ries, Youth going carolling,
Congregation's love-notes, Choirs rehearsin',
Sermons that run too long!
Advent Candle lighting, Craft Group a-hangin',
Lizzie recruitin', and a Wolff gorgeous Christmas tree!

For all these things and more, we are all most grateful. Thank
you all so much!

Echoes of That First Christmas
NEWS from Lenape Valley Presbyterian Church,
New Britain, Pennsylvania, December 1981

There is something about the beauty, the purity, the joy in our proper celebration that doesn't quite ring true. Don't get me wrong: I wouldn't change the way we do things for anything. I love our pageant, the application of Chrismons to the beautiful tree, the lighting of the Advent candles, the Christmas Eve Communion, the gorgeous music sung so well, it's tremendous, and we need its beauty, purity, and joy.

But it doesn't quite ring true. Because so often, in participating with such fervor in the traditional programs and activities of Christmas, we think that the *original* participants in Christ's birth were also filled with beauty, purity, and joy. And nothing could be further from the truth. Jesus was born to an oppressed people (He was Jewish, you may remember). Rome was a reasonably benevolent despot, but there were limits. Read the antics of the Herods or of Pontius Pilate, and you have to remember that one needed always to tread carefully.

Jesus, therefore, was born to a people who knew what fear was. What was the first word of the angelic chorus to the shepherds? *"Fear not!" (Luke 2:10).* (The shepherds, by the way, were a persecuted minority group because their livelihood prevented their observing all the proper religious laws.) And remember what happened when the wise men came to Jerusalem? *"Herod the king was troubled, and all Jerusalem with him" (Matthew 2:3).* And in the "slaughter of the innocents," described later in verse 16 of that Chapter, we understand why. Jesus came to a people who evidently knew what anxiety was. Half of Matthew Chapter Six (or, about one-sixth of the Sermon on the Mount) deals with His antidote to anxiety and, likewise, many other of His teachings. (What was His Upper Room legacy? Peace [e.g., John 16:33]) And of course, women had no rights whatsoever, making all of them oppressed, fearful, and anxious.

In other words, Jesus was born into a world not much different from the world many people know today. Oh, to be sure, His coming has produced many changes. His love has inspired ongoing attempts to eliminate slavery, oppression, the subjection of women, fears and anxieties of the most basic kind. But not for everyone. Many who will read these words may feel trapped in one way or another. Many are torn apart by fears and anxieties. Some may even feel oppressed. Some know not the beauty, purity, and joy Christ can bring to a human life. (Note: this was rewritten during both the pandemic and the racial tensions of 2020.)

Friends, it is for you Christ came. It is into your heart He wants to be born each Christmas. As He Himself put it: *"Those who are well have no need of a physician, but those who are sick..." (Luke 5:31).* If there were but one gift that I could give to each of you, whose lives are anything but beautiful and pure and joyful, it would be this: Christ within you, transforming, remolding, shaping, rebuilding, putting Himself at the center, and casting out anything that prevents your being what He would have you be. God offers this rebirth in the manger of your heart every day. Will you accept it and have a *really* Merry Christmas? I pray that you will!

Some Thoughts on Lent and Easter

A Lenten Meditation
NEWS from the Presbyterian Churches of
Claremont and Kasson, Minnesota, Easter 1966

> *Mary…sat at the Lord's feet and listened to His teaching. But Martha was distracted with much serving; and she went to Him and said, "Lord, do you not care that my sister has left me to serve alone? Tell her then to come help me." But the Lord answered her, 'Martha, you are anxious and troubled about many things; one thing is needful."*
> *(Luke 10:39–42)*

There is something quite contemporary in this scene. It is the persistent question, "Do I have time to listen to Jesus when I am so busy? Is it right that I continue to have a dirty house, dishes piled in the sink, just because there is an opportunity to receive further revelation of God's will?" One would think that Jesus settled this for all time with His short but loving remark: *"One thing is needful."* In the final analysis, when suddenly we are brought face-to-face with the living God, we will be judged not on our faithfulness as tidy homemakers, nor our regularity at attending "club," nor the amount of goods we have stored up, but simply on this: "Have you taken the time to discover God's will for your life, and have you done it? Have you loved God and your neighbor? For *that* is what is important."

Yet, we tend to forget this little vignette so quickly, if we ever really remembered it to begin with. So it gets repeated over and over, like a broken instant replay, as almost twenty centuries later Marthas are still trying to prove that Mary's place is more valuable in the kitchen than at Jesus' feet. And when the church attempts to provide new opportunities for sitting and listening, by His feet, the cry is raised, "But we're so busy! Lord (or "Pastor"), do you not care that my (wife, son, sister, check one) has left me to serve alone?"

In reflecting upon what we are busy with, which mirrors pretty accurately what we think is important, I did a little arithmetic with regard to the activities of our typical third grader. I made up a weekly chart of what he normally does during the school year, in a minister's home, where the child does not have the choice as to whether he "wants" to go to Sunday School and church, and where family devotions are not old-fashioned.

Even with this emphasis, obviously not found in homes where Sunday is the day either for visiting or sleeping, and where few meals are eaten as a family, note the small portion taken for the "one thing needful."

78 hours, 50 minutes per *week* in bed

38 hours, 30 minutes in school

11 hours at play (not including school recreation)

8 hours sort of watching TV (often while doing something else)

7 hours, 30 minutes eating (plus five school meals, one "TV supper")

6 hours, 5 minutes dressing and undressing, bathing, cleaning teeth, etc.

5 hours, 20 minutes of Sunday School and church, devotions, prayers, etc.

4 hours, 45 minutes of extra reading

4 hours of homework

2 hours, 30 minutes of chores and errands

1 hour, 30 minutes for Cub Scouts

The point is, of course, that out of the 168 hours given each of us per week, we are all "busy," but only minimally are we busy with the work of the Kingdom. With only so much time available, how easy it is to shortchange the one thing needful in order to be anxious and troubled about many things that really aren't that important. It is significant that even a third grader spends more time each week in keeping the outside clean than the inside.

It isn't that our other activities are sinful. Christ doesn't force us to choose at this point between the evil and the good, but between the good and the best! He died, not that we might be nice, but rather "new creatures"! And at this season especially, when we reflect that Christ died for ungrateful, self-centered folk like you and me, how shallow seem our lives, "distracted with much serving," and how we need to emphasize the "one thing needful...the good portion" of God.

Christ Died for Whom?
NEWS from the Presbyterian Churches of
Claremont and Kasson, Minnesota, March 1969

Each of us, whether we work regularly with the public or not, spends some of his or her life living in the land of Iphonly. We have our own minimal standards for the conduct of others and frequently lament the lives of those we feel have fallen short. "Iphonly that boy would cut his hair, he'd be nice-looking." "Iphonly that girl would quit tearing around in that hot rod, she'd be more useful." And so it goes down the whole roll of our friends and acquaintances: "Iphonly her dresses weren't so short... Iphonly his grammar were better..." and on and on through all the substandard (at least to us) practices and habits in others we can find. One is almost reminded of the old Quaker who was supposed to have said, "No one has any intelligence but me and thee, and sometimes I wonder about thee."

If this were simply a matter of selecting our friends, perhaps it wouldn't matter so much. But sometimes it affects the way in which we, as the Church, reach out to the unchurched: we much prefer people who think and talk and dress and act as we do, rather than those living over in the land of Iphonly. ("Iphonly he wouldn't chew gum, what a fine usher he'd make.")

The curious thing is that nowhere in the New Testament do we find Jesus Christ visiting the land of Iphonly. He visited many towns and villages and homes throughout Palestine but somehow never got to Iphonly. Instead, Jesus had a way of accepting people in whatever condition it was that they came to him: four fishermen, with the smell of the sea on them; a tax-collector, in the midst of counting his ill-gotten gains; an adulterous woman, caught in the act; and countless others. In fact, He said *All that the Father gives me will come to me; and him who comes to me I will not cast out" (John 6:37)* Paul, in

127

amazement, echoes this in Romans 5:8: *"God shows His love for us in that while we were yet sinners Christ died for us."* Isn't that incredible? Not when mankind was cleaned up and receptive, all bright-eyed and bushy-tailed but while we were sinners, at the very height of our disobedience and rebellion! It was then that Christ died for your sake and for mine.

Nothing points up more the difference between our normal attitudes and "the mind of Christ." We set our minimal standards, as it seems good to us, and let the world know: "As soon as you come up to what I consider to be a minimal standard of conduct, I will accept you as a person, perhaps even as a friend." Jesus simply says, *"Follow me, and I will make you fishers of men" (Mark 4:19).* Come to me first, *then* I will make of you what you can be. See the difference?

If He had waited until X number of people subscribed to minimal Christianity, there would have been no crucifixion…no Easter… no Church…no America. But He didn't! He gave Himself in love to people who abandoned Him and even hated Him, and the shock of that kind of love, rather than the force of coercion, transformed their lives. How hard it is for us to realize that Christ died not only for nice people like you and me, but also for those people we can't stand: the chronic complainers (read Matthew 11:16–19), the lazy, the loud and obnoxious, the whiners, the immature, the stupid, the outcasts, and the drunks and the crooks.

If Jesus died and rose again for such as these (such as we), shouldn't we think twice about *not* caring for these kinds of people? At the same time, for anyone reading this who feels like an outcast for one reason or another, there is great comfort in these words. For Christ does not demand, my friend, that you be socially prominent, or talented, beautiful, or rich. All He demands is that you—and I— be totally obedient when He says, "Follow me."

The words of the old hymn are true:
Just as I am, without one plea
But that Thy blood was shed for me,
And that Thou biddest me come to Thee:
O Lamb of God, I come, I come.

I Don't Like Lent
NEWS from Lenape Valley Presbyterian Church, New Britain, Pennsylvania, Lent 1971

"If you insist on saving your life, you will lose it. Only those who throw away their lives for my sake and for the sake of the Good News will ever know what it means to really live." (Jesus in Mark 8:35, Children's Living Bible)

"Life is like a sewer: you only get out of it what you put into it." (pianist/comedian Tom Lehrer)

I don't like Lent a whole lot. The whole emphasis is on giving—giving time for extra services; giving money and money-instead-of-desserts for the world's needy; giving for others to the limit as Christ did on Good Friday.

What I'd rather do is get!

But you know what? Many summers ago, at a senior-high summer conference, I learned something very important about myself, something which proved the truth both of Jesus' traditional and of Tom Lehrer's rather gross comments. I was director of this conference, had a blue-chip staff, and had returned from vacation just a few days beforehand, looking forward to a week of inspiration, fellowship, and no responsibility. By Wednesday, I was miserable. Everything was in capable hands; the kids were great, and I was miserable. Where was the love I had anticipated? Why wasn't I feeling a part of the fellowship? Why did I feel as if I were on the outside looking in?

Suddenly, I realized what the problem was: I was contributing nothing, expressing love to no one (except old buddies), sharing my faith with no one. And since I had invested nothing of myself, it was inevitable that I was getting no return on my zero investment. So I asked my old song leader buddie Carl if I could take a turn at song leading, and he said "Sure," and suddenly I had joined the camp. "Uncle Dan" became a contributing member of the conference community instead of just a warm body receiving food and other nour-ishment. And from that time on, the week was all I had anticipated and more.

Valuable lesson, wouldn't you say? I had needs that had to be met, and they were met in abundance when I took the initiative and gave of myself to meet the needs of others. It was a lesson I've never forgotten in congregation, community, or Presbytery activities. As Jesus promised, I really come alive and feel as if I am needed and loved in direct proportion to my willingness to throw away my life for Christ's sake and the sake of the Good News. This is what Lent reminds us of, and I really don't like it because naturally I'd rather get than give. But I know I'll never get unless I give first, so I humble myself before the greater wisdom of the Master and get thrilled again and again as His promise is fulfilled.

One more thing I've discovered: The more I give, the less I need. When I'm "down" and want to be stroked, my own needs seem insurmountable. But when I get wrapped up in the needs of others, my own seem to vanish. How do you feel about Lent, about getting by giving, about "throwing away your life" for Christ's sake in order to have your valid needs met? How about making an experimen-tal covenant with God from now until Easter (one month away) to really give it a try? Then, as you find yourself fulfilled and thrilled in so many ways with the truth of Christ's words, how about letting me in on it so I can rejoice with you?

The Disciplines of Lent
NEWS from Lenape Valley Presbyterian Church, New Britain, Pennsylvania, March 1972

There was a time when we knew of the arrival of Lent by the smudges of ash on the foreheads of our Catholic neighbors and by the relentless commercials about food for "meatless Lenten meals." Typically, we Protestants reacted with low-grade humor, announcing that we were giving up something we never did like anyway (such as maybe swallowing goldfish). In recent years, Roman Catholic discipline has eased considerably; our low-grade humor is about the same as ever. And yet, there is something to be said for discipline. Every time I read of a champion in any sport, or of a championship team, I read of the discipline that was required. Hours upon hours of practice, of repetition, or of programming the reflexes so that certain actions and reactions become second nature. And in a crisis, it was the split-second saved by a reflex becoming automatic that made the difference.

I'm not suggesting anyone try for a club championship in things spiritual; yet, even Paul saw the parallel between sports and Christianity and spoke of us ultimately becoming "more than conquerors" through and for Jesus Christ. Surely there must be some discipline involved in that! A casual study of the life of Christ reveals three points (at least) at which His own personal discipline showed through. Luke 4:16 tells us: *"He went to the synagogue, as His custom was, on the Sabbath Day."* So the discipline of regular worship was a part of Christ's life. And remember: it wasn't a question of whether or not He liked the minister: He had an ongoing battle with the leaders of the temple and synagogues themselves! Yet even He felt a closeness to God and a need for corporate worship that evidently even He could find nowhere else. Do you suppose He was trying to tell us something?

On another occasion, we read in Mark 10:1, *"Crowds gathered to Him again; and again,* as His custom was, *He taught them."* This to me implies two disciplines: that of study and of witness. For how can anyone teach without having something to say? If you know anything of the Gospels, you know of Christ's thorough knowledge of the Scriptures. But note also how eager He always was to share, illustrate, and apply those teachings to the questioning men and women who followed Him around. Is there anyone following us around? Perhaps, if we have nothing to say, it's because we haven't studied!

Then at last, on the night of His betrayal, *"He came out, and went,* as was His custom, *to the Mount of Olives" (Luke 22:39).* And there, in the Garden of Gethsemane, Jesus wrestled through the horrible possibility of crucifixion; there Judas knew for sure He could be found. Why? Because Jesus led a disciplined life of prayer, and a major part of His lifestyle was slipping away to "check in" with His Father as to the next steps in the divine plan.

We talk sometimes about imitating Christ's lifestyle, and because it's so much higher than ours, we feel doomed before we begin. But for the next weeks of Lent, let's concentrate on these three disciplines which Christ made part of His own victorious life: regular worship, an appealing witness based on regular study, and regular times (as well as places) of prayer. Let these disciplines become habit, second nature to you! And see if victorious living isn't yours as well.

Easter, When Christ Gave In…and Won!
NEWS from Lenape Valley Presbyterian Church, New Britain, Pennsylvania, March 1979

I was reflecting upon many hours of conversations with many of you in recent weeks, all of them productive in their way, as we who are in so many stages of growth try to understand one another, love one another, and help one another over the rocks that often make our pilgrimage difficult. Suddenly, I saw Easter in a whole new perspective: victory through surrender! And perhaps that's the whole point: reminding us that God's power is so fantastic that He wins even when He seems to lose. He lets the world do whatever it wants to to His incarnate Son: beat Him, spit on Him, crucify Him, lay Him in a tomb; and even then, a stone rolled across the opening, sealed and guarded, could not contain Him!

What makes this so startling in the present context is the realization that while we who are "inside" look down at those trying to run their own lives "outside" and preach to them, saying, "Why don't you let God take over your life?" we have much difficulty living by the same rule-of-thumb once we are "inside"! We often get upset and really begin to put each other down within the fellowship whenever we suspect that something is not being planned or carried out according to Scripture as *we* have perceived it. And in our less-than-total perception of God's truth, in our spiritually myopic insistence that the piece of Christian elephant we are fondling is the whole beast, we miss the basic point that Jesus Christ is Lord even *within* the Church: that God's victory on Easter Sunday means that in no way, in no circumstance, can He ever lose, and that even includes within the local congregation.

To be specific: Jesus Christ first of all *surrendered to church leaders* who were on the wrong track. It was leaders who believed they were doing God's will who delivered Him up to be crucified. And God let them. They even arranged for guards for the tomb and lost! The victory lasted only forty hours before Christ arose and confounded them. Why then should *we* get so upset with church leaders and each other, anyone who hasn't the insights, perspective, and/or maturity we have? Let them go, let them win, for a time, because one way of another, God *cannot* lose! Surrender to Him, as Christ did, relax and anticipate the ultimate victory.

Jesus also *surrendered to the political power play.* Quite a play. Pilate to Herod to Pilate to Calvary, if you're scoring at home. Not a word in His own defense, just a word which sealed His own doom. Yet, how often do we fight anger with anger instead of love, fight power with power instead of weakness, and generally, by our words and actions, give a witness opposite that of the Christ we claim to serve? Feel squeezed out, unjustly put upon, ignored? Surrender, *for so persecuted they the prophets which were before you (Mathew 5:12b).* The ultimate power is God's; He cannot be overthrown. Be at peace with Him and expect the victory.

Finally, Jesus *surrendered to pain and death.* He saved others; He refused to save Himself. Certainly, He could have come down from the cross, but where would you and I be then? The key to the open door of eternal life rests in the fact that Jesus of Nazareth, fully human (as He was also wholly divine), surrendered to pain, suffering, and death and came back to tell us it really wasn't all that bad. And yet, how many hours do we spend trying to convince God that *we* really have the key as to who ought to be healed, restored, made whole? It's a little scary: that's the same package the Devil offered Eve in the Garden! Our mandate is to surrender ourselves and our loved ones, together with their problems, to God; even as Christ surrendered that Good Friday and won! Yield to Him! And receive the joyous freedom of the much-loved servant of the victorious Master.

Gamaliel once saved the necks of Peter and John by using the words found in Acts 5:39: *"If it is of God, you will not be able to stop these men; you will only find yourselves fighting against God."* These words spell out Christian surrender: Letting go and letting God. It is the hidden message of Easter. May it be your watchword and joy all year long!

Echoes of Easter
NEWS from Lenape Valley Presbyterian Church, New Britain, Pennsylvania, May 1988

"For to me to live is Christ, and to die is gain" (Philippians 1:21). Have I remembered to tell you that I was dying? (I'll bet *that* got your attention!) Hopefully, not in the near future (although that isn't something that I can determine. Each of us the capacity to shorten, but not lengthen, life.) And each of you is in the same situation as I am, like it or not. This may come as a shocking realization in a culture committed at whatever cost to denying the aging process in order to stay "younger." Rinse the gray away! Get rid of those horrid age spots! Work out at our spa and add years to your life! Do whatever you can to deny one of the central realities of life: each of us is mortal and must someday die.

But now, let's put away the boxes of Kleenex and think about this rationally. If in fact I learned (as every day people learn) that some bacterial instrument of Satan within me was going to deny my reaching the anticipated threescore years and ten: what would I do? (This was somewhat prophetic, written thirty-two years before the devastating effects of Covid-19.) The *first thing* that comes to mind is to be sure to tell my family and friends how much they mean to me, and how much I appreciate them. Say it in person, say it in letters, "reach out and touch someone" (and thank you for using AT&T). We don't do enough of this with those we are close to. Oh, we plan to do it someday when this current crisis is over. But the truth is that "someday" doesn't come often enough. We criticize at once; we affirm when we get around to it. And, oh yes, include God on that list. And sometimes, we may also need to apologize and ask for forgiveness.

A *second thing* that comes to mind is to "make today count" (to borrow the theme of a leading cancer support group) with spouse, children, and (if you're fortunate enough to still have one or both) parents. Our onetime landlord at a summer home at Barnegat Light confided sadly our last evening there two years ago that his wife would never spend any of the money they were accumulating to take the trips he wanted to take. Then, suddenly, she was gone, and all he had was the bank account. Make today count! Knock off work early and go on a picnic! Take your kids to the zoo or just stay home and *listen* to them. And, as the popular song goes, "If you should survive to a hundred and five, think of all you have gained just by being alive!"

And of course (and some might put this first): to *make sure that life's proper priorities fall into place.* No one has ever said it better than Jesus: "Do not lay up for yourselves treasures on earth, where moth and rust consume and where thieves break in and steal; but lay up for yourselves treasures in Heaven, where neither moth nor rust consume and where thieves do not break in and steal. For where your treasure is, there will your heart be also" (Mathew 6:19–21).

I guess, by modern standards, we were terrible parents. We never took our four kids to Disney World/Land. They didn't have their own credit cards. They didn't have their own cars in high school. We didn't dig for them and their friends a pool in the backyard. I'm surprised the county didn't take them away from us, deprived as they were! Praise God each one had Jesus, and we're grateful for that and proud of them.

That's what I mean by priorities. Jesus never said riches or material things were evil or bad. He just said that they tend to get in the way of putting Him first! And if we realize that one day (only the Father knows when) we will see Him face-to-face and begin to spend eternity with Him, then perhaps putting Him first now isn't such a bad idea. Paul's words in Philippians 1 (quoted above) are mind-blowing if you're not a Christian. If you are, who would want to stay here? If, like Paul, you've had an appetizer of love, joy, peace, and power here, and know how much better it's going to be at the promised banquet in heaven, well, where would you want to live? Let's not be in a hurry, but neither should we be unprepared.

An Attempt to Contain Easter
NEWS from Lenape Valley Presbyterian Church, New Britain, Pennsylvania, May 1992

"So they went and made the sepulchre secure by sealing the stone and setting a guard" (Mathew 27:66). For the benefit of those of you who couldn't make it (as well as those who did but don't mind reruns), I'd like to recap the last portion of my Easter Sunday sermon. (You might want to reread Matthew 27:57–28:10 before you get started.) The first portion of the sermon dealt with the futile attempts of the religious authorities to dispose of Jesus and how, in fear that His disciples might steal the body from the tomb and then claim resurrection, they went to the Roman leaders, with the results summarized in the text above. And of course, it didn't work. There was another earthquake (the first was Good Friday); the stone was rolled away, and the tomb was found to be empty! We then, in the sermon, spent the rest of our brief time together exploring the significance of all this, viz.:

1. *The stone was rolled away, not to let Jesus out, but to let the witnesses in!* Surely, the same Jesus Who appeared through locked doors to the disciples cowering in the upper room (John 2:19) could easily have appeared through the stone that sealed the tomb. But then, how could we have known for sure that the tomb was indeed empty? With the stone removed, it was easy for Mary Magdalene, the other women, and then Peter and John, to witness personally that Jesus no longer lay there. John's personal account (20:1–10) is particularly revealing: he and Peter ran to the tomb, with John (the younger) outrunning Peter but stopping at the

entrance; Peter (the impetuous one) brushing by him to enter; John joining him to share in the sight of the cloths which had once wrapped Jesus' body being collapsed, as if what they had once contained had simply dematerialized (which, in truth it had. Jesus simply changed His mortal body for the resurrection body to which we can all look forward.) The stone was rolled away, not so Jesus could get out, but so the witnesses could get in.

2. *The angel was there as a guest preacher to remind them of what they already knew but had forgotten.* Matthew tells us that *"an angel of the Lord descended from Heaven and came and rolled back the stone, and sat upon it" (28:2).* The word *angel* comes from the Greek *angelos* or "messenger." His message was simply to remind them of what had been told them before: *"He is not here; for He has risen, as He said" (Mathew 28:6).* And isn't that what we preachers do? We are certainly not angels, but surely should be messengers sent to remind you of what you have already heard and believed but have perhaps forgotten. And that is why regular attendance at corporate worship is so important: we need constantly to be reminded of the truth of what we believe, of who we are, and Whose we are! The angel was the guest preacher sent to remind them of what they had already been told.

3. *When Christ appeared, it was not to His enemies, but only to those who had believed beforehand.* We're not sure of the exact order. The Gospel writers agree that Mary Magdalene was among the first at the empty tomb; different writers list different women with her (or, in John's case, none). Luke tells us of the two, Cleopas and another who is unnamed (perhaps the wife of Cleopas, in Luke 24:13–35) to whom Christ appeared on the road to Emmaus. Paul, in 1 Corinthians 15:3–8, typically omits the women but gives additional information: *"He appeared to Cephas (Peter), then to the twelve. Then He appeared to more than five hundred brethren at one time... Then He appeared to James (Jesus'*

brother), then to all the apostles. Last of all, as to one untimely born, He appeared also to me." (Jesus' only appearance to one who at that time was an unbeliever). Never does Jesus yield to the temptation to return to those who had crucified Him in order to say "Aha! You didn't get me after all. The laugh's on you!" No, other than Saul/Paul, He only appeared to those who had believed beforehand. And even today, He will become known to any who truly seek Him and want to enter into fellowship with Him. Remember the Old Testament story of Asa, King of Israel? He and his people *wanted God above everything else, and they found Him! (2 Chronicles 15:15).* So it can be for us today with our living Lord.

4. *Not even a "Master" could hold the Master!* The tomb, sealed and guarded, was the New Testament equivalent of today's master lock. Jesus's enemies had done everything humanly possible to stop Him, to defeat Him. One of His own (Judas Iscariot, of the original twelve) had betrayed Him. Those claiming to be God's exalted rulers violated many of their own sacred laws in seeing to His execution. He was humiliated by being spat upon, insulted, and falsely accused. He was beaten to a pulp with the cruel scourge; collapsed while carrying His own cross to the place of execution; and nailed to that cross, where for at least three hours, He hung in agony. Then, as a final straw, His corpse was guarded by infidel Romans. He took upon Himself everything that can possibly happen to any of us: deceit, humiliation, reception, false accusation, insult, heartbreak, physical cruelty, even death, and overcame them all! Through all of this, He just...kept on going!

That's why we rejoice at Easter. Easter is not an Energiser Bunny that "keeps on going." It is the One who loved us even as we resisted and rejected Him, who took upon Him all that can possibly ever befall us, and was victorious, not as a rabbit, but as a King! And the glorious truth of Easter is that all who commit their lives to Him will share His victory, not just over death, but over life itself! Hallelujah! Let us rejoice!

Reflections on The Way
NEWS from Lenape Valley Presbyterian Church,
New Britain, Pennsylvania, April 1993

"And they were on the road, going up to Jerusalem, and Jesus was walking ahead of them; and they were amazed, and those who followed were afraid" (Mark 10:32). During these past Sunday mornings and Wednesday evenings of Lent (spring of 1993), we have been on The Way, following after Jesus with amazement, perhaps some fears, but always seeking to increase our faith. Because of illness, our cluttered schedules, and some bad weather (cancelling Sunday the fourteenth and Wednesday the seventeenth), not everyone has been able to attend everything. To assist in your preparation for Easter Sunday, here, briefly, is what we have said: We began with the *Call to the Mountain* (Mark 9:2–8); the Mount of Transfiguration where Moses and Elijah appeared to Jesus, with Peter, James, and John looking on. This was literally a time of confirmation, God saying, *"This is my beloved Son; listen to Him" (Mark 9:7b).* For the disciples, it was a time of commissioning. They were in faith to proceed, having been reassured that Jesus was in fact the promised Messiah.

Yet, as inspiring as these mountaintops may be, we cannot stay there (read Mark 9:5). We have to leave and return to the valley, where, inevitably, by way of a letter, a message on the answering machine or an urgent conversation, we meet the modern equivalent of the epileptic boy (read Mark 9:14–29). This necessitates our embarking on *The Way of Faith*, for it is only through the faith enhanced on the mountaintop that we are given the spiritual strength to overcome the hidden obstacles that await us each day. How often have we, like this boy's father, cried out *"Lord, I believe; help my unbelief" (Mark 9:24)*? Such a cry inevitably is answered in the affirmative.

If we go regularly to the mountain (a pilgrimage our daily devotions and worship may fulfill) and there receive strength for the valley below, why then does not everyone follow in The Way? Probably because it is also *The Way of Self-Denial* (read Luke 14:25–33). As Tom Lewis put it succinctly in our midweek study guide: "We are not people who are naturally drawn to self-denial." It is, in fact, counterculture. We must put Christ first materially, morally, and magnetically (that is, in the people we are either drawn to or repelled by). Since the call of the world is so strong, small wonder that the words of John 6:66 can apply regularly today: *"After this many of His disciples drew back and no longer went about with Him."*

Complicating our discipleship is the next step on the Way: *The Way of Love* (read John 13:31–35). Why is that so? Because Christian love (love *agape* way) is not given as an option just for days when we feel so inclined. *"This I command you,"* says Jesus firmly the night of His betrayal, *"to love one another" (John 13:34)*. It is in addition a new context for love: *"As the Father has loved me, so have I loved you...as I have loved you...love one another" (John 15:9, 12)*. The love we are to have is sacrificial, unconditional, and empowering (SUE, if you prefer). In addition, we now have a new concept of religion because of this new commandment. It has nothing to do with external trappings (read 1 Corinthians 13:3). It has to do with relationships: *"By this all (persons) will know that you are my disciples, if you have love for one another" (John 13:35)*. Love thus becomes not what we say, but what we are.

Now, if we master that part, the next is not so difficult: *The Way of Service* (read John 13:1–16). If we do not have love, service is a chore. But if *the love of Christ controls us* (as Paul puts it in 2 Corinthians 5:14), nothing is beneath us, no one unworthy of our care. If in love, Christ died for me, unworthy as I am, should I not be willing also to serve you, another sinner for whom Christ died? Once again, we are at a difficult spot on the Way. We now have faith, love, and are willing to serve. We're home free, right? Not always. For some, there is also *The Way of Suffering* (read Luke 22:39–64). Not that we must all suffer as Christ did—there are other pains. In school or work, perhaps even at home, we may take verbal abuse for our stand along the Way. Others fall under the demonic power of the Enemy and are subjected to physical or social or emotional problems they simply do not deserve. Yet, even as Christ found strength to face the cross, so also we are given strength. Read John 9: the great story showing how God does indeed have the power to bring light into darkness, good out of evil!

If we have persevered thus far, we can with confidence approach our ultimate destination: *The Way of Eternal Life* (read Luke 24:36–49). You see, this Way has been a time of testing; God testing us, we testing God to see if His promises are true and sure. And they have been! Knowing this, we can with confidence approach that which awaits each of us: our mortal death, knowing that it is but a change of address: the fulfillment of our pilgrimage, the graduation to that which is pure and perfect. Does not this assurance make the journey worthwhile? My conviction is that it does! Come, join us on the Way as we follow Jesus to glory and victory!

Reflections
on Marriage

[Note: in my sixty years as an active pastor,
I conducted 402 weddings.]

Sharing an Important Secret
NEWS from Lenape Valley Presbyterian Church,
New Britain, Pennsylvania, June 1979

Somehow, Amy and I would like to express properly our thanks for the lovely reception and remembrance you gave us following the service on June 17 in honor of our twenty-fifth anniversary. It was a complete surprise and an event we shall long cherish. It was really quite a day, starting early with the fine Daybreak (teen choir) service at Salem United Church of Christ in Doylestown at eight-thirty, concluding with their part in the Neshaminy Presbyterian (indoor) lawn service, and containing such unique components as the unexpected visit of two Claremont, Minnesota friends (Andy Dodds and Lyle Lyke, complete with their huge North American Van Lines van!); your approval of bringing to fruition our dreams and plans for a new building; Bob Wherry's eloquent presentation of the meaning of the hymn "Blest Be the Tie That Binds"; the beautiful coffee service and the lovely cakes; the dozens of you who made it a point to be present that Sunday and share love with a word, a glance, a hug, a card. We were, and are, much moved and appreciative and pray that all who had any part in this serendipitous subterfuge will accept this faltering attempt at thanks.

The irony of all this is that even as some of us are celebrating, all that is involved in sharing nearly 9,200 days and nights of one-on-one bed and board, through our Spiritual Life Committee, we are, with a sense of urgency, exploring ways to strengthen the marriages of couples who may not even know they have a problem, as well as ways to minister to those who in rapidly increasing numbers have resolved that strength lies in separation rather than in union.

In reflecting upon all this in recent weeks, it occurred to me that someone might ask, "What is the secret of surviving twenty-five years of marriage?" No one did, so, rather than waste an effort at simple profundity, let me share briefly my conclusions. (They are indeed mine; Amy, who, being married to me, had a more difficult task, might suggest others.)

To keep a marriage afloat requires sailing daily on three C's: Compassion, Communication, and Cuddling.

Compassion, a stronger word for Christians than the overworked word *love* (*agape* is what we're talking about), simply means respecting and caring for your partner as a person with needs and not simply as a conjugal consort under contract to scratch *your* itch! William Barclay's familiar definition of *agape* as "that conquest of self that enables us to develop an unconquerable caring for other people" is nowhere more vital than within the intimacy of marriage.

Communication is the *sine qua non* of marriage. A husband/wife ought to be before anything else the other's best friend with whom dreams, hopes, insights, frustrations—indeed all of life!—can be shared, even as in the days of courtship! Husbands, run through your mental shredder that false "macho" image that inhibits your sharing your hurts with your wife, lest you "lose face." No one wants more to be an instrument of healing. And wives: don't get so over-involved as a mother that you forget to be a wife! You need periodically to abandon your children (without guilt!), in order to be alone with your husband, in order to reopen the stifled, inhibited channels of communication.

Cuddling is the most fun: why should we ever outgrow it? Why does the honeymoon have to end? "Touch my hair as you pass my chair; little things mean a lot" is a line from an old popular song with timeless implications. You see, human dynamics being as they are, one can be physically intimate without being close; and being close is what we need most. This means, of course: being of a size and shape and aroma that is cuddlesome! When "He's/She's twice the man/woman I married" means more than growth of character, there's a problem that needs attention.

There's much more, of course, but this is a little bit gleaned from our first twenty-five years (of which the first ten years were the hardest) of wedded bliss. Sail on these 3 C's, with Christ the fourth, the perpetual unseen guest holding all together, and you won't go far wrong.

"Dearly Beloved, We Are Gathered Here..."
NEWS from Lenape Valley Presbyterian Church,
New Britain, Pennsylvania, May 1983

Remember how many times I have said, as we have continued to baptize and confirm more girls than boys in Lenape Valley Church, "Someday, someone is going to have a lot of weddings." Well, that someday is now, and the someone is me! Seven so far this year (versus six for all of 1982), with another *fourteen* scheduled through the end of October. It seems that every time I publish for the benefit of organist Charles and secretary Mary Ann, another "revised" list, someone else calls! All of which simply means that weddings and marriages are much on my mind; so perhaps, thinking of no one in particular and everyone in general, it is well to make a few observations. (Incidentally, the third edition of the *Marriage Manual* is now on the literature rack, which means we have given out two hundred in less than five years.)

First of all, I want to say the obvious: *marriage is for adults.* I say this not only because marriages of those under the age of twenty-one have always made me nervous but also because the bulk (if not the totality) of marriage counselling I do with couples in trouble involve at least one of the two partners who married before the age of twenty-one. As Amy and I discovered at the "mature" age of eighteen that each was the one the other had been looking for "all those years," my mother used to warn me about how much one changes between the ages of eighteen and twenty-one. Mark Twain once observed something like this: "It's amazing how much smarter Mother has gotten the last thirty years." Mother was correct! And the only way still-maturing couples make it for a lifetime is when they recognize they *will* change, they plan to change, and they commit themselves to change together. And needless to say, to marry simply to get away from home, finding a "father-figure" or a "mother-figure" is to create problems too complex for this page. How long can one enjoy being, or being married to, a child? Marriage is for adults.

Secondly: marriage is for the honest. I have often said that I wished I'd kept a record of all the reasons given for wanting to get married, not on the original schedule, but a week from next Thursday. Some are really far-fetched! And in each case, within a few months, the truth was apparent: the stork arrived a bit earlier than had been planned. By the same token, a more modern phenomenon involves those couples (generally over thirty, with at least one partner previously married) who are timid about mentioning the fact that they already share the same address and have decided to seek God's blessing upon their union. (In the years since this was first written, this has almost become the norm.)

Not being an ordained snoop, I never ask "Are you pregnant?" "Are you living together?" But I would appreciate knowing either (or both, in some cases) of those facts. Why? Two reasons: first, I can perhaps then be a more effective premarital counselor. Generally, there is guilt involved in either or both situations, and it would be healthy to deal with that along the way. But second: if there is not complete honesty in the wedding plans, what assurance is there that there will be honesty in the marriage afterward? One tends to wince at the words at the beginning of the wedding ceremony: "If anyone is joined together other than as God's Word allows, their union is not blessed by Him." God prefers honesty. [Since originally writing this several decades ago, I once had the misfortune of performing a ceremony following which every check: to me, the organist, the sexton, the church, bounced! I have often wondered how a marriage built on deception turned out. The couple moved from the area shortly after the wedding.]

Third: Christian marriage is for the spiritually minded. I have frequently said that I am not a magician. I can do no tricks, card or otherwise. (I even have trouble shuffling a deck of cards!) The water I apply at baptism does not—presto, chango!—produce instant saints. And a marriage in a church no more guarantees a solid marriage than living in a garage makes you a Rolls Royce!

It is simple. We are born self-centered, always insisting on our own way. Until we are changed, we retain vestiges of that selfishness. And it is selfishness, more than anything else, that destroys marriages. Only the love of Jesus Christ within us enables us to love others more than self (and God more than either), thus giving us the patience, tolerance, understanding, love, and inner peace that are the foundation for a lot of joyous tomorrows. It is not the wedding in the church that makes a marriage work, but Christ in the marriage!

Five Steps to a Successful Marriage
NEWS from Lenape Valley Presbyterian Church,
New Britain, Pennsylvania, June 1985

It's that time of year again. Including our own daughter Sally's wedding here on July 29: there are ten weddings of various sizes on the schedule in an eleven-week period. At the same time this is happening, the distraught voices again and again on the office phone alert me to the prevalence of what, for want of a better term, I would call the "splitsville virus" attacking far too many of our couples and families. (Close to a dozen at that time were on my daily prayer list. I'm sure that didn't include all the marriages that were having difficulty of one kind or another.) So, for what it might be worth, I feel led to summarize what I like to share with couples immediately prior to their marriage. Based upon our own nearly forty-one years of experience (and mistakes!) in attempting to define the answer to my question "How can you stay married the next fifty years?" I suggest five ways (at least) in which a couple ought to relate in marriage.

1. The first and most basic area is that of *Friendship*. Two people meet; they are attracted to one another, feel comfortable with one another. They find they are willing to be vulnerable with one another. They enjoy each other's company: in fact, prefer one another to anyone else. However, there is in this dimension of the relationship a caution. In my experience, the friendship between husband and wife is the most difficult part of the marriage to maintain. As with any other friendship with acquaintances outside the family, it has to be worked on constantly. Parents need time away from their children on a regular basis simply to maintain (or sometimes reconstruct) the all-important basic dimension of friendship.

149

2. At some time in the development of the friendship, perhaps at a time neither partner can identify, it is decided that they want to be more than friends. They want to enter into the *Marital* stage of the relationship. But as Burt Reynolds and Goldie Hawn discovered in the old film *Best Friends*, something seems to happen to a friendship when it deepens to the marital level. (Statistics show that couples living together before marriage have a higher divorce rate than those who do not.) One reason may be the psychological effect of expressing their feelings publicly before God, parents and family, friends, and the officiating pastor(s). Another reason may be symbolized in the oft-used nuptial candle: the implication suggested in two becoming one, not just physically, but as well in hopes and dreams and goals! (This symbolism is even more powerful if one of the partners comes from a Roman Catholic background and in effect is using his or her baptismal candle, given many years before, to light the unity candle.)

3. I also have come to firmly believe that there needs to be in a good marriage a relationship on the *Parental* level: both husband and wife need to be willing at times to parent the other or be parented by the other as the need arises. This requires the dual ability to be both sensitive and vulnerable. Remember how, when you had a really bad day at school, you guys came home and dumped on Mom? Or you gals came home and cried on Dad's shoulder? They couldn't fix the problem, but they could listen, affirm, comfort, and reassure you that whatever else might have gone wrong, you always had a haven of love there. No matter how old we are, there are times when we still need this, except that, with parents grown old or gone, we look to our spouses instead.

4. There is also the all-important *Sensual* (sexual or erotic) dimension in a good marriage. "Dear Abby" once referred to sex as "one of God's most generous gifts," which it is—a gift to be shared within the bonds of marriage to the fullest

extent. However, for better or worse, it is also a need, sometimes even an appetite, which we have, and when that need is unmet, problems can arise. (A good parallel: never go food shopping when you're hungry!) While this may seem strange to a young couple chomping at the bit for the honeymoon, as situations change, children arrive, and jobs are more demanding, this dimension, like that of friendship, needs to be worked on, with time scheduled and set aside for its enjoyment.

5. Finally (though it forms the foundation upon which all the other dimensions should be built), there is the *Spiritual* dimension. The typical couple today has spouses of differing religious backgrounds or perhaps none at all. Yet, experience has shown that the spiritual dimension is the "glue" that holds everything else together. We can apply that familiar law of physics which states that two objects, as they are drawn closer to a common object, are inevitably drawn closer to one another. When it is to God, through Jesus Christ, that they are drawn, their own closeness necessarily follows. Or perhaps you prefer the acronym JOY from "Brian's Song": Jesus first, Others second, Yourself third. Great formula for a solid and long-lasting relationship.

I generally close this little talk by suggesting that if the couple can do really well in three of the five areas, they should have a long and loving relationship. In any event, it has worked for us for over forty years!

An Exercise in Latin Weddings
NEWS from Lenape Valley Presbyterian Church,
New Britain, Pennsylvania, September 1987

With the increasing numbers of weddings we've had and will continue to have, and with the seriousness with which we take them, whether the couple involved is from our congregation or not, I got to thinking over the summer months about the different kinds of weddings I've observed over the years and the relationships (or lack of same) they inaugurated. Here are some of the kinds I can recall, alphabetized according to their ersatz Latin titles. By the grace of God, the vast majority of these marriages survived *anyway!* But it wasn't always easy.

Autos obsolescencos: the typical American GM syndrome. Buy it, use it up, replace it with something better and/or more modern. Okay for cars and trucks (or even TVs): devastating for mothers, fathers, and especially for children.

Borus Weekendus: Had a fraternity brother who once pulled this trick. You bored too? Let's run down to Maryland and get married. Have often wondered what happened in that relationship. In my experience, getting married is not the ultimate answer to boring weekends. (Alternative: Try giving of yourself…)

Condo Rento: Similar in many ways to *Autos obsolescencos* but infused with more Yuppiedom. This is the "starter set" syndrome in marriage, seen a lot among showbiz and sports hero types, but not limited to them. "She's/he's fine for now; but I'll need someone more cultured and sophisticated the further up the ladder I climb." (Somehow, that is seen as easier than *growing together* through life.)

Haftus Hurriuppus, the virus from which no family is ever completely immune, in which somehow travel plans gets reversed, and the stork gets there slightly before Cupid and the minister do! When the combination of love and human frailty produce this condition, many solid, long-term marriages are produced anyway, despite the double adjustment (parenthood and marriage) initially.

Homus Escapus. Someone (typically, but not exclusively, the girl) can't stand it at home and takes the first offer that comes, frequently from a boy or girl who can't stand it at home either! The chief problem here is that marriage is not an A-frame building. If two run to each other in order to lean upon each other, and neither is strong (make that "mature") enough to stand alone, what happens when one falls? Some of the most difficult relationships often come out of this kind of situation. Remember: marriage is for adults; teens running away from home don't qualify.

Socialis Eventis: my least favorite type and the one for whom I have the least sympathy (as opposed to the last two where there is obviously a lot of emotional pain). The focus here is neither the sacred vows nor even the two lives being intertwined; rather, the total effect of the staging (time of day; quantities of flowers; numbers of candles, attendants, and guests; drama of the getaway: stretch limo? Carriage and stretch horse? and, most important of all, the extravagance and place of the reception.) But you know: I've watched these from the first month of my first parish and have yet to see even the slightest correlation between the quantity of funds expended for weddings (gowns, flowers, and reception) and the *quality* of love in the relationship (as well as the durability of the marriage).

But there is one other I would hope all would consider: *Theos Ordinatos,* the relationship ordained by God. Adam, in that ancient Eden story, was incomplete. Therefore, Eve was created and brought to him. Doesn't that tell you something? The prologue to our old, traditional service reminds us that God "has established and sanctified marriage *for the welfare and happiness of mankind.*" Isn't that awesome?

The point is really quite simple: our Christian faith teaches that our loving and personal God has a stake in our marriages, as well as the homes and families they produce. When, through Jesus Christ, we commit our way to Him, thereby finding out who we are and what He has in mind for us, and *then*_(hopefully, only then) find that person He wants us to share that plan with, Wow! That's love, permanence, joy, and much peace.

An Old, Recurring Virus
NEWS from Lenape Valley Presbyterian Church, New Britain, Pennsylvania, March 1989

An epidemic has been sweeping our nation in recent years and has of late been touching our congregation in frightening proportions. It is a virus that too often seems impervious to any antibiotic. It is a disease from which the carriers all too often seem not to want to be cured. No, I'm not talking about the flu. I'm talking about the painful scourge of divorce.

Pastors are sometimes asked, "What's the problem? Why do so many couples who begin their relationships with high hopes all too soon reach the point at which they feel it would be in everyone's best interests if they separated, even knowing that not only they, but their children (if there are any) will to some extent carry the painful scars for life?" There is no one answer. Sometimes, marriage is entered into for the wrong reasons. Gert Behanna said that she quickly said Yes to her first proposal because she was afraid no one else would ask her. Oftentimes, it is the immaturity, their unwillingness to take responsibility, of one or the other (or perhaps both) of the partners that is the cause.

But I have not felt led to write this in order to analyze causes. Rather, I want to share God's original plan for making these relationships work. The point is not to add pain to the many who are already hurting but, rather, to strengthen the bonds of those already committed to one another. That plan is found in Genesis 2, in the second of the two creation stories. There we find the three elements God has shown us are prerequisite for a strong and lasting marriage union: Completion, Contentment, and Commitment.

First, there was *Completion*. Adam was alone, and as God observed, *"It isn't good for man to be alone. I will make a companion for him, a helper suited to his needs" (Genesis 2:18, Living Bible)*. Surely, in an ideal marriage relationship, each partner finds his/her completion in the other. Being alone is the one thing God referred to as "not-good." Being whole, in harmony, in community, is what Scripture is all about. We find our completion in that person from whom we receive, and *to whom we give*, whatever is necessary to make each other complete.

Secondly, there was *Contentment*. Verse 25, which we usually omit when reading this passage at weddings, says *"The man and his wife were both naked, and were not ashamed."* That, friends, is contentment. We wear clothes for a lot of reasons: because most of us look better with them on, or because by their finery we want to impress someone, or because they are necessary for warmth (or, in some cases,

154

safety. Legally, they are also required.). But clothes can also be a barrier, a fence, a way of not being completely open, a way of protecting ourselves. I won't attempt to apply that to twentieth-Century living, except to point out that in that perfect Garden of Eden setting, there were no barriers whatsoever between the partners of that first married couple. That complete lack of self-consciousness, of self-protection bespeaks the kind of contentment one with another which God also wants for us.

Finally, and making the previous truths possible, was *Commitment:* a brief, total commitment to their Creator for as long as they were obedient. (Bethel students will remember that when disobedience shattered their commitment, their disharmony with God produced disharmony between them, symbolized by their felt need to be dressed!) If you would make a triangle, with Adam and Eve (or perhaps you and yours) at the bottom angles and God at the apex, you can quickly see that the closer you draw to Him through your increasing commitment, the closer you draw to each other.

Think about, pray about, and perhaps come in and talk about these things (if you like). They are God's initial formula, never improved upon, for two becoming one, not just in the initial thrill of the honeymoon, but 'til death do you part.

A Word for Husbands and Fathers
NEWS from Lenape Valley Presbyterian Church, New Britain, Pennsylvania, June 1991

In Matthew 13:44–46, Jesus told these parables:

> *The Kingdom of Heaven in like treasure hidden in a field, which a man found and covered up; then in his joy he goes and sells all that he has and buys that field.*
>
> *Again, the Kingdom of Heaven is like a merchant in search of fine pearls, who, on finding one*

*pearl of great value, went and sold all that he had
and bought it.*

While on our personal spiritual journeys, we may not feel that way about the Kingdom, certainly we can relate in each case to the excitement of, in one case, the finder of the treasure; and, in the other, the dealer in pearls. And at the same time, we would wonder at the sanity of either, had they taken home a chest of treasure or a pearl of great value and then ignored them, putting them aside, permitting them to become covered with dust and cobwebs, ignoring what once was so important in favor of the interest-of-the-moment. What man would act in that way?

That's a question that has come to mind again and again in recent years, as over and over I have listened to tales of marriage that, if not broken, are at least on shaky ground. Substitute in Jesus's parables above the word *marriage* for the words *Kingdom of Heaven,* and you can understand my confusion. Because you see: without exception, in the weddings I am asked to perform, the groom looks at his bride as if she were a treasure which he has discovered, and he is willing to invest his whole life in making her his own. Or she is to him the pearl of great value, more valuable than any other pearl he has ever seen, the one pearl worth giving up everything (or at least everyone) else to obtain.

But then what? Too often these days (and I'm thinking in general, not of any specific situation), I am told of these same men who behaved like the strange folk we described above, taking the treasure or pearl home, and then, over a period of years (or in some sad cases, almost immediately) putting those treasures aside, ignoring them, letting them lose their original lustre, all the while pursuing other superficially alluring treasures.

Husbands and fathers: please listen to me. Don't cast aside your "pearl of great value" in your preoccupation with other things. You may have forgotten what a treasure you really have. Even King Solomon, at last becoming wise after somehow surviving seven hundred wives and three hundred concubines, wrote in his Proverbs: *"A good wife who can find? She is far more precious than jewels. The heart of her husband trusts in her, and he will have no lack of gain... Charm is deceitful and beauty is vain; but a woman who fears the Lord is to be praised" (Proverbs 30:10–11, 30).* Even as so often, through our outside activities, we get distracted by different fads, let me suggest FADS for Father's Day, four gifts you husbands and fathers can and should give your wives and children that day and every day.

First, be a *friend* to your wife. Almost every marriage relationship starts out as a friendship, yet the element of friendship is one of the most difficult things to retain in a marriage. Even as you have friends at work and in your various other outside activities, make your spouse your *best friend.* Some wedding bulletin covers carry the simple line, "Today I will marry my friend." You already have! Maintain that friendship..

Second, be *affirming.* One of the easiest (and least productive) things to do in a relationship is to criticize, to put someone down. One of the greatest gifts we can give is the gift of affirmation, the gift of encouragement, the concept we have talked about of "being in your family's balcony": cheering on the efforts of your wife and children. (I recently heard of a family that gives standing ovations at dinnertime for significant accomplishments!)

Third, be a real *daddy.* One of my treasures, and perhaps it took me too many years to learn this, is a counted cross-stitch hanging on our bedroom wall that our (middle daughter) Brenda gave me many Father's Days back. It reads: "Any man can be a father. It takes someone special to be a Daddy." Take those words seriously.

And finally, as we complete our FADS acronym: be a *soul mate.* Share with your spouse the deeper things of the spirit. Share your feelings, your concerns, your dreams, your frustrations (which is the kinds of things friends tend to do anyway). And be willing to talk together about how the Lord is (or at least should be) part of your relationship, the real Head of your family, and what dependence upon Him can mean for you all.

Men, you have in your home a pearl, a valuable treasure. Treat her accordingly.

"How do you keep the music playing...?"
(A closer look at Ephesians 5:21–33)
NEWS from Lenape Valley Presbyterian Church,
New Britain, Pennsylvania, Spring 1996

It's getting to be that season again: the marrying season. In a sixteen-week stretch, May through August, a dozen weddings are scheduled. Each time, handsome groom and beautiful bride will promise to be loving and faithful: "in plenty and in want, in joy and in sorrow, in sickness and in health, as long as we both shall live." Beautiful words spoken in sincerity at the time. But time changes things, and all too often, the promises are forgotten or broken. A quick count of our resident members at this time revealed *thirty-six* who are divorced, separated, or who are otherwise single parents. (When we began here, twenty-five years ago, there was *one!*) That doesn't count at least that number who are remarried after broken marriages, the children of broken homes whose parent is not a member, the marriages which at best are on shaky ground (and a matter of daily prayer), nor the single parents who are visitors but not yet members.

Because of the way it begins, that passage in Ephesians 5 beginning at verse 21 doesn't get chosen a lot for readings in the wedding ceremony. With equality between the sexes now something to be coveted, most brides don't want to hear *"Wives, be subject to your husbands, as to the Lord."* Yet, a closer examination of the verses which follow give us some inspired clues as to how to build a strong and lasting marriage: "how to keep the music playing" in the words of a current popular song. Let's explore a bit!

Let's begin with verse 25: *"Husbands, love your wives, as Christ loved the church and gave Himself up for her..."* The key implication here is *sacrifice*. Skip over those first verses about wives being subject to husbands, and husbands being head of the wives. When we zero in on this key thought in verse 25, we find a first guideline for keeping the music playing that helps bring everything else into focus. One of Jesus' constant temptations was to be a ruler. It's the third of the temptations in the wilderness (Matthew 4:8–10 and parallels);

it's what Jesus rejects after the feeding of the five thousand (John's account: 6:15); it's what Jesus eliminates by example in the well-known foot-washing ceremony (John 13:1–17). It's also what Jesus wants for us in a text from His great prayer for the Church: *"And for their sake I consecrate myself" (John 17:19).*

If I were twenty-one again, knowing what I know now, and getting married once more (to the same girl, of course), my attitude would be completely different. At that time (and I'm sure this is true for a lot of hotshot guys newly graduated from college), I must confess that one big reason for marrying that girl of my dream was that she seemed capable of meeting all *my* needs. That *she* might have needs to be met as well is not something I can remember considering. If we were starting over, with the wisdom of almost forty-two years behind us, I would hopefully be thinking "What can I *bring* into this marriage? What can I give her?" rather than "What's in it for me?" I think that's what Paul is talking about: loving sacrifice, as Christ did for the Church.

Then, in verse 28, Paul writes, *"Even so husbands should love their wives as their own bodies. He who loves his wife loves himself."* The magic words implied here are *pride* and *respect.* Do you remember how Jesus responded when asked what the first and greatest commandment was? Loving God with all that is in you was first, *"and a second is like it. You shall love your neighbor as yourself" (Matthew 22:39).* The assumption is that one loves him- or herself. Unfortunately, that is not always true. There is a great crowd of people out there who don't like themselves a whole lot, much less love themselves. And, psychologically, it is a fact that unless you love yourself, you have no love to give to anyone else. That's what happens in many marriages-gone-wrong: one or other of the partners has no self-love, and that transfers to disenchantment for the mate. If you see yourself in that situation, get some help, and soon! It is only as you have pride and respect for yourself that you can take pride in and respect your mate.

Finally, in verse 31: *"For this reason a man shall leave his father and mother and be joined to his wife, and the two shall become one flesh."* Now we are addressing the issue of *unity.* Not just physical unity, which tends to be less a priority over the years, but spiritual, intellectual, and emotional unity. That's what the candle-lighting ceremony in a wedding means: The two (candles) become one, yet without losing their unique individuality. It means the "I" becomes a "we." One in aims, goals, priorities, but most important of all, one in the spirit. It is a law of physics that two objects drawn closer to the same object are inevitably drawn close to each other. Thus, as husband and wife, each are drawn closer to God through Christ; inevitably, they are drawn closer to one another. Paul is speaking to husbands especially when he says: Seek above all spiritual unity with your wives. Sacrifice, pride and respect, unity: Christ's model for the Church, and for us. Above all: *Make love your aim (1 Corinthians 14:1).*

Some Thoughts on Stewardship

Note: these meditations reflect thoughts that results from the writer's chairing Interpretation and Stewardship Committees for four years in the old Sheldon Jackson Presbytery in Southeastern Minnesota, and three more years in a similar capacity immediately after moving to Philadelphia. He also was involved in four building campaigns: A new sanctuary and classrooms in Kasson, Minnesota (1965); A narthex connecting two older buildings in Claremont, Minnesota (1971); A new sanctuary in Lenape Valley (1980), and A fellowship hall and adjoining classrooms in Lenape Valley (1992).

The messages which follow reflect God's hand in these successful ventures.

From My Remodeled Basement Corner
NEWS from the First Presbyterian Church,
Brewster, Minnesota, November 1961

I am writing from my remodeled basement corner, newly cleaned, thanks to a recent miserable day; and newly waterproofed, thanks to the board of trustees. I feel a bit guilty, in that the first issue of the NEWS this year deals primarily with money. Isn't that just what people say: "The Church is always asking for money!"?

I won't attempt to explain what happened to the two previous unprinted issues, except to say that there were things of greater importance to do that just couldn't wait! But as far as the money is concerned, let's be realistic. With half of the world's wealth here on our doorstep, aren't we being rather selfish about things? With half the world going to be hungry each night, how can we explain the fact that Americans eat *72 percent above* their maximum food requirements? Why are we so blessed? Is not this a challenge to sacrificial stewardship?

Last Friday evening, your elected representatives on the session and the board of trustees sat down to prepare a budget for 1962. We were fully aware that this is a dying community, with young families moving away and older saints finding rest at last. Yet, after almost three hours of dedicated study, a *5 percent increase* in the total budget was produced! Now, just what does this mean for you, a member or friend of this congregation?

The obvious implication is that each contributor should increase his or her pledge at 5 percent over this year. To do otherwise would be mathematically absurd and spiritually irresponsible. But more than that, realize that at very point, this was a *minimum* goal! Many times in the midst of considering our mission, at home and in the world, we were brought up short by the question: where will the money come from? It must come from you and me! There is no limit as to what could be done if you and I, as dedicated Christians, could in faith catch the vision of a world that needs Jesus Christ almost more than bread itself. If we will let ourselves be carried away with enthusiasm for the work of the Kingdom, no boundary can be drawn that can halt the spread of the Gospel.

Will you accept this challenge? Will you, when you pledge on November 19, think not in terms of this budget but in terms of the countless ways God has loved and blessed and prospered you? Think it over carefully and prayerfully. He sacrificed His Son for you. What have you sacrificed for Him?

Four Years in Retrospect
NEWS from the Presbyterian Churches of
Claremont and Kasson, Minnesota, May 1967

Before the next issue of the NEWS disturbs the dust in your mailbox, we will have completed four years of service among you. That may not seem like much of an accomplishment; yet it is amazing how few of my predecessors lasted that long! In Kasson, only J. J. Ward, who served from 1874–94, surpassed that record. Bob Chalmers fell a trifle short, with three years and eleven months of service.

Claremont has experienced a little more experience of tenure: with George Hollinger (1925–34) the pacesetter with eight years and eleven months and George Ainslie close behind, at eight years and four months (1876–84). Bob Chalmers, Don Hansen, Raymond

Johnson, and Floren Schendel, in that order, also passed the four-year mark of service.

It is interesting to look back to that point in the spring of 1965 when we felt that God was calling us to "Go down there and work yourself out of a job!" (serving the two congregations). We're a long way from doing that, but some wonderful things have happened during that period. For example: in the parish as a whole, membership shows a net increase to date of 18 percent. Finances from January 1, 1963, to January 1, 1967, (including the new building in Kasson but excluding the Claremont Fifty Million Dollar Fund) have increased a whopping 63.75 percent.

In Kasson, where dedicated local leadership has kept alive the Adult and Youth Fellowships, the only real addition to program has been the Men's Bible class, requested (and still largely supported) by the Kasson men. The church building, which will be two years old come September, is of course the most obvious accomplishment; also of interest is the fact that 35.5 percent of the current resident membership of eighty-five people are folks who have united in the past four years.

In Claremont, the Spirit has also been moving in some remarkable ways. Since mid-1963, the Adult Fellowship, the evening circle, Sunday School and Youth Fellowship for senior highs, and Youth Fellowship for junior highs have either been added to or restored to the program. Membership is nudging near the three hundred mark. Finances have grown from the indebted days of late 1962 to the great stride of the Fifty Million Fund campaign. And, through it all has been the growth of many individuals. Now, lest any of this be misunderstood, it is to God that all glory is due, for as the Psalmist long ago wrote: "*O give thanks to the Lord, for He is good; for His mercy endureth forever*" *(Psalm 118:1).* Each of us who has had a part in this spiritual, financial, and numerical growth is but an instrument of His will, a channel of His power. And it is this very truth which tells us how far we will go as we look to the future: how far we will grow spiritually, numerically, financially. For all of this hinges upon the measure of our continued faith in Him who has already brought us this far together.

"But what do we still lack?" Ah, to be able to answer fully that question. But here are some areas of need:

1. At least thirty-four of our able-bodied resident members *never* shared in the Sacrament of the Lord's Supper the past twelve months.
2. Less than 50 percent of our women, and only nine of our men, are engaged in *any* form of Bible study group.
3. We are offering nothing to the single, working high school graduate.
4. We have no regular prayer meeting or prayer group.
5. We have no organized outreach to the unchurched in our communities.

I suppose I could go on, but I'm sure you get the point. But I hope you also get the point that this is *our* ministry rather than *my* ministry! Because, to paraphrase Charlie Brown, "I need all the help I can get!" First of all, let me state that these areas above are not options ("things it might be nice to do something about") but mandates if we are truly to be the Church of Jesus Christ. But having said this, I must immediately state that I have reached the limit, physically; and that if we are to move into some new areas into which God may be calling us, someone will have to step forward to care for many of these old areas now under way.

This has been a frustrating year in the sense that I have too often felt tired and devoid of energy. This has affected primarily the area of calling, either because on crabby days I thought it better if I stayed home or because lack of motivation in arising with the chickens pushed office work and studies back into hours best for visitation. If at some time you expected me and I didn't get there, I apologize. Now you know why. So what is the answer? Well, for one thing, I am hopeful to rearrange the schedule next year so that each Monday is indeed a day off, including the evening. For the first time in my ministry, I have had to concede that this is essential for my long-term well-being. But in addition, since the work won't go away by being ignored, I shall be inviting many more of you to participate in one phase or other of our ministry. For example, one of our greatest needs at this point (looking to the fall) is someone to give a few hours per week to answer mail and file in the Claremont office! The reason the office is generally such a mess is that there are always more important things to do than to play with administrivia.

In a couple of months, we shall be going on vacation, primarily for the purpose of sleeping and relaxing. I would hope that you too would be sleeping on the needs of the parish, with an eye to a more efficient witness to our Lord next fall. I do hope you will understand my frankness in letting down what hair there is left in this way. "Cutting back" or "slowing down" are not options for, realistically, we are not even now doing as much as we should as followers of Jesus Christ. In a few words, my own frustration is the realization that nothing we are now doing should be eliminated; yet, there is so much more lurking in the wings (primarily my own ministry to persons, the heart of the Gospel), which continues being put off or simply left undone.

We have come far in but four years. Will you pray with me that we may progress at least as far in the next four by being obedient and faithful stewards in our use of the time God has given us?

Many, many thanks for your ongoing help and encouragement and prayers.

Where Are We in the Fifty Million Dollar Fund?
NEWS from the Presbyterian Churches of Claremont and Kasson, Minnesota, October 1969

As the Claremont congregation approaches the last six months of the three-year Fifty Million Dollar Fund campaign, it seems good to give a detailed report of just where we are at this point.

Nationally, the picture is very exciting. As reported to the most recent General Assembly: $63,587,047 was pledged, and as of December 31, 1968, $45,799,670 has been received from participating congregations, of which all but $10,000 has already been put to work. Our congregation, far exceeding its goal of $7,200, pledged

$11,008 over the three-year period May 1, 1967 through April 30, 1970. As of September 30 of the current year, $7,927 has been paid on those pledges, leaving a balance of $3,081 to be received on or before May 1. (It should be noted that at the last meeting of the Synod of Minnesota, the Claremont congregation was recognized as having the highest pledge amount among smaller congregations.)

One of the more attractive aspects of the FMF as originally presented was the opportunity for small congregations such as ours to designate specific areas or projects toward which we wished to contribute. Accordingly, we designated $4,500 toward a Cooperative Medical Center in the Philippines, and an additional $6,000 to renovate the basement of the Lexington Parkway Presbyterian Church in St. Paul. The difficulty with this kind of practice is manifold. Sometimes projects are oversubscribed when they seem attractive to a number of congregations. This happened to us with the Cooperative Medical Center. Other projects change in importance and are no longer of high priority for receiving funds. This also happened with the Lexington Parkway Church, which has now merged with another St. Paul Congregation (Merriam Park) with the buildings no longer in use.

It has therefore been necessary to change the designation of our funds so that they could still be put to work in areas with which we felt a common bond. Accordingly, the initial $4,500 was transferred to another Philippines project: the Church Erection Challenge Fund, also in the Philippines. This has been received by that project, and in a letter dated August 7, 1968, the General Secretary of the United Church of Christ in the Philippines (of which we are a part), Cirilo A Ricos, sent his thanks in these words: "On behalf of the United Church of Christ in the Philippines, I wish to thank you and your congregation for this generous contribution. Oftentimes, typhoons visit our country, and as a result many of our church buildings are destroyed. Due to lack of funds, it is really difficult for us to rebuild our church buildings. This help coming from the Fifty Million Fund Project toward our Church Erection Fund will greatly help meet this need. Please accept our deepest appreciation and profound gratitude." Specifically, the Church we are helping rebuild is the Batangas Evangelical Church on the island of Luzon, south of Manila.

The Minnesota project toward which our funds have been redesignated is a new chapel at Warba, Minnesota. This is one of the many little congregations and chapels long served by Rev. Herb Peters, our Mobile Minister in the logging country of Duluth Presbytery. Warba is located on Highway 2, about fifteen miles southeast of Grand Rapids (currently served by our former pastor, Floren Schendel). So far, we have been able to contribute $3,200 toward this additional project.

As we also consider our pledges for 1970, we need to remember two things:

1. Only four months remain after January 1 in Fifty Million Dollar Fund pledges. Thus, when figuring your percentage for next year (and we encourage your giving at least 3 1/3 percent of expendable family income), please keep this in mind.
2. At the same time, we do not want to fall short of the total amount pledged to the Fifty Million Dollar Fund. With the possibility of this, you might want to overpay your pledge. Thank you for your faithful and ongoing support.

On Eagles' Wings
NEWS from the Presbyterian Churches of
Claremont and Kasson, Minnesota, March 1970

The minister drones on, redundantly explaining for the umpteenth time why we should give generously to. What is it this time? Great moment of sharing? Well, anyway, here's my quarter. Hope the sermon isn't as dull as the announcements! Then suddenly, in my borderline world of fantasy, I was riding on the very eagle on that quarter I'd tossed into the plate, actually going with my offering to see it at work! And there I was in Biafra, swooping down on a nation technically at peace but still feeling the effects of starvation. And I wondered: How many starving children can a quarter keep alive?

Up again, and now to Palestine, with refugees as far as the eye could see. My chief complaint here at home has been a lack of hot water, after eight loads of wash and five showers before mine. *Their* complaint: no place to live. How many blankets and tents will a quarter buy? And now in India, where in arid areas people were desperately drilling for water. And so on around the world, seeing the desperate hunger in the eyes of people dying for want of food, medicine, clothing, blankets. I can't get from my hearing the sounds of babies crying, whining constantly in their hunger, their mothers' breasts dry because the mothers too are starving. What a bad trip!

"One-half of the world lives in the shadow of need." I'm back in my comfortable pew. It's the minister still talking: "Your help today; self-help tomorrow." Boy, I'm for that! After what I've seen, I couldn't live with myself after such a tiny gift. In which pocket is my check-book? I want to show these longing people (God's children) that this American Christian at least cares about something more than color TVs and sports cars. He cares about *persons!* (You can show that you care also by giving generously to the *One Great Hour of Sharing*, to be received on Easter Sunday.)

This should also serve as a reminder that May 1 marks the end of the three-year Fifty Million Dollar Fund campaign in the Claremont congregation, with $2,500 remaining to be paid on pledges as of January 1. If you haven't completed your pledge, please do so as soon as you can. If you haven't as yet pledged or contributed, your gift would be greatly appreciated. Let's not falter now with the finish line in sight!

That 10 Percent Challenge
NEWS from Lenape Valley Presbyterian Church, New Britain, Pennsylvania, January 1977

It's both exciting and startling when someone actually *listens to* a sermon (or at least a part thereof) and acts upon it. And when that someone is the preacher's family, look out! Which is how it happens that we're opening a family tithing (checking) account as of January, promising to put 10 percent off the top into it each payday. Actually, we've been building toward this for a long time. I've been up to my wallet in fundraising ever since leading the student council's annual charity fund drive in college days. Twenty fundraising autumns in local congregations, ten years on Presbytery Stewardship Committees (seven as chairman), a Fifty Million Dollar Fund (missions), building and remodeling funds successfully carried out in previous congregations, with something akin looming on the horizon here. Quite honestly, I'm tired of cajoling, coaxing, interpreting, inspiring, shaming, and/or embarrassing nice, active, friendly church members of all ages into giving a larger share back to God of what He gave them in the first place. After nearly twenty years of being practical, realistic, low-key, and all that, I see our denomination in worse financial shape than ever before, and LVPC's budget growing with such painful slowness that we still must live hand-to-mouth where the future is concerned. (Although I must say praise the Lord for the increase at a time when so many are having to decrease.)

So, with typical reluctance (the Lord has dragged me kicking and screaming into every new adventure in the faith I've ever had!), I have reached the conclusion that to preach and exemplify tithing is the only solution. Clearly, it's Scriptural! The prophet Malachi said it best: *"Bring the full tithes into the storehouse, that there may be food in my house; and thereby put me to the test, says the Lord of hosts, if I will not open the windows of heaven for you and pour down for you an overflowing blessing"* (Malachi 3:10). (See also Jesus's update in Matthew 23:23.)

Some of you are way ahead of us on that score, and we thank God for you! But we need so many more of you/us that we may multiply our mission in the days ahead. Think of some of the possibilities: Suppose, for example, we would return to a two-compartment weekly envelope, one side for "us"; the other for "others" (Mission beyond LVPC). You could then tell the session, through your divided pledge, how far you'd like to reach out in mission, but it could only work in a tithing congregation where there would *also* be enough for the considerable expense of maintaining our church programs, properties, and staff. By the same token, should we adopt (as I hope we will in '78) a mission-project-of-the-month (which of course would include One Great Hour of Sharing, the Christmas offering, special people or programs we'd "adopt" as well as provide opportunities to respond to world crises), we could easily offer this kind of voluntary "mission plus" giving, over and above the approved budget, knowing that tithing families had funds waiting to be used for such a purpose.

In addition, there is the challenge of future capital needs, beginning with the unresolved challenges of organ and parking lot. We are still not in a position to deal with future expansion. Our budget for '77 shows increases in almost every area (there were decreases in '76), and we thank you for making this possible. But we still can't afford a line marked "Building Fund." And until we have enough to do that, the mound of expansion looks like a mountain indeed!

In 1964, as you were building, so were we, in a small Minnesota town. A congregation of less than forty families and one hundred members was planning a $60,000 building to replace an 1888 structure about to be condemned. Impossible? Not for them. A leader who later spent many Sabbath mornings on his knees (cutting and laying floor tile) confidently told me: "Any of us would mortgage ourselves for $20,000 or $30,000 for a new home. Why can't we together mortgage ourselves for $60,000 for a new church?" And that's exactly what we did!

With this kind of spirit, and the faith that you can't outgive God, we too can get out of our pecuniary doldrums and really grow in spirit, outreach, and facilities! Let's make 1977 a 10 percent New Year—and to God be the glory!

Letter to the Praise and Prayer Community
Sent from the Pastor on February 11, 1979

Dan Reid, servant of Jesus Christ, to the Praise and Prayer Community of Lenape Valley Church:

Grace to you and peace from God our Father and the Lord Jesus Christ. You know of my love and support, and my appreciation for your love and support offered in return, together with your prayers.

You have been a great leavening influence in bringing Lenape Valley Church to where it is today: a growing community in which spiritual seekers find warmth and spiritual nurture.

This is the reason that it is of deep concern to me that we are on such different wavelengths regarding the proposed expansion of our current building. Of even deeper concern is the fact that, knowing our differences, none of you has (in the spirit of Mathew 5:23–24 and 18:15) asked to sit down with me to seek a better understanding of one another's perspective. (To be sure, nor have I sought this dialogue but only because I felt no call to make home visits in order to sell a building program).

As I wrestled with this concern late Wednesday night and into Thursday morning, there began to form in my mind a message I was called to share with you. The words were more clearly dictated during a time of uninterrupted prayer on Friday morning, a time in which I was filled with much love and peace, as well as the Spirit's presence. It came to me that I should remind you that for my first years in Lenape Valley, I too was opposed to the whole concept of building, for all the same reasons some folks are opposed to it today (cost, extravagance, funds for self instead of others, etc.). The event the Lord used to turn my thinking around 180 degrees was the first Sunday morning Praise and Prayer Service (March 14, 1976). When I returned from the senior high retreat and was told that perhaps two dozen of our members came forward in response to an invitation for dedication and renewal, it immediately came to me that if this was to be the direction our ministry was to go, we needed different worship facilities that would help, instead of hinder, that ministry. (Note: at that time, we worshipped on folding chairs in a fellowship hall.)

(Parenthetically, I should add that on many occasions since we have had two services, I have been asked whether I would do a certain thing at eleven that we had done at eight. The most recent occasion for that question was January 14. In each case, I have had to say No because the current structure with its inadequate acoustics does not lend itself to the same informality with a large crowd that it does with a small one.) I believe it also needs to be said that those who have been responsible for promoting this building program also love the Lord and this congregation and have been motivated solely by a concern to develop a facility better equipped to minister to a growing community. Much prayer has gone into what is being presented next Sunday afternoon. I believe the committee has acted responsibly, and I am gratified that, quite unlike the first building committee (years ago in the '60s), this one has bent over backward to listen to everyone and to turn no one away empty.

Unlike most committees of the church, this one was not chosen. It is composed solely of those who felt led by the Lord to step forward and serve. This has led to a level of dedicated participation unrivalled by any other committee in the church.

I Think I'm On to Something
NEWS from Lenape Valley Presbyterian Church, New Britain, Pennsylvania, November 1979

"Love your neighbor as yourself" (Mark 12:31). I think I'm on to something. I was preparing for this column a message that was probably not very nice, saying in essence that I believe that all too often in LVPC, *mission* is just a word, not a commitment: a word used as part of sinful man's PBP ("Pocketbook Protection," the generic name for our defensiveness when we are asked to contribute). The rationale for this is the ongoing circular experience of never being able to meet certain demands. For example: "I won't give to the parking lot/lawn mower/organ/new building (check one or all) because that's not "mission." All right, then will you contribute to the Major Mission Fund? "But we don't know where that money is going." Come to next week's family night and find out. "I'm sorry. That's *our* family night. We stay home with the children. And that's what I'd like my mission money to do: stay right at home." Fine, there are several families around who need help. "But can't *their* families help? And what about the various agencies of welfare?" And so on and so on.

When you reach this point, you know you've been had. What all the verbiage amounts to is that until you and I reach a certain point of spiritual maturity, we don't really want to give to *anything*,

174

and in our guilt and defensiveness use these dodges to keep others from knowing the real truth behind our self-centeredness. I originally wanted to elaborate on that theme until last Sunday, when, after the second hour of preaching on the text above, Christ's assurance that we can't love our neighbor (missions) until we love ourselves, it suddenly hit me: if this is true of self, why isn't it true of the congregation, the corporate self?

You may recall that last Sunday (October 21), we quoted from Nancy Covert Smith's book, *Of Pebbles and Pearls* (1974, Word Books, p. 91: "When I had to spend all my time trying to save myself from despair, I had no energy left for anyone else. When I gained inner peace and no longer needed to direct the majority of my time to my own survival I could reach out.") Suddenly, a lot of things began to make sense to me. We have over the years been made to feel so guilty about loving our corporate self (spending money on LVPC property) that we finally stopped doing it. And like the down-and-outer who doesn't wash or shave, and who wears threadbare, dirty, ill-fitting clothes because the healthy pride of self-love is long gone, we have let little things slide. Hardly anyone shows up anymore for workdays at church or manse. Our teenagers (not their parents) now do the midsummer landscaping and manicuring. And were it not for the great dedication of Bob Fry and his family, restoring the building from the general air of abandonment that is prevalent during the week, we would be ashamed and disappointed each Sunday.

While this attitude was developing, our benevolence-giving tumbled, sometimes half of what it had been with half the membership. Like faltering, insecure adolescents, we couldn't love our neighbors because we really didn't love ourselves. Then something happened. A couple of years ago, you decided it was okay to buy a new organ and began thinking of a new sanctuary, and our benevolence-giving doubled ($5,021 to $12,253!). Last year, we were just under $13,000 (1965's all-time high); this year we should surpass that, and next year, by God's grace and your generosity, we should increase even that figure substantially.

I'm not sure what all this means. For one thing, it contradicts the old teaching: your church only comes alive as you give to others.

Yet, we know that individually, there can be no love for others without the prior security of self-love. Perhaps this all simply underscores my conviction that, with the pride that will come with our new building, if we dedicate it as a springboard for mission here and throughout the world, we will be richly blessed. And "mission" will not be a part of PBP nor a lamentation for past priorities, but a vital way of life here at Lenape Valley that makes a difference across the entire church!

"I Just Called to Say 'I Love You'"
NEWS FROM Lenape Valley Presbyterian Church, New Britain, Pennsylvania, November 1981

Remember that song? Once there was a father who loved his son. While he never did that, or said so, he just did things that proved it. He gave his *time*. With a fairly large corner property to maintain, there was always a lawn to cut, hedges to trim, roses to prune, and all the other time-consuming preoccupations of a perfectionist. Yet, in the face of this, and the need for any hardworking provider to just flop from time to time, a small boy's question, "Dad, could we go to the ball game?" was never answered in the negative. Whatever else was pressing could wait. There was always time for really important things, like taking a son to a ball game.

He gave his *talent* also. And it goes without saying that time and talent are intertwined. Among his several skills (including music and horticulture) was a never-lost skill at baseball (the father had been a semi-pro catcher as a young man. A forever-crooked nose testified to what happens to a batter who stands in for an anticipated curve ball and gets a high inside fast ball instead!) The son had merely enthusiasm, little skill. But when the son got tired of being chosen last game after game and sought help, the father took two or three summer evenings each week at the end of a busy day to drive to an open field and hit fly balls by the hour until at least the son at last was able to catch anything that a human could catch.

He also gave his *treasure*. There was never a new car in the family after World War II, when the classic 1937 Studebaker President

died. "Why do I need a new car, sitting in traffic, waiting for the light
to change?" he would say. The truth of the matter was that by cutting
back on his own treasure/pleasures, the entire family could enjoy a
month's vacation at the seashore each year. (He also always took the
last piece of meat at dinner, frequently the smallest piece.) There are
different ways to say "I love you." Some say it with words. (There is
an old saying, "Say it with flowers".) This particular father found it
easier to say it with his gifts of time, talent, and treasure. I know. He
was my father. I was the son.

How do we return God's love to Him? It is so easy to say, "O
Lord, we love you so much for all that you have done for us on the
cross, saving me from sin and giving me a whole new life." And we
are sincere. But all too often, judging by that state of affairs in the
world (as well as in too many congregations and communities), that's
as far as it goes.

John, who significantly describes himself in his Gospel as "the
beloved disciple," says this in his First Letter: *"Little children, let us
stop just saying we love people; let us really love them, and show it in your
actions" (1 John 3:18, Living Bible).* That's what our annual autumnal stewardship reminder is all about. It is a chance to indicate to our
God just *how much* we love Him by sharing that love with others
through tangible commitments of time, talent, and treasure. There
is so much not being done (even with all that *is* being done) because
too many say "I don't have time." Or because a beautiful talent is not
being invested.

And we tend to treat our treasure as if it were ours! "I don't
pledge to LVPC because I don't approve of what the World Council
of Churches does." Or whatever your pet peeve might be. Listen:
when I started dating, my dad didn't approve of all the girls I dated at
the Shore, but we still went back each August! Think about it. How
do you show your love to members of your own family? In word or
sacrificial deed? And how do you show your love for the God who
gave you Life in Jesus Christ?

Rev. Daniel W. Reid

Reflections on a Good Year
NEWS from Lenape Valley Presbyterian Church,
New Britain, Pennsylvania, May 1984

"And they sold all their possessions and goods and distributed them to all, as any had need" (Acts 2:45). As we continue our studies and reflections upon the characteristics of that first Christian church and their relevance for us today, let me first of all commend you for a number of things over the past winter and Lenten seasons. Actually, we could begin with Christmas weekend. I don't remember when I last had as many "warm fuzzies" (a greater sense of the real love of Christ) as I did that Saturday night and Sunday morning. It is so neat when we can minister to each other in that way. This then became contagious through the winter months, and I am sure has been a factor in a remarkable growth spurt during that time. Including the nineteen members of the Confirmation class; we have received into our membership fifty-three new friends since Thanksgiving! And that is *your doing*, my colleagues. You radiate the love that makes them feel at home; we simply help them confirm what you began. Never forget that a first-time visitor gets an impression from those in the narthex, those in the next pew, the ushers and deacons on duty, before ever there appears a pastor in the chancel. Thank you for per-petuating Christian love.

The Joyce Landorf series during Lent also was exciting. You brought your friends and told your neighbors, and we hope and pray that these humorous yet inspiring messages each week touched some needs and healed some hurts (besides adding some interesting items to grocery lists! You hadda be there for that one.) Then you topped it all off with an absolutely incredible One Great Hour of Sharing offering, not just edging over but blasting through our $3,000 goal! And of course, your attendance Easter Sunday (three-hundred-plus twice) after the one hundred or so in the chill of the 6:00 a.m. service outdoors was an inspiration to all.

As one who finds himself so often cast in the role of the moti-vator, the prodder, the nudger, the one who may produce guilt or anger, I wanted to begin these notes by thanking you for responding to all those Holy Spirit nudges (from whatever source) over these past months. Lenape Valley is more and more becoming such an exciting place in which to work and grow. Like the early church. What fanatics they must have been! The study and worship and communion were okay (Acts 2:42); even the sharing of themselves and their possessions (2:44). But to give everything away? Isn't this where the parallel stops?

There have been successful communes (Christian) in which this has happened. I have to say in all honesty it's up to you how far you believe the Lord wants you to take this literally. I am simply going to say this: I believe that for us, the operative phrase is "as any had need." When someone came with a need, it was met. The hungry were fed. The naked were clothed. The bereaved were comforted. The lonely were loved. The sick were ministered to. There was no need that early group of believers ignored, even to the point of sacrificing their own worldly goods.

This is the part I believe we need to take seriously. We are a young congregation with many real "secular" needs (mortgages, educating our children). Yet, at the same time, we are richly blessed. Is *sacrifice* a word in your Christian vocabulary? Are we as individuals and as a congregation totally committed to needs-meeting? Think and pray about it. How would God have *you* interpret and apply Acts 2:45?

Responding to His Call
NEWS from Lenape Valley Presbyterian Church, New Britain, Pennsylvania, November 1985

"Bring your Campbell labels..." (frequent bulletin announcement)

"Him who comes to me I will not cast out" (John 6:37b).

There were two bags of them this time, two grocery sacks filled with several month's accumulation of Campbell labels. And since I've never gotten around to asking someone else to do so, I took them along on our recent trip to the Poconos, so they could be trimmed and organized for mailing. Doing so provided an interesting study in human nature and the different ways people respond to the same request: "Please bring your Campbell labels for the House of Samuel (in Tucson, Arizona). They are there turned into playground equipment."

Some folks are neat to a fault. The labels are trimmed so that any excess verbiage is removed. Some are not trimmed but cut neatly on a straight line at approximately the same point in each label. Others, at the opposite extreme, are obviously in a hurry, some to the point of making it appear that they have first torn off the label in their hunger, then torn apart the can to get at the contents, the conventional opener being too slow! The bottom line is, or course, that no matter how they were brought in, we were and are grateful that so many took the time to do so because in the midst of meal preparation, it is indeed one more thing to remember. And there really isn't a *right* way; some methods are simply more convenient.

The thing that grew in my mind was the realization that we respond to Christ's invitation, *"Come, follow me"* in the same variety of ways. Some are very neat about it; others in the big rush that produces sloppiness. Some are open and flat for all to see; others are all rolled up tightly into themselves. Or if we might be a bit more theological, some are clean and neat when they respond to His invitation, with few, if any, imperfections showing; others drag along a whole luggage set of guilt and problems, as well as skeletons in the closet. And probably, you and I are somewhere in between, with various combinations of neatness and skeletons.

But the bottom line is the same: it doesn't matter *how* we come. It only matters *that* we come. "Just as I am, without one plea" is not only a familiar hymn but a Biblical truth. God loves us in Christ just as we are, knowing all our warts and inner struggles, and invites us to drop our agendas and adjourn, just as we are, into His Presence, as obedient disciples. Then, as we recognize we are accepted and loved and forgiven in spite of what we are, instead of because of what we are, we are motivated for service. This is what prompts real Christian stewardship, of our time, our talents, our financial treasure: recognizing that we are loved even when we neither desired nor deserved that love. That's what keeps my motor running. Isn't that what jump-starts you into deeper Christian service?

"Him who comes to me I will not cast out," Jesus told His followers. Just like Campbell's soup labels! Doesn't that knowledge cause you to rethink your priorities, your lifestyle, your investment of self, in gratitude?

Inspiration from a Dumpster
NEWS from Lenape Valley Presbyterian Church,
New Britain, Pennsylvania, September 1986

Have you ever noticed how, when you've made a commitment to the Lord, you may forget, but He doesn't? I'm thinking specifically of my idea, expressed in a spring issue of the newsletter for members of the congregation to match the amount eating out with a contribution to Lenape Valley's Hunger Fund. Subsequently and following endorsement by the Mission Committee and the session, I just plain flat-out forgot to say anything further in these pages, although I had promised to outline a procedure for fulfilling its objective.

Then while waiting for the plane to bring me back from General Assembly in Minneapolis, I was perusing the June 18 edition of the *Minneapolis Star*. Suddenly, I spotted an article on folks injured, some seriously, while "dumpster diving"! Imagine! In the "City of Lakes," clean, beautiful Minneapolis, there are starving street people who survive by scavenging in dumpsters. And some, in jumping or diving in, have landed upon glass or other sharp objects, and have been seriously injured. And then I remembered my promise. But the Lord didn't stop with that. A month later, we were headed to Barnegat Light, in the early afternoon, since affairs of business had detained me through the noon hour. Ahead of us on a back road over around Florence, NJ, a pickup truck loaded with unsecured hay bales hit a bump, scattering a dozen bales over the roadway. Naturally, we slowed down in order to get around them. But we didn't stop to help. After all, we were on vacation and running late (see Luke 10:15–37).

The next morning, we were Lutherans (since there is a Lutheran church a half-block from where we stayed the previous three summers). Pastor John is John Madden in clerics (although he has lost some weight over the years). He has a machine-gun style of delivery but always hits a nerve somewhere.

This year, the lectionary provided the familiar parable referred to above as the lesson for July 13. And as Pastor John was going on at some length about being a neighbor (and who is my neighbor?), I had to fight down the urge to get up, leave, drive back to Florence, and help that farmer pick up his bales. Obviously, that would neither have been practical nor timely. Surely by Sunday morning, they were picked up and restacked. But once again, I was reminded of something I had said.

So, having now made my confession, here 'tis. The idea is this: as an ongoing way of trying to do something tangible about hunger in the Philadelphia area, my proposal originally was that (for any who feel so led) whenever we eat out, we set aside an equivalent amount of the meal to be given through Lenape Valley for Presbytery's Hunger Fund (or, should it seem good to you, an equivalent fund). Simply mark your check *Hunger Fund* and put it in the offering plate. The counters will see that it is transferred to Elaine Benner's Benevolence account, and each month, she will send a check to Presbytery. Simple? Let's try it and see what happens. The Lord bugs me that way when it's important. That's how He got us tithing. But that's another story...

With Apologies to Channel 12
NEWS from Lenape Valley Presbyterian Church,
New Britain, Pennsylvania, October 1986

The other morning, during my devotional time, I was in my prayer sharing my concern for our fall stewardship campaign, which is so subtle and low-key that many may not even realize we are in one! Certainly, the low attendance at the three family stewards meetings would lend credence to that idea. Anyway, it was during that time that the following hit me. And while we know that the Lord has a sense of humor, it's a little scary to think that He has the same perverted twists as mine! Nevertheless, this is what I shared this past Sunday morning.

"Have you ever stopped to consider what it would be like should we go at fundraising like Channel 12 (or whatever your local public television station might be) does? If we did, then something like this might happen: "In the middle of the sermon, someone from the Stewardship Committee would come to the lectern, interrupting the preacher, and say to the congregation: 'Isn't that a great sermon? I know you can't wait to hear the end of it. I just wanted to let you know that this is just a sample of the kind of great worship services and preaching you get here at Lenape Valley *every* Sunday morning. But: we can't do it without your support! Now, if you send in a pledge of at least $25 per week, we'll send you this really tacky bag that has John 3:16 on one side, and "God loves you, and so does Lenape Valley" on the other. For $50 or more per week, we'll send you this album, *The Cherub Choir's Greatest Hits, and a Few Misses*, each album personally autographed by the choir director. 'For those of you who have been throwing a dollar into the offering plate every Sunday for the past forty years, we have a bumper sticker: "I am trying to get something for nothing at Lenape Valley Church." Even now our operators are standing by, awaiting your call. There are sixty-six of them, one for each book of the Bible. They are all members of St. Jude's Church and attended Saturday night mass so they could be here this morning! As soon as every phone lights up, we'll get back to another outstanding sermon. Thank you for your pledge of support!'

Then I said: "Isn't it good that we don't do things that way? And yet, in many ways we are like public radio or television, totally dependent upon your support for our program and mission." [Note: we actually did his on an appropriate Sunday.] As you reflect upon your investment of time, talent, and treasure for 1987, I would ask you to keep in mind three things: (1) how thankful you are to God for all His unmerited gifts to you; (2) how you should translate that thankfulness into your pledge of time, talent, and treasure in 1987; and (3) how committed you are to furthering the program and mission of Lenape Valley Church.

Next Sunday, during the last hymn, you will have opportunity to come forward and lay upon the Communion Table your pledges for 1987. May they accurately reflect your thankfulness to God and your commitment to deepening the quality of our program and mission here at Lenape Valley.

Investing in our Heritage
NEWS from Lenape Valley Presbyterian Church,
New Britain, Pennsylvania, November 1989

When we watch a movie at our house, we naturally want something deep and intellectually stimulating (say what?). Therefore, it didn't come as much of a surprise to learn that a few weeks ago, my wife purchased our own private copy of *Bambi*. And one quiet Monday evening, watching that classic film once again was the depth of our intellectual stimulation. There's a scene in *Bambi* that is guaranteed to at least moisten the eyes of all but the most cynical and hardened of viewers: that time when, at least by implication, we realize that Bambi's mother has been shot by man. And suddenly, mysteriously, Bambi's father, the Great Stag, appears, telling Bambi he must now grow up and be on his own. That's the toughest part of growing up and/or growing older, isn't it? Realizing suddenly that whoever it was we had leaned on, learned from, looked up to, just isn't there anymore, and we must go on without that person. And even more, we must grow up to be whatever that person represented and keep alive whatever good influence that individual had in the world.

This underlying truth has been one that has forced me to continue to try to grow as a pastor. Those whom I looked up to in earlier years have now become part of the eternal communion of saints, and who is to carry on their work if not us of the next generation?

To give a complete list of examples would be both impossible and tedious. But just to cite a few: the pastors under whom I grew up in First Church, Germantown, Sherman Skinner and John Clark Finney. The pastor through whose ministry in Amy's church (First Presbyterian in Lancaster, PA) God finally got through to me that He wanted me in His service as a Minister of the Word, John Gordon. Most of those under whom I studied and learned from at Princeton Seminary, giants of the faith such as John A. Mackay, Emile Cailliet, and Howard Tillman Kuist.

It goes without saying that in every parish we have served, we have come to know and love and eventually lose (however temporarily) friends who have also contributed much in their little corners of the Kingdom. To name just two from Lenape Valley whose contributions were unique and irreplaceable: John and Sue Zwaan and the Rev. Harvey Miracle. And, of course, with both sets of our parents gone to glory, there is another impetus to grow up and walk responsibility in the world. The reason I write this is that our congregation is in the Presbytery (if not in the denomination as a whole) in that same position. We are twenty-seven and a half years old, reasonably mature by human standards. We have gone from zero to over eight hundred souls in that time, a time when all around us, the majority of congregations have gotten smaller, are dying, or have already died.

The General Assembly book of 1988 statistics, which arrived in August, told the tale: we are now the fifteenth largest congregation in the Presbytery. Our membership exceeds such former powers as my home church, First Germantown, as well as Ardmore, Overbrook, First in Philadelphia, and Grace Church, Jenkintown, among many others. The pattern is all too typical, the members of the congregation grow older and die; the composition of the neighborhood changes; and there are no longer the people (and therefore no longer the resources) to be in ministry as effectively as before. Who is to carry on? We as a congregation are heirs to the promise, just as we as individuals are heirs to the promise of our families and mentors and must carry on responsibly. Remember this as the Pony Express (stewardship campaign) envelope comes to your door. There are many reasons for giving, thanks to God being paramount, but one I would

185

offer is the unavoidable realization that if we who are the next generation of congregations do not continue to grow up and exercise our responsibility to support the total mission of Christ and His church, one day there may be no mission. Or as Jesus put it so succinctly: *"Every one to whom much is given, of him will much be required; and of him to whom men commit much they will demand the more"* (Luke 12:48b). Thanks be to God for your continuing generous support.

Living in the Best of Times
NEWS from Lenape Valley Presbyterian Church,
New Britain, Pennsylvania, November 1991

Charles Dickens, you all probably will remember, began his immortal *Tale of Two Cities* with the familiar words, "It was the best of times; it was the worst of times." There is a sense in which these same words could be used to describe the present state of affairs in America, or at least, in our small corner of it. "It is the worst of times" financially, for many of you to consider a major capital funds campaign. Some of you are unemployed; some of you are underemployed; some of you are concerned about the possibility of having to move; some of you are single parents literally taking life "one day at a time." You don't want to hear anything about sacrificing or "second-mile giving" because you are already stretched to the limit. We hear you, and we understand all that.

At the same time, "it is the best of times" because many of those involved in the various phases of construction are looking for work and will seek to bid contracts that are appealing. It could be that we will be able to accomplish what we hope to accomplish at significant savings because of the financial climate in which we find ourselves. How do we know for sure? We don't. And we won't, unless we try. In discussing with one of you this very point, an Old Testament story came to mind that I felt was relevant. It is found in the Book of Joshua, Chapter 3, beginning at verse 7. (I'll wait while you look it up.) The situation is this: after forty years of wandering in the wilderness, it was time for the Israelites to cross the Jordan River and set foot on the Promised Land prior to actually fighting the battles to take it. So in verses 12–13, we read this: *"Now therefore take twelve men from the tribes of Israel, from each tribe a man. And when the soles of the feet of the priests who bear the ark of the Lord, the Lord of all the earth, shall rest in the waters of the Jordan, the waters of the Jordan shall be stopped from flowing, and the waters coming down from above shall stand in one heap."* And it happened. Look at verse 17: *"And while all Israel were passing over on* dry ground, *the priests who bore the ark of the covenant of the Lord* stood on dry ground *in the midst of the Jordan."*

Try to put yourself in the place of those privileged to assist in carrying the ark. The river was running swiftly: *"The Jordan overflows all its banks throughout the time of harvest" (v. 15).* Can you not hear yourself saying to Joshua (or at least to one of the other eleven): "This is definitely not a good time to cross the Jordan. I think we ought to wait, either for the river to recede somewhat or for God to give us some sign that this crossing will be successful." I'll be honest: I could hear myself saying that, not being of a particularly adventurous sort. Can you also hear echoes of your own voice?

You see, our very human tendency is to hold back from anything a bit scary, praying something like "Lord, give us a sign that this is what you want. If you will, then we will." But throughout Scripture, it works in reverse. God says to His faithful, "No, it works the other way. If *you* will, in faith, then I will. Step into that raging stream. *Then* I will dry it up." So also Abraham believed God, and Sarah, in her nineties, gave birth to their firstborn son, Isaac. Gideon, hopelessly outnumbered, believed God, and his strange army of only three hundred (armed only with trumpets, jars, and torches, see Judges 7) defeated the Midianites. And in the greatest example of faithful obedience, Paul writes of Christ: *"Being found in human form He humbled Himself and became obedient unto death, even death on a cross, Therefore God has highly exalted Him" (Philippians 2:8–9).*

Each of you that has a reason for holding back, for waiting, for not doing quite so much now, has a valid reason for believing that way. We hear you, and we respect your feelings. We're family here, and family members listen to one another, even if they don't necessarily agree. I would simply urge you all to add to your thinking the dimension of the kind of faith exhibited by those twelve ark-carriers, willing to step out into the torrent, believing that somehow God would dry it up. I think it's neat that our task seems, by many standards, to be logically impossible because that will mean that when it is accomplished—and it will be (and it was!)—we'll give to God all the glory and praise. These next few weeks, let's all, in faith, step out into the flood, one step at a time, confident that if this is to be God's plan and purpose, all obstacles shall be dammed in a heap somewhere upstream, and we shall cross on dry land.

Thanks for Everything?
NEWS from Lenape Valley Presbyterian Church,
New Britain, Pennsylvania, November 1993

"Always and for everything giving thanks in the name of our Lord Jesus Christ to God the Father" (Ephesians 5:21). It's late, and I'm tired. I have just finished the exhausting task of composing a most carefully worded two-page letter in dealing with a problem on the Presbytery level. I will go home to an empty house because Amy is in Allentown for two days helping our Deb take care of three-year old Bekah, who has chickenpox. What better time to spend a few moments with you, the week before Thanksgiving, wrestling with some of the implications of Paul's text? For *everything*, give thanks? Is he out of his gourd?

Well, for starters, let's check out that possibility. The recap of the highlights of his ministry are found in 2 Corinthians 11:24–28:

> *Five different times the Jews gave me their terrible thirty-nine lashes. Three times I was beaten with rods. Once I was stoned. Three times I was shipwrecked. Once in the open sea all night and the whole next day. I have traveled many weary miles and have been often in great danger from flooded rivers, and from robbers, and from my own people, the Jews, as well as from the hands of the Gentiles.*

*I have faced grave dangers from mobs in the
cities and from death in the deserts and in the
stormy seas, and from men who claim to be brothers
in Christ, but are not. I have lived with weariness
and pain and sleepless nights. Often I have been
hungry and thirsty and have gone without food.
Often I have shivered with cold, without enough
clothing to keep me warm. Then, besides all this,
I have the constant worry of how the churches are
getting along. (Living Bible)*

Heard enough? This is a man who would seem somehow to
have the right to say, "In everything, give thanks." Now, the question
is how was this possible for him, as well as possible for us? *First,* note
that in the next chapter of 2 Corinthians, following this catalogue of
persecution, he talks about this nebulous but oft-referred-to "thorn
in the flesh." Paul writes:

*Three times I besought the Lord about this,
that it should leave me, but He said to me, "My
grace is sufficient for you, for my power is made perfect in weakness." I will all the more gladly boast
of my weaknesses, that the power of Christ may rest
upon me. For the sake of Christ, then, I am content
with weaknesses, insults, hardships, persecutions,
and calamities; for when I am weak, then I am
strong. (2 Corinthians 12:8–10)*

Boy, there's an attitude for you, one that can produce thanksgiving in all situations. "Lord, thanks so much for this situation in which
my weakness is exposed. It gives me an openness to receive your great
strength!" How's that for a beginning Thanksgiving prayer?

Second, in writing from prison to the Christians of the congregation in Philippi, Paul gives us this clue: *"I have learned, in whatever
state I am, to be content. I know how to be abased, and I know how to
abound; in any and all circumstances I have learned the secret of facing*

plenty and hunger, abundance and want. I can do all things in Him Who strengthens me" (Philippians 4:11b–13). There's a counterculture statement if ever there was one! "I have learned, in whatever state I am, to be content." Man, that would put the whole advertising industry out of business, wouldn't it? But think about it: one of the reasons we don't live more in a state of gratitude is that we are conditioned to be perpetually discontent, to want more or want better or want larger. Paul, operating in the strength of his Lord, Jesus Christ, simply learned to give thanks when he had and give thanks when he hadn't. Thus, contentment in all situations.

Third: in one of his letters to Timothy, Paul gives the best clue of all for how to give thanks regardless of conditions and circumstances. He wrote: *"I know Whom I have believed..." (2 Timothy 1:12).* There's more to that verse, but that's sufficient. Read it again: "I know *Whom* I have believed," not "I know what I have believed" or "I believe all those orthodox doctrines about Him," just "I know Him." You see, when we actually know Jesus Christ, His love and joy and peace (and all the other fruits of the Spirit, actually) so fill us that we can say, with Paul, *"We are afflicted in every way, but not crushed; perplexed, but not driven to despair; persecuted, but not forsaken; struck down, but not destroyed; always carrying in the body the death of Jesus, so that the life of Jesus may also be manifested in our bodies" (2 Corinthians 4:8–10).*

Are you feeling any of those things this season of Thanksgiving and joy? Do you feel afflicted, knocked down carrying a heavy burden? You too can give thanks because when you know personally Jesus of Nazareth, you are given strength, peace, and contentment and are moved to respond accordingly. I know. I read the end of the story. He wins!

How Much Does the Church Cost?
NEWS from Lenape Valley Presbyterian Church,
New Britain, Pennsylvania, September 1994

We passed the forty-year mark back on June 12. Amazing. Four decades since we stood at the chancel of First Church, Lancaster, in front of John Gordon (Amy's pastor and my mentor) and John Clark Finney (imported from my First Church, Germantown), both of whom long ago were called home, and our respective parents, who have also joined that celestial party at the marriage supper of the Lamb, which is in heaven. I remember we were thinking ourselves terribly mature and promised to love one another "'til death do us part." Actually, it will be forty-three years come November 13 since we first found each other, forty-three years some time in December since I shared that most important-at-the-time fraternity pin, and we started "going steady." Roughly two-thirds of our lives we have forsaken all others and have been committed only to one another. Incredible! How could anyone put up with me that long? (The *real* me, not the *professional* one you see after I've taken my "industrial strength nice pills"!)

The response to this kind of commitment is, I suppose, a combination of love and gratitude. The response takes tangible form often in the form of *things* (as well as words). Want to go out for dinner? Sure, no problem. Want to take a trip next summer? Sure, we'll find the time and money somewhere. Need some medical or dental work done? Go ahead, anything to keep you healthy and comfortable. In other words, whatever it takes as a tangible expression of love, commitment, and support, if it's at all feasible, you do. One doesn't attach a price tag. That's what it means to be involved in a lifelong relationship with someone you love.

These thoughts were triggered by a clipping someone recently sent to "Dear Abby" entitled "Is the Church Costing Too Much?" It reads:

> Let me share an experience with you. On June 2, 1940, a little girl was born to us. She cost us money from the time she was born. As she grew from babyhood to girlhood, she cost even more: her dresses and shoes were more expensive, and we had to have the doctor through all those childhood diseases.
>
> She was even more expensive during her school and teen years. She needed long dresses to

go to parties. When she went to college, we discovered, along with other parents, that all college expenses are not listed in the catalogue. Then, after graduation, she fell in love and married. She was married in a church wedding, and that too cost a lot of money.

Then, five months after her marriage, she suddenly sickened, and within a week, she was dead. She hasn't cost us a penny since we walked away from her grave.

As long as the church is alive, it will cost money. And the more alive a church is, the more money she will cost. Only a dead church, like a dead child, is no longer expensive.

Think it over. Is the church costing too much?

Powerful, isn't it? We tend to view our financial obligations backward. All preachers have wild stories illustrating this. I can recall trying to give my farmer/every home visitors out in Brewster, Minnesota, a pep talk on the meaning of true Christian stewardship, only to have Al Wehler, chairman of the trustees, say on the way out, "We'll just ask them to give more because the budget's up." So much for the theology of stewardship. On other occasions, folks have asked, "What's the per capita? I want to keep (fill in the blank) on the roll."

You're going to be reading and hearing a lot these next couple of months on the subject of our financial stewardship responsibilities. We are finishing up (already!) the first three-year campaign for our Tools for the Task: the new building, organ installation, and $10,000 denominational BiCentennial Fund pledge. Thus, it's time for the next (the second of three) three-year campaign, coupled with the 1995 operating budget campaign. With a growing congregation and its expanded needs (especially in the areas of spiritual nurture and growth), it goes without saying that each of us needs to take seriously our obligations.

But that's the backward way of looking at it. The real question, thinking back to the introductory paragraphs above, is How much do you love God? How much do you love Christ and His Church? How much do you love Lenape Valley Church? Can we set limits on our giving of ourselves when we really, *really* love? How will that love be expressed in our investment of self this next year: our time, our talent, and our treasure?

With Apologies to Columnist Mike Royko
NEWS from Lenape Valley Presbyterian Church,
New Britain, Pennsylvania, October 1994

It was just past the middle of the afternoon. It would be a while until dinner, and I was running early for my next appointment, so I succumbed to my baser instincts and stopped at my favorite watering hole. Seating myself at the counter, I ordered my normal indulgence: "One Peanut Buster Parfait, please." As I awaited the crafty creation of caloric content, I noticed someone vaguely familiar out of the corner of my eye. Carefully preparing the proper wording, I asked, "Excuse me. You look so familiar. Aren't you Slats Grobnik, well-known friend and advisor to the famous Minneapolis columnist Mike Royko?"

"That is correct."

I asked him what had brought him to these parts from Chicago, and he replied that he was passing through on a business trip, and, like I, needed a quick pick-me-up. His was a banana split, double cherries. He of course asked who I was, and when I identified myself as the senior pastor of the Presbyterian church next door, he really took off.

"The church!" he exploded, whipped cream flying. "All you people do is ask for money. That was the only piece of first class mail I got before I left Chicago, some dumb request for a pledge for 1995."

I was tempted to tell the story of the man who complained about his wife's constantly asking him for money: $10, $20, $50. When a friend inquired what she did with it all, the man replied, "I don't know. I never give her any." But I decided that would not be helpful. Instead, I inquired innocently, "And how do you plan to respond?"

"I never pledge. I just give whenever I go."

"I see. And how often do you attend?"

"Oh, once or twice a month. In the winter, that is. Can't get there much in the summer."

"Interesting. Twice a month for, let's say, eight months. Sixteen Sundays out of fifty-two. And if you don't mind my asking, how much do you give when you do attend?"

"Why, a buck, just like everyone else. Just like my father and grandfather before me!"

"Uh, huh. You support your church, which presumably is always there for you in times of need, to the tune of not less than $15 but probably not more than $20 a year. How far do you think that goes in these inflationary times?"

Slats seemed to ignore my math while asking the girl behind the counter for a couple for cherries for his banana split. I figured I'd blown it, but then he growled something else: "I just can't understand why it's so expensive to belong to a church."

In a moment of inspiration, I parried with "Let me ask you a question. Do you happen to belong to a country club?"

"Of course," he snapped. "Doesn't everyone?"

"And don't they charge an annual fee of some kind?"

"Now there's a brilliant question. Naturally they do! How else can they survive?"

"I rest my case."

"Now wait a minute." I seemed to have attracted his attention. The spoon combining cherry and dripping ice cream paused halfway to his mouth. "Are you suggesting the church is like a country club?"

"No, although sometimes there may be similarities. All I'm suggesting to you is that there isn't an organization in the country that will accept you as a member without requiring you to pay an entrance fee, as well as annual or monthly dues. If you stop paying, you will lose all privileges. Yet, for some reason, too many church members see a congregation in a different light."

"Well, that makes sense. A congregation is different."

"Yes. In more ways than you might think. There is no entrance fee, gifts are solicited but not required, and the services (whether pastoral, educational, or a simple thing like a monthly newsletter) are administered regardless of regularity or size of the gifts of the members."

"Let me get this straight. You're saying that if I don't pay my annual fee at the country club, they'll kick me out, but if I don't give my church anything, they'll still take care of me?"

"That's right."

"That's crazy!"

"Not really. Just good theology. You've seen that John 3:16 banner folks sometimes hold up behind the goal posts at football games?"

"Yeah. Buncha kooks."

"Perhaps. My point is that that verse means God gave us something, His love, before we ever had a chance to do anything. Everything we do should be a proper response to that love. And since His giving was unconditional and without reservation, we are encouraged to respond in that same way."

"Hmph. I'll have to think about that. Maybe I ought to put $5 in the plate…"

A Tithing Fantasy
NEWS from Lenape Valley Presbyterian Church, New Britain, Pennsylvania, September 1995

I dream a lot. They say that's conducive to mental health, so I'm not going to knock it. Most of them I can't even remember by morning to share with my wife, but there are a few which made a memorable imprint. There was one in the adventure category: a rogue wave on the heels of a killer hurricane is about to swamp Ocean City, New Jersey, and I'm trying to awaken my wife (who tends to sleep through just about anything) and get her off the bed before it was washed out to sea. (The front wall of the house had already been demolished.) Then there's the GP-13R type, a romantic tryst with some female with whom I'm scarcely acquainted. And, inevitably, the business-related kind: I come out to church on a Sunday morning without my clothes, and, totally unconcerned, stand around greeting people in the nude during coffee hour. (Everyone else, of course, is properly dressed.) I don't know whether that one is better or worse than the recurring nightmare I had in my early years in the ministry, when we lived next to the church out in Brewster, Minnesota. I dreamed of oversleeping on a Sunday and waking up to look out upon worshippers already there while I was still in my jammies! Needless to say, none of these fit under the heading of fantasies I would like to have come true.

There's another dream I have, one which involves you. It's the dream that God has so powerfully touched the heart of each of our members and friends that simultaneously all decide to tithe! Just think of the possibilities! To give you a rough idea: according to the 1990 census, the median family income in Bucks County was $48,851. Now, since it tends to be a bit higher in Montgomery County, where a significant portion of our congregation lives, and since that figure is five years old, let's conservatively round it off to $50,000 per family. Multiply that by our roughly four hundred family units, and you have a congregational income of—are you ready for this?—$20,000,000. Twenty *million dollars*! And, of course, a tithe of that would be—ta-da—*two million dollars*! That's a *conservative* estimate of what our church budget could be if everyone would respond to God's gifts according to the scriptural admonition to give back 10 percent. (In my dream, I am awakened by the elders in a session meeting squabbling over what to use and what to invest of this marvelous windfall.)

Pause for a moment and reflect upon what uses we could make of an amount almost six times our current budget. The most obvious area is that of *mission*. At the October session meeting, we will have a team of visitors from Philadelphia Presbytery come and plead with us to give greater support to Presbytery mission causes. You see, Lenape Valley is not typical of the congregations of Philadelphia Presbytery, especially the city churches. We are growing; they are not. Many of the congregations that used to support the Presbytery's mission causes with great generosity are no longer in a position to do so.

With our growth comes responsibility. As one of the largest twenty congregations in the Presbytery (out of 158), we are being asked to increase our support of Presbytery's mission, but we cannot without your help. (The same can be said of Synod and General Assembly causes.)

The second area is that of *staff.* Key to our growth has been the influx of families with young children. That is the reason we needed to expand our facilities three years ago. But if we are going to continue to have additional children and young people coming to us, we need to provide the programs for them. Thus, the need for two assistants is growing more apparent: a youth director to assist Steve Gribble in these areas and a choir assistant to work with Charles Frischmann and enhance a music ministry, which already includes seven choirs. We are also going to need additional office help as we grow.

A third area is our *facilities.* There are several areas which had to be cropped because of budget considerations a few years ago but are still on the "wish list." In no order of priority, they include (1) finishing the changes in the office wing to complete the refurbishing of the old office and to give Steve a larger office (with a closet!); (b) the air-conditioning of the sanctuary; (c) a room for storage off the sanctuary and to house the blower for the pipe organ; and (d) an attached, heated garage for our lawn tractor, and other equipment needed to care for our six acres.

I'm sure you can think of other things as well, but these are some of the key areas that come to mind in seeking to interpret and apply my dream. The key here of course is that we focus on God and all His gifts, the greatest of which is the forgiveness, salvation, love, and eternal life we have through our faith in Jesus Christ. In response to that, and to the Scriptural commands, we give back *at least* 10 percent of our riches, in addition to a proportion of our time and talent, to Him in gratitude. When that happens, all kinds of other exciting things can be accomplished. My first dreams mentioned I really don't want to come true. But can this one? That's entirely up to you. Thanks for what you are already doing and have done.

The Challenge of Growth
NEWS from Lenape Valley Presbyterian Church,
New Britain, Pennsylvania, September 1996

*And day by day, attending the temple together
and breaking bread in their homes, they partook of
food with glad and generous hearts, praising God
and having favor with the people. And the Lord
added to their number day by day those who were
being saved. (Acts 2:46–47)*

*So the Church throughout all Judea and
Galilee and Samaria had peace and was built up;
and walking in the fear of the Lord and in the comfort of the Holy Spirit it was multiplied. (Acts 9:31)*

As one reads the Book of the Acts of the Apostles, one of the most exciting elements is the fantastic growth of the early church: three thousand baptized on that first Day of Pentecost, for example. When the saving message of Jesus Christ was proclaimed with power and sincerity (though not necessarily with eloquence, read Paul's self-deprecating comments in 1 Corinthians 2:1–5, people would respond with a desire to commit their lives to Him. This growth is happening everywhere in the world today, in China, especially, *except* among name-brand denominations in the United States.)

Lenape Valley is a denominational phenomenon, though surely not the only one. At a time when the denomination as a whole and Presbytery as well have lost members by the gross, we have quietly tripled our membership in the last twenty-five years, going from zero to 960-plus in less that thirty-five years (we were organized March 25, 1962). (Also, in the past twenty-five years, the Peachtree Presbyterian Church in Atlanta has grown from 1,800 to 11,250 members, doing basically the same things we try to do here.) This should be cause for great rejoicing; yet, from time to time, one hears murmurs of "We're getting too large." Since, while I understand the concern, I don't find that verse in the New Testament, let's take a quick look at the phenomenon of growth.

To begin with. As stated in the texts above, growth is *Scriptural.* From the beginning, God has wanted His people to multiply. Remember God's promise to elderly, childless Abraham? *"Look toward heaven, and number the stars, if you are able to number them... So shall your descendants be" (Genesis 15:5).* The growth of the church as told in Acts shares this refrain again and again. As Paul began his missionary journeys, *"So the churches were strengthened in the faith, and* they increased in numbers daily" *(Acts 16:5).*

Secondly, church growth is *our calling.* Remember the words you probably memorized in Sunday School, Jesus' "Great Commission": *"Go therefore and make disciples of all nations, baptizing them in the name of the Father and of the Son and of the Holy Spirit, teaching them to observe all that I have commanded you; and lo, I am with you always, to the close of the age" (Matthew 28:19–20).*We try to obey this commission both locally and worldwide. For example, as a result of the Mission 21 India funds you raised, 526 people have made decisions for Christ in the first year alone!

Third: growth is both *natural and desirable in* living organisms. Its opposite is death. Since moving to our present home almost nine years ago, many of the original trees have died, their root systems smothered by fill. Each has been replaced by a young tree, each of which is growing nicely. If they were not growing, it would be evident that something was radically wrong (the same can be said of small children, of course). The same also can be said of congregations in areas like ours. We were "planted" here by Philadelphia Presbytery in order to minister to a growing community. Something would be radically wrong if we were not growing.

Finally, growth is *not without challenges.* We read in Acts 6:1: *"Now in these days when the disciples were increasing in number, the Hellenists murmured against the Hebrews because their widows were neglected in the daily distribution."* Out of this challenge came a wonderful new concept: the first board of deacons! Over the years, Lenape Valley's growth has presented many challenges, to which you have responded marvellously each time: the expansions of the boards, the need for more officers, three building programs, the wonderful ways in which you have responded to various mission challenges (many special offerings, Mission 21 India, the BiCentennial Fund, to name a few).

Now, as you should learn from the various materials available at the fellowship fair (or which you will receive in the mail), the next biggest challenge is funding for additional staff. An additional large challenge is the investment of time on the part of volunteers to assist in the many programs which all need to be expanded to meet the needs of the children, youth, and adults who come to us for love, nurture, guidance, and support. You see, a larger membership doesn't mean we each have less to do. It means that if each of us does *something*, we have the resources to make a tremendous impact for Christ in our community, Presbytery, and world. We need the investment of time, talent, and treasure of every able-bodied member of our congregation if we are to fulfill our purpose for having been planted here.

In these next weeks, please make a commitment to do three things: to attend the fellowship fair, October 6 or 13 (between the services), to see what great things have already happened and will continue to happen as a result of God's gift of growth. Second, to fill out the Time and Talent brochure, even if you've done it many times before. We are trying hard to improve our response to this essential part of our church's life and work and to plug you in wherever you feel most comfortable. Third: pray seriously about your financial commitment to Christ and His church through Lenape Valley. Thanks much for your proportionate giving.

Personal Reflections on Family

Side-Dressing for Healthy Families
NEWS from the Presbyterian Churches of
Claremont and Kasson, Minnesota, June 1970

It's been a rough old year for teenagers. Alcohol, sex, and cars have exacted a high price for their use. And at that, we're at this point fortunate in not being touched here by drugs or runaways. And so it's only natural that most concerned parents are asking some questions: "Pastor, How in the world can you raise children properly in days like this? What have I done wrong (or right)? Aren't you worried about what's going to happen when yours grow up?"

Well, I'm not as yet convinced that it's anymore difficult today than when we were kids. The opportunities for trouble are counterbalanced by opportunities for good I never knew about: retreats, work camps, and the like. And to know what was wrong in a specific situation, I'd have to live with you for a couple of years, a bit of an impossibility. And as far as worrying about the next five or ten years, this is the ultimate in futility when you can't anticipate the future, and there are immediate solutions and problems that *can* be dealt with now. Quite frankly, I don't have any simple formula with which to solve the generation gap, teenage rebellion, or parental inadequacy. And you'll have to check back with us in fifteen years to see how well we did with our own.

But as I look back, I think my parents did pretty well in our family: three sons with high school and college degrees and master's degrees in the bargain (older brother Ted, in English; younger brother Jack, in sociology; me, the BD from Princeton Seminary). Ted served in Germany toward the end of World War II; none of us were ever thrown out of any place or locked up for anything; all of us are married to the same wives we started with, are reasonably successful in our chosen fields, and I suppose you might say we are card-carrying, respectable members of the silent majority. Now, how did my parents do such a better-than-average job through the Depression, World War II, and the Korean War amid the temptations and difficulties that were a part of the world even then? Well, as I, in trying to do at least as good a job with our four as they did with their three, reflect back on my years at home, I recall some elements that might have done the trick, elements that unfortunately are not to be found in all homes in this or any age recently.

To begin with, there was a very rigid and healthy set of priorities, both of time and possessions. For example, recognizing the need for the spiritual undergirding of the family, time was organized around essential church functions. We rarely had such a thing as a Saturday night party because we had to be up and going Sunday morning, both to Sunday School and worship, all of us together, and we needed to be rested. Not that the folks were squares, not at all. In those days, they were part of a permanently established floating bridge game, which met frequently and enjoyably, but never on a Saturday night. And there was none of this nonsense about giving us a choice about going to Church Sunday morning: that was the number 1 and major priority for the day, and we just went, no questions asked! And if we were too sick to go, well, we'd better still be sick in the afternoon as well!

The family itself was a high priority also. None of this fragmentation of individuals going their own way and doing their own things while living under the same roof: we lived with and for each other and did many things together. My parents were (and are) friends, as well as lovers and partners, and whatever they enjoyed (from bridge to grand opera), they enjoyed together. Nor did we boys ever feel like "intruders." We picnicked as a family almost every Memorial Day and Fourth of July and vacationed together every August. And when, in the inevitable high school crush, I began drawing apart in favor of The Girl (whom, incidentally, I met in Sunday School), I recall Mother reminding me that real love does not divide the family: it expands and adds to it. And there were excellent financial priorities as well. Would you believe my dad's last new car was a 1937 Studebaker President? (Try to find parts for one of those!) When that quit, in 1948, he got a 1946 Dodge and has been driving low-priced used cars ever since. As he explained it to me one time: "I don't need all that power, waiting for the light to change at Greene and Chelten." The money saved enabled us to live in a good home, with quality furnishings we could all enjoy.

A very sensible and sound set of spiritual, personal, and financial priorities were grounded into us and made a very valuable contribution to our lives. Then, as I think back, there was something I can't describe in any other way than to suggest: an absence of phoniness. There was honesty, a reality in the atmosphere and the relationships of our home, which underscored not only the bond between us but aided our instruction, by both teaching and example. What I mean is that my parents lived by the same set of standards they tried to communicate to us. There were neither liquor nor cigarettes in the home; hence, no problem of "You'll have to wait until you're older in order to do what you see us doing now." There were no books or magazines to be hidden from curious little eyes: not one kind of language and jokes for the family, and another when the preacher was invited to dinner. There was nothing to hide.

Such intangibles as honesty, sincerity, and generosity were taught by example as much as by word. About the worst violation of this I can remember was one night, in downtown Philadelphia, when my dad "stole" a parking place by heading in when someone else didn't back in fast enough. But I also remember Mother (and even myself!) chewing him out until he almost went back to move the car! At which point, we dropped the subject (and never referred to it again).

More in character was the nightly ritual: the carving and serving of the meat. (And at its peak, our family numbered seven: my mother's mother and my dad's father lived with us until their deaths in the '50s, as well as us three boys.) There were nights when the portions seemed a little slim, and I can still hear Mother asking, "Dear, do you have enough for yourself?" and the inevitable answer, "Yes, this is all right. I have plenty" as he scooped some fragments from the meat platter onto his plate.

In every phase of life, my parents saw to it that the needs of my brothers and I were met before they worried about themselves. There was no phoniness at our house. And of course, there was discipline, but of two kinds: punitive and positive. The punitive discipline served the same purpose as the 2 × 4 cracked over the head of the stubborn mule—it served as an attention-getting device. Each parent had his/her own technique. On my rare bold days, I would some-times venture (as a boy) to talk back to my mother. Her response was to attempt to clean up my language by washing out my mouth with soap (until she used Fels Naphtha one day, and I threw up all over her). My Dad never used a brush or a belt on me. Not even once. He didn't have to: his right hand was powerful enough. And along with that was a psychological gimmick: "Get up to the bathroom and take your pants down!" And you'd stand there with your little bare bottom already trembling before Father ever hit the bottom step in his ascent!

No problem of punitive discipline: a word spoken was meant, it was fair, and it was followed through. What better preparation for the discipline required for an education and for life itself? But there was also the positive discipline of routine. Part of this was the by-product of living in a dentist's home, to be sure, with every day pretty much on schedule, but part of it was the security and logic of a well-ordered household. Things were always done on time, usually ahead of time, and were done right. Many are the illustrations, but the fondest memories are of Sundays. I mentioned earlier the Sunday School and worship ritual. Dinner at noon followed. While Mother sorted Monday's wash (so my dad could carry it downstairs and spare her back), then it was concert time: my dad on his violin; me on the piano. Then the violin packed away for another week, and wash in the basement for Monday. In all but the worst weather, my dad and I would go for a walk (while Mother napped) in the woods, along the Wissahickon Creek, by a golf course, to inspect a new home or an old abandoned one. And while I admit there were occasions when I wanted to break out of that routine, and was restrained from it only because I knew it would hurt someone's feelings, that routine is now one of my most cherished memories of growing up at home.

Finally, and most important of all, there was religion in our home: the Christian religion. I've mentioned regular attendance, but that was only a part of it. Both parents spent time on their knees, sep-arately, every morning of the year, praying for guidance and strength for the day, and help for friends in need. Then, together by their bed at night, they gave thanks for the blessings of the day. And I am certain that they still adhere to some adaptation of that routine.

We had, and still have, when we're there, family devotions each evening at dinner. And both parents taught Sunday School, adult classes of their respective genders, with perhaps two nights each week devoted to an almost sermon-like preparation of the material. In fact, I believe that if I could spend as much time on my sermons as my folks did on their adult class lessons, I'd be a better preacher!

We were not *sent* to Sunday School but *taken*, nor were we ever discouraged from participating in the extra activities the church offered. And if you've ever wondered about when and where I learned some of those curious little Old Testament stories, they undoubtedly date back to nighttime readings by my mother from *Egermeier's Bible Story Book*.

A good set of priorities, an absence of phoniness, punitive and positive discipline, and the faithful application of the Christian faith: these were some of the things that I believe were vital in starting the three Reid boys off on the right track. Sure, we all rebelled at one time or another. And I argued with my folks, and fought to grow up and be independent, and had (and still have) certain differences of opinion with them. It wouldn't be normal, otherwise. Neither one of us is perfect, and there is that generation gap.

But I grew up upon a solid foundation for life, amid security, understanding, encouragement, much loyalty and joy and love, common sense, and the presence of Jesus Christ. I had (and have) much respect for my parents and have always liked to come home (while at the same time being quite content to be head of my own home). And regardless of the temptations and tribulations that I know lie ahead, I am yet convinced that if I can provide the same kind of home environment for our four as my parents provided for their three, we really aren't going to have a whole lot to worry about.

And neither would you.

[Note. My father, Dr. Theodore M. Reid, DDS, died on October of 1975. My mother, Emma Cogill Reid, died in October of 1983. Older brother Ted, Jr., died in November of 1993. *Blessed in the sight of the Lord is the death of His saints.*]

Reflections upon Turning Forty
NEWS from Lenape Valley Presbyterian Church, New Britain, Pennsylvania, March 1973

"I'm worried about my dad. Every night, he sits in the kitchen eating cold cereal and looking at the pictures in his old high school yearbook."

"How old is your father?"

"I think he just turned forty…"

"Nothing to worry about…he's right on schedule! Five cents, please…"

(Exchange between Charlie Brown and Lucy in *You're a Pal, Snoopy!*)

Actually, it wasn't all that bad turning forty earlier this week. To be sure, I'll never run a fifty-four-second quarter mile again, and I get more tired sooner than I used to, and I find I really can't stand Doris Day anymore. But otherwise, the bulk of the reflections are positive!

An initial reaction has to be thanksgiving. I made it this far! Not everyone does, you know. There simply is no guarantee of longevity in this world. Debra Hinton was only seven weeks old when she died in Duluth of "quick pneumonia." Dick Ebenhoh was seventeen when he drowned while swimming in a gravel pit north of Claremont, Minnesota. Sgt. Bill Griffith was twenty-four when he was thrown out of and flattened by that half-track in 'Nam (son of our Claremont organist). Skip Anderson was thirty-four, with four children and another due, when he was chewed up by that augur in a grain bin outside Brewster, Minnesota. There's no guarantee of reaching forty! Life is a gift, and we must always receive it with gratitude because it's not based upon merit.

At this point, one thinks about life's priorities, what really has been important over the years. A lot of things were accomplished long ago which don't really seem so important now: being high school valedictorian and college student council president; winning the third place medal in the mile relay in the 1952 Penn Relays, other awards and prizes tucked away in some box buried somewhere—significant milestones at the time, but not really of much value over the long haul. This isn't false modesty. The truth of the matter is that the greatest thing that has ever happened to me was coming to have a personal knowledge of Jesus Christ and His love because that love turned me around and gave me a depth, a message, a standard, and a purpose I'd never had before, with all my apparent "success." How true are Paul's words to the Christians at Philippi (read Chapter 3): *"Indeed I count everything as loss because of the surpassing worth of knowing Christ Jesus my Lord."*

At the same time, I confess an increasing impatience: there's so much yet to be done. Life is slipping away, let's get going! I find I'm not as patient as I used to be with adults who weren't paying attention, resulting in the needless repetition of something already explained, with kids fooling around in class. Class time is too valuable to have to spend it on discipline with long speeches and pointless meetings and salesmen who try to sell me something I don't want. I fight the battle but seem to lose more often than before. If I've ever been sharp or short with you as a result, I am sorry. In retrospect, trying to capsulize twoscore years in one paragraph: while there have been minuses, there have been far more plusses; and in general, I feel I have received far more than I have been able to contribute. I have been blessed with a solid background in home, church, and school. I have a wife and family I am proud of, priceless treasures by themselves. I like my work and my coworkers, another rare blessing, and I have been privileged for over fifteen years to share in the joys and sorrows and anxieties of hundreds of real people for whom I have been pastor: men and women and youth of every educational and socioeconomic background, some easy and some harder to love, but people nonetheless, struggling as I have been to discern personal meaning and purpose in the vastness of God's creation.

I have personally experienced the truth of many Biblical promises, one of particular relevance is Paul's *"in everything, God works for good with those who love Him…" (Romans 8:28)*. While never satisfied (especially with myself), I am content and look forward with enthusiasm to the next forty years, grateful for the knowledge that they'll only come one day at a time!

Thoughts on a Christian Funeral
NEWS from Lenape Valley Presbyterian Church,
New Britain, Pennsylvania, February 1974

"But we would not have you ignorant, brethren, concerning those who are asleep, that you may not grieve as others do who have no hope" *(1 Thessalonians 4:13)*. Apropos of nothing in particular, and yet anticipating the glorious Good News of Easter (the cornerstone event upon which our Christian faith is built), I would like to share with you a few thoughts on the Christian funeral. And so as not to seem, even by implication, to be treading on anyone else's ideas, I would simply like to share what I would like to have happen at my own, and why, in the hope that this might in the future provide some productive food for thought and discussion.

Let's talk first about our attitudes toward such planning. I cannot say "If something happens to me..." because some day it *will!* Thus, planning becomes not morbid but realistic. We plan for graduations, marriages, retirement. And we know that each of us will one day die: why not plan for that occasion as well? Not that I'm eagerly looking forward to death: there are too many things I'd still like to accomplish here on earth! But neither do I fear death. Every page of the New Testament reassures me that because I have committed my life to Jesus Christ, death is merely the key that unlocks the door to *real* living! And that promise is good enough for me. So then, when death comes to one Daniel Reid, what should be the prevailing atmosphere? Surely, a certain amount of sadness is not only normal but necessarily therapeutic, but let it not be the prevailing motif! For the Christian, the so-called knell of death is in reality the glorious chord of victory! All that we battle here, the hates and the hurts, the infirmities and the inabilities, are suddenly behind us, vanquished! Is not this cause for singing Hallelujah?

I hope that whenever this new opportunity presents itself before me (all the while recognizing that sometimes death comes too suddenly to be anticipated), I will feel no regrets, no sense of "Why me?" I have already received so much more than I ever expected, and a great deal more than I have deserved so that each new day is a bonus, a gift for which to be grateful, a blessing to be used well. It simply would not be honest for me to say, at 41 or 101, "Why so soon, Lord?" For as one who as a Christian has known from the beginning that "I'm just passing through," it really isn't up to me to establish the duration of my journey.

So then: how does one plan properly within such a context? Well, to begin with, by dispensing with the viewing. If, in over forty years of living, my friends and family couldn't take time to see "How nice I look" on occasions when I could share the joys of reunion, I'm not really excited about being stared at when I can no longer respond. And also, keep flowers at a minimum. Memorial gifts (to get whatever church I'm associated with at the time something it needs but can't afford) are so much more practical than the extravagance of flowers which get viewed in the service and then abandoned at the cemetery.

I want a memorial service *in the church*, with the *cross* central, not the casket. I have been baptized, confirmed, married, ordained, and installed several times in the church and have spent there some of the greatest moments of my life. So I want the final service there too, even if only a few people come. I would hope the officiating pastor would meet with my immediate family the night before; the funeral chapel is an excellent place for that kind of personalized comfort. But as a servant of God, I refer that the public memorial service be held in the house of the Lord.

And I would like the service to be truly "a witness to the resurrection": positive music, Scripture, and prayers; a minister who knows how to communicate eloquently the Good News of Christ's victory over death; with the congregation joining in two hymns which over the years have meant much to me personally, "Guide Me, O Thou Great Jehovah" and "When I Survey the Wondrous Cross." Afterward, I should like my remains cremated. I much prefer my Father's kind of "perpetual care."

I am sharing these thoughts so that you may know what I would like *for me*. That does not mean this is necessarily right for *you*, nor will I ever force my views upon anyone. But if this has stimulated some thoughts and ideas on your part, I'd be real happy to discuss them with you whenever it is convenient.

[Note: In the nearly half-century since this was written, the author's thoughts have changed somewhat in certain areas.]

Praise the Lord Anyway... I Think...
NEWS from Lenape Valley Presbyterian Church,
New Britain, Pennsylvania, Summer 1975

So there we were a couple of weeks ago, cruising at a leisurely pace on a delightful day on Route 9, travelling from Ocean City, NJ, to Smithville when there was an ominous "ping," back in that "mammoth" VW van power plant, followed by a grinding sound, followed by a loss of power and some red lights on the dash. So there we were, drifting at a decelerating pace, nothing on the road (nor off the road), wondering whether we could drift far enough to find a gas station, a phone booth, or any vestige of civilization.

The M-M Hotel loomed ahead, and into it we coasted, one dead VW van and two apprehensive occupants. At times like this, one's faith is put to a bit of a test, to say the least. One tends to breathe prayers of deep theological insight like "Why me, Lord?" "What am I being punished for?" Then there was the positively paranoid motel mistress who wouldn't even let us use the phone (gotta remember to find material imprinted with Celtic crosses for the next curtains in the van) and tried to order us off her property. "Love to, ma'am, but it doesn't run!"; who really didn't increase our spirit of "Praise the Lord, anyway!"

Since we received no help there, we walked the remaining half-mile to Smithville, called AAA in Absecon (who couldn't come until one, which gave us time to eat as planned). I walked back and met the tow truck while Amy toured Smithville alone (getting some funny looks: *no one* tours Smithville *alone*. Guess they thought she'd escaped in disguise from a Senior Citizens' tour), was taken in the dead van to Heinz' Precision Motors in Absecon, where Grandpa Strohman's brother's diagnosis was (a) blown engine, (b) couldn't get at it for at least two weeks, (c) it would cost $700–$900 to replace; and (d) no, we don't have rental cars. (The reader invites us to review the prayers in the last two paragraphs uttered between clenched teeth while kicking tires.)

Now this is the point at which our Christian faith really needs to speak to us. Not at the point of giving us a security blanket to protect us from any and all problems, but at the point of getting down with us in the real, demanding, agonizing, hurtful, even expensive problems of everyday living, and calming us while showing us the answer. This is what incarnational theology is all about: this is what it meant for God to become human in the person of Jesus Christ. He *knows* all the frustrating problems of being human and can and will comfort and guide us even on such an unspiritual matter as a VW engine blowing up while on vacation.

As Mr. Heinz went off about his business and I wandered about his parking lot, gradually a plan and a direction became clear as I tried (with difficulty, I must admit) to "praise the Lord anyway." Looking back, the course of action that unfolded was the only logical thing *to* do: take a bus to Atlantic City, rent a car from Hertz (Avis didn't have one), call Mark's Garage back home in Chalfont and ask him to come get the van, pick up wife in Smithville, and resume vacation. Which is what we did, having, I might add, a restful and peaceful week from then on. By the following Wednesday, the van was fixed and back in operation. All of this autobiography is simply by way of reminder that no matter who you are, faith in Christ does not necessarily prevent you from having problems. It *does* help you deal with them and overcome them, becoming, to use Paul's words, *more than conquerors.*

As you may find yourself dealing with problems both of far lesser and of far greater importance than an engine failure while on vacation, may you be given faith to "praise the Lord anyway," and, through that faith in Christ, to emerge victorious over even the worst life can throw at you.

Rev. Daniel W. Reid

Post-Thanksgiving Thoughts
NEWS from Lenape Valley Presbyterian Church,
New Britain, Pennsylvania, December 1980

"Always and for everything giving thanks" (Ephesians 5:20). I
don't know how it is with you, but somehow, the older I get, the
more things I feel thankful for. And even though the official day for
Thanksgiving is now past, I thought I'd share this beginning list of
things for which I feel thankful.

- For the battles of my youth, which taught me what it costs
  to win. (Somehow you most often learn that after you've
  lost a few.)
- For parents who believed the peer pressure that was important came from family and church and significant adults,
  not from schoolmates. Although I couldn't always see it at
  the time, they were right.
- For a value system at home that had Christian principles
  interwoven so that truth, honesty, caring, and diligence
  were a way of life, supported by prayer, devotions, and
  attendance without fail at worship, Sunday School, and
  other special events.
- For education and its spin-off—sports, music, newspaper
  work, social life—considered important as a means to the
  end of making a contribution to life and never seen as
  ends in themselves (as, for example, grades for their own
  sake).
- For a first boss who showed by example what it meant to
  work a sixty-one-minute hour and the moral importance
  of trying to do a perfect job for a customer you may have
  never liked nor respected.
- For a crazy fraternity (football players, Marines returning from Korea, party boys, and one or two scholars) that
  taught me how to get along with people I may neither have
  understood nor approved of.

214

- For a large church that wrapped its warm, loving arms around this college boy and gave him a home away from home. I met my wife there. And God met me there.

- For a pastoral pilgrimage that wandered through the highest of mountaintops and the deepest of valleys into situations of ever-increasing "degrees of difficulty," each event in the hand of the Master Steward, a preparation for a more challenging one later.

- For a plethora of patient parishioners who, godlike, knew I was neither as wise nor as capable as I might have thought I was, told me so but loved and accepted me anyway.

- For some fantastic teenagers (now church leaders and parents in their thirties) who taught me about love, and fellowship, and Christian hilarity, and faith-sharing, and who let me be me.

- For some giants in the faith named Gordon and Beeners and Macleod and Chappie and Chalmers and many others, who, early on each in his own say, made a profound impact into molding something useful out of this lump of wet clay.

- For a wife who has put up with so much for over a quarter century yet keeps coming back for more.

- For four quite different children, for whom it is easy to be proud, and who are fun to be with.

- For a congregation more motivated to battle with the enemy than with itself or me, and accordingly keeps rising to new spiritual heights, with the end not yet in view—a congregation very easy to love.

- For a patient, loving, forgiving God, easy to please but hard to satisfy, Who keeps breaking through human resistance and comfort with new insights, discoveries, revelations, and inspiration—a God Who really does keep His promises and is really like Jesus Christ (see John 14:9); a God for whom all sacrifices are worthwhile, not only because of past gifts received beyond description, but because the prospect of spending eternity with Him makes anything and everything wise and exciting investments.

There could be lots, lots more. It's hard to stop once you get started. How about you? We speak so often of "counting our many blessings"; have you done it lately? Maybe that would be a good spiritual exercise this coming Advent Season in preparation for the coming to earth of God's greatest gift in human flesh, Jesus the Christ.

Thank you for you.

You Never Stop Learning...
NEWS from Lenape Valley Presbyterian Church, New Britain, Pennsylvania, June 1983

"The Counselor, the Holy Spirit, whom the Father will send in my name, He will teach you all things..." (John 14:26). Sounds so easy, doesn't it? Yet, one of the major challenges of our Christian pilgrimage is discerning and applying God's teachings. This is a theme that is emerging from our Sunday morning studies in the Revelation: much of the imagery and prophecy was designed to help the Christian readers in that early, persecuted Church listen to what God was saying to them in and through their suffering.

On a recent Saturday morning *Sesame Street* show (our minds begin very slowly on Saturdays), Big Bird was telling Snuffy that one of the things you need to be able to do in first grade is listen. Funny: that's a lesson for us first graders, little spiritual children, in prayer as well. At any rate, all of this got me to thinking about the ways in which God has used different experiences, specifically parishes and their people, to teach me some things He knew I really needed to know at the time (even though (1) I didn't necessarily know I needed to know these things and (2) often the learning process was painful!).

Brewster (my first congregation in Southwest Minnesota) taught me to communicate on the level of the average person. One comes out of seminary (any seminary, I am sure) with these neat words like "kerugma" and "Septuagint" and "anthropomorphisms"; and while a rural congregation may be tremendously impressed that *you* both understand and can pronounce such words, they in all probability can do neither; hence, no communication takes place. Having to lead monthly women's circle Bible studies for the leaders (who were intelligent but generally had only a high school education) in such deep spiritual books as John and Romans was one of the greatest disciplines I could have had early on. Learning how to reduce Scriptural truth and doctrine to their simplest terms has been invaluable ever since.

Duluth taught me how much I didn't know. (I was going to use the word *humility*, but don't you stop being humble once you call yourself humble? Whatever...) It was very painful, many times. It was also very necessary. You see, the devotional life often proceeds out of desperation, an extension of everyone's favorite prayer: "*Help!*" It is only when one truly feels inadequate, weak that one taps into the spiritual strength that is oh so very available (read 2 Corinthians 12:9). Yet, once in our weakness, we learn how to plug in to spiritual strength on a daily basis—the sky's the limit!

Paralleling these two addresses, one must hasten to add that my work on both the Presbytery and Synod levels with senior highs taught me love—how to give it and how to receive it. Here my Presbyterian reserve broke down. Here I learned to give a quiet testimony of faith amid the sincere questioning of impressionable youth. And it was within this context of discovering the emotional dimension of Christianity that one moving summer conference communion I met Jesus Christ for the first time (three years out of seminary. I'm a late bloomer).

With these gifts of grace, we went back into the country again, and in Kasson and Claremont (again, in Southern Minnesota) we learned the many facets of patience. If a city boy is to survive in the country, he must learn patience. Hurrying a farmer is like pushing a string! And yet, learning patience with people helps us appreciate God's patience with us. Part of patience is waiting in prayer. Another is learning to keep one's mouth shut and not react, for the Lord in His own time will indeed bring vindication on His foes. We also became more disciplined. The only way to survive with two growing congregations fourteen miles apart: disciplines in prayer, in work habits, in being more organised. Here I discovered I functioned better in six days if, like the Lord, I rested on the seventh. And the other gifts continued to grow...

It's too early to tell what Lenape Valley has taught me the past dozen years. You are perhaps in a better position than I to judge. I simply share all of this in order to ask: What is God trying to teach you? Have you learned to listen, to hear, and to apply?

Receiving Priceless Gifts
NEWS from Lenape Valley Presbyterian Church,
New Britain, Pennsylvania, November 1983

> God setteth the solitary in families. (Psalm 68:6 KJV)

> I thank my God in all my remembrance of you...thankful for your partnership in the Gospel. (Philippians 1:3, 5)

I am writing this the afternoon of Mission Sunday, while these words are still very fresh in my mind and heart. It has been an interesting morning, emotionally speaking. We had a long, though pleasurable (and profitable!), day yesterday at the flea market; I slept extremely well and spent most of the 9:15 a.m. service attempting to wake up. With the rain, my head was full of cobwebs, and thinking was an effort. But even more, the wait for my mother's imminent call to glory was much with us. She did not recognize us Thursday, or last evening, and talks (when she can) of long-gone relatives, mistaking us last night for her brother Clarence, whom I never knew, and his widow.

It's within this context that I felt so ministered to by so many of you in so many beautiful ways. Of course, one's immediate family is vital at such a time. The words in the marriage service, "comfort one another in sickness, trouble and sorrow" take on new meaning, as spouse becomes equally a sounding-board and a leaning-post (as well as, often, the intermediary). Children are also helpful, except that we don't have many around anymore.

So it's at this point that you, the extended family, were so helpful today. You see, we have many fellowships within the greater fellowship, and sometimes, I begin to realize how many of them I am able to move into and out of. I covet and appreciate the love and fellowship of our teenagers and young adults, whose freshness and enthusiasm so often provide a much-needed shot of adrenalin. Our gracious God has also seen fit to provide perhaps half a dozen "children in the Lord" whose smiles, love, and hugs provide an incomparable brightness in an otherwise drab and gloomy day.

At different times, I have felt the supporting care of the neat guys (and their wives) with whom I have often shared different kinds of joys and sorrows on the softball field. It felt so good to be able to relate in this deeper way. Fellowship with the choir(s) also provides a special kind of closeness, and there is a lot of caring that takes place in those brief moments prior to the eleven o'clock service. One thinks also of staff support: Tom and Charles and Mary Ann, the surrogate parents of Forever Young and Pine Run; the members of session and the board of deacons; and the many, many others who perhaps don't fit into any of the above categories but who are expert at the ministry of caring.

Anyway, what happened was that when you all got through with me between and after the services, I felt all manner of warm fuzzies: the love and concern and support that can only take place in Christ's Church. And as I was thinking about all this (I must confess during Newt Thurber's sermon at eleven. Well, I had heard it once before...), I really got sorta choked up a couple of times. It's so great to be part of such a caring family. I should add that the family doesn't end with Lenape Valley. Our family beyond, represented by the different folks at the mission fair, added their words of support, encouragement, and understanding also: friends like Brenda Tucker, Herb McClain, and so many others that have come to feel at home here.

All of this is simply to say that I love and appreciate you all very much, and the answer to that age-old question about being a Christian apart from a fellowship is answered on a day like this. There is simply no substitute for a family.

Toward a Moderate Christmas
NEWS from Lenape Valley Presbyterian Church,
New Britain, Pennsylvania, December 1985

Killing time recently while watching one of the cable channels, I was amused by an old Charlie Chaplin rerun from the silent days. The poor little guy was simply trying to get into his second-floor room, but everything conspired against him. The final blow (quite literally!) was a wall clock next to the door to his room, one which sported a pendulum with an exaggerated swing. Every time Charlie approached his door, the pendulum would swing out, crack him a good one, and send him tumbling back down the stairs again.

Pendula (I guess that's the plural) tend to do that in life as well. Once things have gone too far in one direction, we tend to swing too far in the other, and sometimes people get knocked over in the process. One such incident is what increasingly I have been hearing regarding our celebration of Christmas. We are tired of commercialization, tired of Santa Claus coming in mid-November (someone the other day advertised his arriving via hot air balloon!), tired of boring Christmas letters, and all the rest. Now, certainly I understand the problem and have no intention of saying to anyone, "You're wrong." I simply felt led to share my own experience of Christmases past, and why I haven't gotten on what seems to be a kind of "anti" bandwagon.

Santa Claus was really big in our house when I was a kid. According to my mother, he helped with wrapping gifts and helped also with setting up the trains, the tree, and all the rest. (We were living in a home in which the living room could be blocked off, so these preparations went unseen as we walked past in the hallway.) And when I grew beyond the stage of believing, I don't ever remember feeling I had been betrayed or lied to. I just remember thinking that my mother and father must have really loved me to go to all that trouble in order to make Christmas special.

We always made a big thing out of gift-giving. We never had all that much money, so Christmas became the one time in the year when it was okay to splurge, within reason, and show the other members of the family what you really thought of them. You might even say it became an excuse for saying "I love you," which was more implied than spoken the rest of the year. The other thing I recall was that Christmas was the one occasion, other than vacation, when my dad spent quality time with the family. Until I grew old enough to take over, he spent hours setting up the tree and the old classic Lionel trains and even took an extra day or so off work in order to do so!

All of this is simply to say that somehow, my folks seemed able to use the best the secular world had to offer without ever letting me forget the real reason for it all: God's gift of self in Jesus Christ. It was a happy blend of moderation which hopefully we have been able to pass on to our own kids. Never forget that Scripture reminds us over and over that God is capable of using anything to His glory. If the props were a teenage girl, a stable, a star, and an undistinguished supporting cast, that's what He used! And rather well, one might add. Let's continue to proclaim Christ to a Christless world; let's continue to love in a loveless world; let's continue to give in a world that doesn't want our gifts; and trust that God is even now overcoming that same world.

Thanks for Some Special Christmas Gifts
NEWS from Lenape Valley Presbyterian Church,
New Britain, Pennsylvania, December 1986

I have a feeling that if I ever make it to senior citizen-hood, I'm going to be an emotional mess because I find that every year I live, I get a little more emotional (as in borderline blubbery) at special times of the year like this when I reflect upon all the undeserved riches that have come into my life. Let me just attempt to share some of the major things for which I am thankful, in some sort of order or priority. Hopefully, you will be able to relate to some of these things. Add many of your own or perhaps see some of these as goals for which to strive.

I must start with *the joy of believing*. I am daily humbled and in awe of the extent to which our great Creator-God cares for *me!* (I know me far better than you do.) For His calling me into His service in the first place, for His infinite patience with me as I have staggered and stumbled through almost thirty years in that service, for the sense of purpose and fulfillment this all has given, for the undeserved gifts I have received at each crucial point in the journey, and for a never-ending process of growth, I am truly grateful.

Next, I must list *my partner* in that journey: a relationship which now goes back more than thirty-five years! When I speak premaritally to couples about the five ways in which married couples should relate (best friends, marriage, parentally, sensually, and spiritually), I do so out of our own positive experience in each of these areas. I am so thankful that home is for me a place I love to go back to.

Then there is our superlative *family*. When they were young and I was active in senior high work in the Synod of Minnesota, I considered myself an expert on raising teens. Twenty-five years later, if you would ask me what we did right, I could only point to the grace of God. To have four neat kids who have stayed in the church and are all involved in one way or another in caring for other people is nothing short of miraculous, and we can never adequately express our thanks.

And I am thankful for *my work*. Of course, it is demanding. Of course, the hours are long. Of course, I get tired. That's all "part of the territory," as the late Harvey Miracle used to say. Yet, your response, your growth, your support, the feeling that we are all in this *together* makes it all worthwhile.

We have so many "problems" here most pastors would give their right arms to have: an increasingly overcrowded Sunday School, for example. How to involve constructively (without overloading) the many fine new members who are led to us each year. How to invest and use well your generous contributions. The hunger for spiritual growth and renewal that is heard and felt everywhere we turn. These are just some of the things that make me give thanks for *you* and make this an exciting place in which to labor.

Needless to say, this does not exhaust the list. I have been blessed with endurance and uncommon good health, with a lot of folks upholding me/us daily in prayer, with a lot of love everywhere I turn. All of which provides a motivation for the Christian life. How can we give thanks for all this bounty? By faithful, loving service to Him who has made it all possible. Happy belated Thanksgiving!

Reflections on Thirty Years in the Ministry
NEWS from Lenape Valley Presbyterian Church,
New Britain, Pennsylvania, May 1987

(As a member of this year's thirtieth anniversary class of Princeton Seminary, I received a form to fill out, inviting us to share thirty years of reflections. I thought you might also be interested in what I had to say.)

Once when I was a little fellow, I received a somewhat complicated game for a Christmas gift. I remember that subsequently my dad sat down to play it with me (which in itself made the occasion memorable!) but *insisted* on reading the directions first! And I can recall being impatiently annoyed at the inconvenience of having to wait while he was finding out how to play the game!

I share this long-forgotten incident because it really is my ministry in a nutshell. This is the attitude the Lord always had to overcome. Whenever I patiently awaited His instructions, all went well; when I blundered on without waiting for His directions, I inevitably got into difficulty. Looking back over thirty years in rural, urban, and suburban parishes, I can't think of one instance when the hot water I had gotten into couldn't have been avoided had I "waited on the Lord." Of course, one of the things that happens when one blunders ahead in one's own weakness instead of His strength is this: in being insensitive to God, one often becomes insensitive to God's people as well, and that, of course, compounds the problem.

Now let's suppose someone had early on picked up on my tendency toward impatience, toward rushing ahead to play the game without waiting for the instructions. Suppose this someone was a person I admired and trusted, who was skilled at constructive criticism devoid of judgment. What might I have done differently had I had that sort of mentor, either in seminary or in the first few years in the parish afterward?

For one thing, I would have prayed more. Despite all the years of sermons, good teaching, and the fine example of my parents, it took me too long to realize what power I was missing. I'm talking here about three kinds of prayer: the "creative listening" that comes with mornings or days apart with God, praying *for* people, and praying *with* people.

It took burn-out a couple of summers back before I began the discipline of a monthly "Day Apart" for prayer, meditation (and some planning). The initial response to my carefully written prayers seemed to be: "I thought you'd never ask!" And even before that, it took too many years before I fully believed the old E. Stanley Jones image of the Christian as a camel who kneels at the start of the day to receive the burden for the day, and kneels again at day's end to have the burden removed.

Praying for others goes beyond the obvious (the ill, for example). One cannot remain angry or upset with anyone for whom one is praying. And I wish I had done more praying *with* people. Amazing and beautiful things happen when you do. I also wish I had written more thank-you notes and less "poisoned pen letters." Little notes of appreciation, encouragement, and affirmation are so helpful in the upbuilding of individuals in their faith, but it takes a little time and thought to do that. The other kind of notes are generally thoughtless. They are generally impatient overreactions to a situation in which too often, not all the facts are known. Along with things I wish I hadn't said (or should have said), there are letters I wish I had never written or should have written.

The miracle of all this is that I have felt richly blessed throughout my ministry. I feel I am living proof that, while we are sinners, Christ loves us and died for us (Romans 5:8) "'Tis grace has brought me safe thus far, and grace will lead me home." My hope and prayer is that, in the portion of the last active decades that still remain to me, I will be able to remember and apply those things which I took so long to learn.

Thirtieth Anniversary, Part 2
NEWS from Lenape Valley Presbyterian Church,
Ne Britain, Pennsylvania, Summer 1987

Reunions are interesting phenomena. I recall returning from my twenty-fifth class reunion at Franklin and Marshall College some years ago, realizing that only those who consider themselves "successful" travel hundreds of miles and spend a couple hundred dollars in order to brag, "I have really done some stupid things these past twenty-five years and generally made a mess of my life." That would be appropriate for counselling or group therapy, but not generally for a class reunion.

But within that rare species known as professional clergy, one's expectation tend to be higher. Surely, there might be echoes of *God, I thank Thee that I am not like other people: extortioners, unjust, adulterers, or even like this unordained layperson! (with apologies to Luke 18:11)* But as we shared in my thirtieth reunion at Princeton Seminary the end of May, I discovered once more that clergy-types are mortal, suffering from the same afflictions (and, presumably, temptations) as the sinner in the pew. One is humbled by this, recognizing anew that the Christian walk, for clergy and laity alike, is a walk of grace. We shall never know in this life what temptations we have not been led into (as we pray regularly in the Lord's Prayer), which dangerous pitfalls and rapids we have skirted, what tragedies we might have avoided, because we did decide to answer that phone call as we were going out the door.

So once again, there is this deeply-rooted sense of gratitude for countless unmerited blessings in general, but (in my mind, at least) four things in particular (although not necessarily in order of importance. It's the order I thought of them.):

First, I am grateful for grace, for strength in the midst of weakness, for staying in the parish ministry these thirty years. We were sitting around in the late Dr. Erdman's living room, perhaps eighteen of us plus some spouses, and only four of us had done nothing else but parish ministry since graduation! A couple had dropped out and have come back (one as, of all things, an Episcopalian!), and one also who had a degree in Christian Education has retired, but the vast majority present in that gathering had for a variety of reasons left the parish ministry for other callings and/or jobs. And perhaps this wasn't all bad: perhaps not all were really called to the demands of the parish in the first place, but I still felt sad that so many had gone that route.

The *second thing* that crossed my mind was gratitude for being married to the same girl I started with a little over thirty-three years ago (approaching thirty-six, if you count courtship). Perhaps I shouldn't have been, but I was surprised at how many who seemed happily married back in those halcyon seminary days didn't make it this long together. And one wonders what happened, even while recognizing the incredible amounts of grace and patience required for *any* marriage to make it these days.

Then I *gave thanks* for having four kids that have stayed in the church! I know a lot less about raising teenagers now, having done so, than I did before we had any! (Boy, did I have advice for parents back in my camp and conference days when all we had were two preschoolers!) I honestly don't know what we did that was right. (I can remember a lot of things we did *wrong*, however.) Suffice it to say that it is only by the grace of God that we have four kids who have now passed twenty-one and are active in congregations. (This was not the case in many of the families represented at the reunion.)

I'm also *glad to be alive.* Not all of my former classmates are. And it hasn't been illness so much as that other modern plague, the traffic fatality. One tragically was shot and killed in his own home. More and more, I realize the extent to which each day is a gift from God. So we begin the summer with hearts filled with gratitude. May our times of refreshment and recreation be such that we begin the fall with even more of the same!

Celebrating a Half-Century Plus
NEWS from Lenape Valley Presbyterian Church,
New Britain, Pennsylvania, February 1988

Sometime soon, Lord willing, I will be celebrating the thirtieth anniversary of my twenty-fifth birthday. And so often, in reaching such milestones, one is moved to reflection about months and years of coming to grips with life, usually winning (in the power of the Spirit) but sometimes suffering setbacks as well.

One of these reflections, looking back over more than a half-century of trying to get along with people, is this: *all* relationships, without exception, are *fragile!* I'm talking about the marriage relationship, parent-child relationships, sibling relationships at any age, relationships between friends, coworkers, pastors and congregations—any area of life you can suggest. Relationships are precious and fragile and need to be cared for with that in mind.

If this were a discussion group rather than a one-page editorial, illustrations would probably be endless. You can be married ten, twenty, thirty, or more years, yet an angry word or thoughtless act can, in a moment, undo all the love that has been built up all that time. When children have reached maturity, they have a way sometimes of reminding parents of a time many years ago when something was said, long ago forgotten by the speaker, that made a lasting impression on the children, and perhaps even left a scar. And it's true as well of all our relationships outside the family. A friendship must be nurtured tenderly, like a plant. Those that are not die.

This is not moving toward any other point other than this: we can never often enough tell our spouses, our children, our parents that we love them; and our friends and colleagues that we appreciate them. Not one of us says this, or is told this, enough (a recent study revealed that the greatest need teens in America feel today is the need to know they are loved). But there is a corollary to this. The one relationship in our lives that is *not* fragile is our relationship to God. Again and again, one returns to and clings to that affirmation of

Paul (who should have known): "Nothing... *will be able to separate us from the love of God in Christ Jesus our Lord*" *(Romans 8:39)*. Nothing you and I have ever done, are doing now, or could possibly do in the future (including even rejecting God's love!) can ever sever the relationship and remove us from His love. Isn't that fantastic? And comforting? And that, of course, is the love Christ tells us to have for one another.

The second reflection (and this is particularly directed at the many parents of young children) is that no matter how old we are privileged to grow, we somehow never *out*grow the self-image developed in our formative years when all we know is our own home and its environment. Again, illustrations could overwhelm us. If you, for example, grow up as the family's psychological whipping boy/girl, getting blamed for whatever goes wrong, getting yelled at a lot, getting called disparaging names, echoes of this will continue to haunt you decades later. It is always expected, even in adult life, that this same treatment will always be given. Now, in Christ, these memories can be healed and overcome, even used productively in working with others; yet the lingering thought is always there. The many, many adults we meet who have low self-esteem testifies to this. At the same time, if one grows up feeling loved and affirmed, *no matter what*, then, regardless of physical attractiveness (or lack of same) or even failures, there is the feeling I'm a person of worth and value. Tony Campolo has shared a study that suggests that our self-image is dependent upon what the most important person in our lives thinks of us. "And," he goes on, "if the most important person in your life is Jesus Christ: He thinks you're great!"

Just a couple of reflections given to me while driving at a speed lower than my age. It is my hope, prayer, and aim that they may be helpful to you in all your love-relationships, including the one with God through Christ.

"Bloom Where You're Planted"
NEWS from Lenape Valley Presbyterian Church,
New Britain, Pennsylvania, February 1989

"Go home to your friends, and tell them how much the Lord has done for you, and how He has had mercy on you" (Mark 4:19). At the 9:15 a.m. service on January 8, I shared some reflections that had come to me during New Year's weekend as we were in Tucson for son Wayne and Laura's wedding. And since not all were able to attend the morning service, and I felt these reflections were worth repeating, I am condensing them herewith.

I began by sharing the story of quite dissimilar ministries we experienced that weekend. The first was at Grace Chapel, where the wedding took place. The folks there have developed an impressive ministry for the handicapped. The bride, her matron of honor and her husband, and three other guests, were all in wheelchairs. Since so many who are handicapped come to Arizona for the dry weather, what a wonderful use of the opportunity for ministry that is there!

Then Sunday morning (the wedding was on Saturday), we worshipped in the congregation pastored by John Fife, who has become sort of the father of the Sanctuary Movement in the Presbyterian Church. It was again a warm and loving congregation, this time encompassing racial minorities. The pianist was black. The liturgist was Hispanic, and we sang (or attempted to) "O Come, All Ye Faithful" in Spanish. The announcements celebrated the successful completion of their building program, which will enable them to build facilities for dealing more effectively and sensitively with Central American refugees. In the prayer concerns, this same issue was touched upon. Once again, we were privileged to experience a part of the ministry of a congregation reaching out to its own community.

And so I raised in that sermon the question: are we doing all we ought to be doing where *we* are? I didn't tell these stories in order to suggest we ought to recruit more folks who are handicapped (although our ramps make it readily accessible for them) nor to get involved in the Sanctuary Movement (although you are welcome to contribute if you feel so led). No, the point is that made by Jesus to the cured demoniac: You don't have to run off to do what someone else is doing. Rather, go home and tell your friends (and even family) how much the Lord has done for you and how He has had mercy on you. Stay where you are! Bloom where you're planted!

Of course (and I somehow almost forgot this paragraph), we have had folks who *did* feel called to leave home: the Knipes (and our son Wayne) in Tucson, Nancy Jensen in Zaire, and more recently, the Kniselys in Nepal, the Ruths in New Guinea, and the Clarks in Japan. But being called to mission doesn't necessarily mean going thousands of miles from home. It may just mean finding new and better ways to be in ministry:

- To single parents and their children
- To teens (and younger) in need of foster homes
- To the transients and the homeless
- To abused women and children
- To those living in BARC homes
- To the students at Delaware Valley College
- To the increasing number of minorities moving into our area
- To any other group close to you

Even as we have had folks who have made Trevor's campaign their ministry, perhaps God is calling you to reach out to one of these groups. Are you listening? If you think you are hearing something, let us know. We are not Grace Chapel or Southwest Presbyterian Church. But let's be the best Lenape Valley we can be!

Reflections on Your Generous Gift Trip
NEWS from Lenape Valley Presbyterian Church,
New Britain, Pennsylvania, Summer 1989

First of all, thanks so much for making a great trip (our thirty-fifth anniversary cruise to Alaska) possible. Had it not been for your generosity two years ago, that cruise would remain what it still sometimes seems: a dream! The slides are back but not edited; you will have opportunity to see them either at the previously-announced October meeting of the Lenape Valley luncheon club or at a Sunday evening to be planned later. I plan to tape a script so you won't have to bring a sleeping bag when you come!

En route by plane to Vancouver (our point of departure), there were a lot of hours, so I absorbed the *Reader's Digest* version of James Michener's *Alaska*, which gave not only a historical but also a cultural background of what we were about to experience. One of the early conflicts noted was that between the Russian Orthodox Church and the local shamans or medicine men who held a mysterious and superstitious power over those early natives. (Perhaps you may recall that we did not purchase Alaska from Russia until 1867.)

Sunday of Memorial Day weekend we were in Sitka, home of Sheldon Jackson College: the Presbyterian college where James Michener stayed while writing his book. We walked quickly through the museum as we headed to worship in the First Presbyterian Church (in the worship service, as we all introduced ourselves, we discovered another visitor was old friend Jean Crassweller from Lakeside in Duluth!) and noted in a glass case many items which had been used by the shamans over the years. I was fascinated by these words on the descriptive card: "The shaman served as link to the world of spirits through his spirit helpers… A shaman needed masks, amulets, rattles, and other items to call his spirit helpers to him for aid and information."

Several things came to mind. One was that dramatic contest between Elijah and the four hundred priests of Baal on Mt. Carmel, recorded in 1 Kings 18. The prophet at one point teased the priests into a frenzy:

> *"Cry aloud, for he is a god; either he is musing,*
> *or he has gone aside, or he is on a journey, or perhaps*
> *he is asleep and must be awakened." And they cried*
> *aloud, and cut themselves after their custom with*
> *swords and lances, until the blood gushed out upon*

them. And as midday passed, they raved on until the
time of the offering of the oblation, but there was no
voice; no one answered, no one heeded...". (1 Kings
18:27–29)

Perhaps they forgot their rattles!

Paul had to deal with somewhat the same problem centuries later in writing to the Christians at Colossae. The problem there was the heresy of Gnosticism, a belief that, like the superstitions of the Alaskan shamans, there were spirits out there ("emanations") that had to be won over in order to make contact with a god who was both distant and aloof. So Paul wrote forcefully:

> *See to it that no one makes a prey of you by*
> *philosophy and empty deceit, according to human*
> *tradition, according to the elemental spirits of the*
> *universe, and not according to Christ. For in Him*
> *the whole fullness of deity dwells bodily, and you*
> *have come to fullness of life in Him, who is the*
> *head of all rule and authority...(God) disarmed the*
> *principalities and powers and made a public exam-*
> *ple of them, triumphing over them in (the cross).*
> *(Colossians 2:8–10, 15)*

As I read the description of the shamans and their "toys," I couldn't help but think back to the emphasis on prayer that we maintained during the pre-Pentecost renewal period back in April and May. How easy it is for *us* to "take everything to God in prayer" without masks, amulets, or rattles; and how often we take it all for granted and neglect this great gift. And now that we have begun the sermon series on the Ten Commandments, the underlying theme cries out to be heard again and again: *"I am the Lord your God, who showed power and love in bringing you out of the land of Egypt, out of the house of bondage. You need no other gods besides me."*

As at last we have even a few weeks (or a few long weekends) in which to catch our collective breaths this summer, can we reflect upon these two great truths? Prayer is God's gift of instant communication: the original cordless phone. Let's not waste it but use it faithfully; remembering that ours is a God of power and love, who in Christ became personal. We need neither person nor thing to attract His attention: just our own sincere, stumbling words (read Romans 8:26).

Another Litany of Thanksgiving
NEWS from Lenape Valley Presbyterian Church,
New Britain, Pennsylvania, December 1989

"Always and for *everything* giving thanks" (Paul to the Ephesian Christians, 5:20). Traditionally, at this time of year, we "give thanks for all our many blessings." And I don't want to knock that. We are well-fed, clothed, and housed, with plenty to share. We are generally employed with many fine benefits. We are free to worship (or not worship) when and where we choose. We are warmed and filled with love, from family and/or surrogate family, as well as Christ Himself. And we live in a land of endless variety and beauty.

But Paul, centuries ago, admonished believers to give thanks for *everything.* And that isn't always easy. At least not for me. And probably, not for many of you either. We all tend to want what someone once described as "lawns without crabgrass." Yet, so often, it is in dealing with the crabgrass in the lawn of life that we grow! Let me share some crabgrass in mind that grudgingly, over the years, I am learning to be grateful for.

I am thankful that my mother sent me off to school a year early ("so I'd have someone to play with," I learned years later), resulting in my being the youngest and smallest of all through twelve years of schooling. This meant enduring being picked on, generally being chosen last for teams, as well as being "class baby." Yet, I have come to believe this bad experience has made me more sensitive to those in similar straits.

I am thankful I developed late as a baseball player. (First starting role, age twenty-four; first all-star game, age thirty-nine!) Had I just a little more talent and confidence, with my love for the game, I'd have probably wasted many vital years in minor league towns, attempting to play professional baseball, awaiting my "big chance." I am thankful the Lord didn't get through to me with his call to ministry until after I'd enrolled in Franklin and Marshall College in Lancaster as a predental student. Otherwise, I would probably never have met my wife, who has without doubt had the strongest positive influence on my personality.

I am thankful for the entire Minnesota experience of thirteen and a half years. Had I left seminary with anymore ability or confidence, I would never have been content to start out so small, make the mistakes and get knocked down but eventually discover what kind of pastor the Lord had in mind for *me*. And I am thankful for all the situations I have gotten into that I couldn't handle on my own, not only pastoral (counseling, bereavement, terminal illness, and the like), but also personal: our son's vision handicap, the loss of both sets of our parents over the years, a very sensitive divorce in the family. These things have not only driven me to my knees in prayer but have helped me better to empathize with others going through the same kinds of problems.

I am also extremely thankful for some things that *didn't* happen. I think of two verses attributed to David: *"There is but a step between me and death"* (1 Samuel 20:3b) and *"The Lord preserves the simple"* (Psalm 116:6a). Over the years, we have driven between four and five hundred thousand miles without serious injury or accident (auto and motor home). I am convinced that doesn't happen by accident (pun intended)! There isn't space to list all the "near-ums" that still make me flinch a bit when I think of them. When one continues to escape unscathed, sometimes with less than a foot separating safety from catastrophe, one is gratefully aware that life's task has not yet been completed. I also recall acutely, a Tuesday of Holy Week a couple of years ago, stopping a well-struck racquetball with my face in a spot that left me uninjured, while an inch or so in another direction could have resulted in a broken nose, broken tooth, or even loss of vision.

For what are you thankful? Can you give thanks for something unpleasant or unfortunate, which the Lord has used or can use constructively? It's so freeing when you can! This year, in *everything* give thanks!

Reflections on a Good Vacation
NEWS from Lenape Valley Presbyterian Church,
New Britain, Pennsylvania, September 1992

I'm not sure how one defines a "good" vacation, but if the definition involves fond memories of meaningful visits with old friends, and of events experienced, along with a complete blotting-out of the mind of those things which dominate the other eleven months of the year, well, it was a good one! All of that happened, and more. We've only been back a couple of weeks at this writing, and I'm sure that as we distance ourselves from the event, other matters of significance will surface and take on prominence. However, from this vantage point, here are some things which I'd like to share, if for no other reason than to get them out of my head so that I can once again concentrate on the challenging task at hand.

First, there is the importance of *prayer,* both yours and ours, in an enterprise such as this (which turned out to be 7,500 miles across seventeen states in the faithful Chevy-American RV). Of the thirty days we were gone, eighteen involved traveling at least two hundred miles per day (over five hundred on a few occasions). To have always arrived on schedule, whatever our destination, and whatever the road and weather conditions, says to me that it was not my cleverness or ability but the inspiration which was given as a result of many prayers that made this possible.

At the same time, there was the *sense of fulfillment* in the third stanza of a familiar hymn, which we gratefully attribute to the undergirding of *your* prayers before and during the trip: "Through many dangers, toils, and snares, I have already come; 'Tis grace has brought me safe thus far, and grace will lead me home." And it did. There were no "close ones" of which we were aware. The timing involved in always being slightly (or sometimes muchly) behind the severe storms that attacked the Midwest we believe was God's timing. Even our learning of the escaped convict terrorizing the Grand Canyon came about because of the neat timing of our being able to have dinner with my brother and his wife (who live in Colorado), their daughter, son, and daughter-in-law, in Arizona, where their two children are settling. Without going into a lot of unnecessary detail, suffice it to say that we always felt we were not alone, whatever the interstate.

Those of you who have recently studied the little brochure "My Heart, Christ's Home" in Inquirer's Class will recall that one area Christ wants to be included in and Lord of is the Rec Room. When that happens, when He is included in vacation plans prayerfully prepared, amazing things can and will happen.

A second area which came across loud and clear, especially during the first ten days of the trip as we visited with long-time friends, former parishioners in three different locations in Minnesota, is *the strength of the laity* in the Church of Jesus Christ (that "holy catholic church" in which we affirm belief in the Apostles' Creed). An uninvolved former pastor becomes a good sounding-board for complaints about present or former pastors, their inadequacy and sometimes (regrettably) hurtfulness. One can but sympathize that there are times when the enemy seems to be winning. What better target for him than that fallibility we all share, clergy and laity alike? Yet, Jesus's promise was that not even the powers of death could overcome His Church (Matthew 16:18), and His power is vested, not in the clergy alone (although it is of course there for us also), but in the faithful believers among laity. To put it another way: across our land and the world, the Church of Jesus Christ is alive and well because of folks like you! We are simply your servants rather than the sole purveyors of that Life.

The third area that goes without saying is that this indeed is *a magnificent land!* Last evening, we looked at the six rolls of slides that just returned. Amy shot at least that many rolls of prints. They tease and sample, but do not do justice to this land in which God has placed us. Let me describe just a few scenes (not all of which were photographed): deer grazing by the side of the road in the lonely forests of the Upper Michigan peninsula; the breathtaking cliffs and deep blue waters of Lake Superior on a clear Sunday afternoon; flourishing crops of all varieties stretching for miles across the Midwest (despite some, in Southeastern Minnesota, having been touched by an unseasonable killing frost the week before we arrived); the incredible varieties of rock formations and mountains experienced while travelling from Colorado through New Mexico to Arizona and return; the transition from cactus to lush pine when ascending Tucson's Mt. Lemon; the stark beauty of the desert; the warmth of a full moon in St. Louis after a dinnertime shower, and so on.

There is a line in one of the funeral prayers in the Book of Common Worship which goes: "Help us to walk amid the things of this world with eyes open to the beauty and glory of the eternal; that so, among the sundry and manifold changes of this life, our hearts may surely there be fixed where true joys are to be found." May this be your vision also, not only during vacation, but throughout the year to come! See you in church.

The Foolishness of Preaching
NEWS from Lenape Valley Presbyterian Church, New Britain, Pennsylvania, November 1993

"For since, in the wisdom of God, the world did not know God through wisdom, it pleased God through the folly of what we preach ["the foolishness of preaching", in the King James tr.] to save those who believe" (1 Corinthians 1:21).

One Sunday last February, unnoticed until sometime this past summer, I delivered my 2,500[th] sermon. That's not separate Sundays, mind you. It counts the same sermon twice each Sunday here during the school season, and twice each Sunday when I served the two congregations in Southeastern Minnesota. 2,500 times standing before people with various joys, hurts, needs, and/or questions, attempting with some mere human words to take a Biblical text: interpret, illustrate, and apply it, and try to meet at least some of the needs of those who have made the effort to come and listen. What foolishness to even consider that something I could say could make a difference!

Paul wrestled in the first chapter of his first Letter to the Christians at Corinth with the same issue. He states the incongruity of it and places the responsibility clearly upon God. *"For Jews demand signs and Greeks seek wisdom; but we preach Christ crucified, a stumbling block to Jews and folly to Gentiles; but to those who are called, both Jews and Greeks, Christ the power of God and the wisdom of God. For the foolishness of God is wiser than men, and the weakness of God is stronger than men" (vv. 24–25).* But aren't great and powerful sermons important, the hallmark of our Presbyterian and Reformed (and Scottish) traditions? Not necessarily. Putting his own ability down (and we have no one to contradict him), Paul said earlier (v. 17), "*For Christ did not send me to baptize but to preach the Gospel, and not with eloquent wisdom, lest the cross of Christ be emptied of its power."*

Ah, perhaps we've put a finger on it. God has chosen the vehicle of "the foolishness of preaching" to illustrate how His great power can overcome even the sinful weakness of the preacher. For the communication that takes place in the course of a sermon is a mystery of God's timing and grace. Consider a pastor, perhaps weeks ahead of a given Sunday, as he is seeking guidance through prayer, is given a text and the germ of an idea. His experiences with the congregation and the world help that idea develop. An illustration may come from his own experience, the six o'clock news, or the world of sports. And *sometimes* (may God be praised for His blessings!) it turns out that someone worships that Sunday for whom that message is a gift, wrapped and personally addressed. As one of our former members, Jim Knipe, used to say on occasion: "You've been reading my mail again." What a miracle! What a mystery.

I share this with you for three reasons (is that a good sermon outline, or what?): *First,* in the early days of this month, I attended at First Church downtown a conference on the new Presbyterian Book of Common Worship. (The one I use for baptisms, weddings, and funerals dates back to 1946, a revision of the 1933 model.) It was healthy to sit and listen to lectures and discussions on what one might call "idealized worship." Sunday worship as it ought to be. Time and space do not permit a lengthy summary. Suffice it to say that we were reminded that preparation for worship is as important for the worshipper as well as for the leaders; that an attitude of expectancy on the part of all is vital; and we all need to remember why we are there—to worship, praise, and give thanks to our generous God.

It is He into Whose presence we come, the best those of us charged with leading worship can do is attempt (however imperfectly) to create an arena in which we feel His Presence above us, Christ's Presence beside us, and the Presence of the Holy Spirit within us. The sermon represents only a piece of all this.

Secondly, we keep waiting to bite the bullet and come to grips with discussing how we can make this experience of inspiring worship available to all. Currently, some of our faithful members must choose between teaching or attending Sunday school and worshipping. (To put it another way: some may go weeks without being fed in worship.) How can we change this? Offering worship at a time other than Sunday morning? Adjusting our Sunday morning schedule? We need your help on this one. Discuss the issue when you get together and start "talking church" and let us know what constructive ideas you have. We'd really appreciate it.

Finally, there are far too many for whom worship attendance is merely a sometime option. "It's the only morning I can sleep in... I had to cut the lawn...wash the car...shampoo the cat..." whatever. But what happens when folks get out of the habit of regular worship is slow, deadly spiritual starvation. It's like missing a meal! It is a mystery of God's grace how imperfect human beings can be channels of God's personal message to so many individuals; yet, it happens! Come and see! Make Sunday worship your top priority from now through Christmas. Through "the foolishness of preaching" God has guaranteed that great things will happen.

Sudden Change in Plans
NEWS from Lenape Valley Presbyterian Church, New Britain, Pennsylvania, November 1994

"There is but one step between me and death." (1 Samuel 20:.3b)

This is not the editorial I had originally planned, but as many of you I am sure have already discovered, serious illness tends to put life in perspective. For the benefit of those who haven't yet been brought up to date: a sudden attack of what was called "unstable angina" (after a couple of lesser attacks over the weekend I had passed off as something else) around 5:00 a.m. Monday, October 3, shot me to Doylestown Hospital; from whence on Tuesday, I was transported down to Presbyterian Hospital for immediate catherization. (This was before Doylestown Hospital had added a heart unit.) The most serious discovery of that exploration was that my main coronary artery, providing 60 percent of the heart's oxygen, was 99 percent occluded. Immediate bypass surgery was necessary, and a triple bypass was performed Wednesday afternoon. Recovery has been fairly rapid, and I was brought home Monday, October 10, where I will be staying for a while.

It is all too fresh for adequate reflection, but there are a few things I wanted to share with you at this time. The first is to echo what Mel Wolff said when she had her surgery a couple of years ago: the tremendous sense of peace that is there when one is aware of all the prayers that are being fired off, literally, from coast to coast. At no time was I anxious or fearful. I just remember saying to the doctors, "Let's get on with it." I thank you all for that, and God for hearing you. I am grateful as well for the tremendous outpouring of cards and lovely notes that are still arriving, including the hand-done, special cards from the different Sunday School classes. The pile is about nine inches high! They also mean a lot.

Of course, it goes without saying that I am so glad we have Martha Bowman (interim associate pastor), who, with the leadership of the session and others who have stepped forward (Carol Sosa for Bethel, for example), will see to it that we don't miss a beat in what is a most crucial time of the year. On a deeper level, part of the shock of this for me (as well, I gather, as for others) is that I have worked hard at taking care of myself over the years: exercise (softball and racquetball), diet, hobbies, relaxation, and so on. An immediate question which crossed my mind was, quite naturally, "What good did it all do?" Well, it kept me alive is the ultimate answer. From what I can discern from the diagnoses, considering the severity of that one closure, there is a pretty good chance that I wouldn't be here otherwise. Or if that hadn't happened, I wouldn't be recovering so rapidly with the heart undamaged. As others in similar situations have said, the gift of each new day means so much more upon the recognition that, conceivably, there might not have been anymore of them. (I also need to add my thanks for the gift of pain. I still remember the story of the Russian skater who had a similar medical problem, but without the warning signs, and died in his late twenties.)

Enough of that. So many have offered their services, and Amy and I are most grateful. Recognizing there's so many more of you than there are of us, it is possible that we might not be able to take everyone up on their offers. The prayers and phone calls are so much appreciated, and the sense of family support is great. What we would really appreciate is for all of you to continue to be supportive of Lenape Valley during this interim period (of probably six weeks): attending regularly regardless of who might be preaching (and I don't think it is realistic to look for me in the pulpit until Thanksgiving time); supporting fully the fine stewardship program being presented to you at this time; and being sensitive to needs you hear in the congregation, so that Martha or one of the deacons can follow through.

We value your love, your friendship, and your prayers and look forward eagerly but patiently to the day when we can again serve you.

One More Litany of Thanksgiving
NEWS from Lenape Valley Presbyterian Church,
New Britain, Pennsylvania, November 1994

"[A]lways and for everything giving thanks in the name of our Lord Jesus Christ to God the Father." (Ephesians 5:20)

"We know that in everything God works for good with those who love Him…" (Romans 8:28)

How many times have we heard these texts read from the pulpit, or read them ourselves in our private devotions, and cuddled up to them as one snuggles up with mate or special friend without their meaning really sinking in? They give us the comfort of familiarity; but do they really make an impression? Have you ever stopped to consider all that Paul had to go through before reaching these conclusions? And how far must we be distanced from a crisis event before they have meaning for us?

At this point, and I'm writing seven weeks after surgery, I can't answer that. An elder who has come back from far more critical circumstances than I suggested that the revelation unfolds a bit at a time, and I appreciate knowing that. At this point, with health pretty much regained and only the energy and strength as yet far from limitless, I only know that Thanksgiving will take on new meaning for the Reids this year. [A parenthetical note. I remember this week, thirty-seven years ago, a few months out of seminary, with a wife of not more than three years, a son four months old, and a new church (for me), sitting at my typewriter attempting to articulate my first Thanksgiving service sermon and having a deuce of a time finding the right words. Life had been so good, so easy for me, that I had taken everything pretty much for granted. Funny how nearly four decades of life's experiences can change that!]

Back to the present. I have been thinking much (with much time to think) these past days and weeks about those things for which I am thankful; and, in hopes this list may resonate with you, I shall attempt to share them. I am attempting some kind of order, although that is dangerous. If it wouldn't be your order, that's okay: it might not be mine next week, either.

At this stage of my life, I am most thankful for:

- The gift of life itself. What a gift we so often abuse and/or take for granted! Yet, how fragile it is. As one who had always planned months in advance and never before failed to keep a commitment, I have a better understanding now of those ominous but true words in James' Letter: *Come now, you who say, "Today or tomorrow we will go into such*

*and such a town and spend a year there and get gain;" whereas
you do not know about tomorrow. What is your life? For you
are a mist that appears for a little while and then vanishes.
Instead you ought to say, "If the Lord wills, we shall live and
we shall do this or that" (James 4:13–14).* Life is a gift. Never
take it for granted. Make each day count.

- The love and support of wife and family. I don't think that
needs to be elaborated upon.

- The love and support of you, the extended family, the
congregation of Lenape Valley Church; and beyond you,
the further extended family represented by Philadelphia
Presbytery, as well as the community as a whole. Not
counting the neat cards from the Sunday School children,
we received almost 350 cards, letters, and notes, and some
are still coming in! Recently, I took an evening to review
them all. It took three and one-half hours! What I'd like to
do is to visit every one of you to thank you personally, but
that is impossible. Perhaps this will suffice to let you know
how deep is our appreciation for your support and love.

- Corollary to this is your prayers. They do work! My conviction is that prayers for an individual help to open that
individual to the gifts of healing God wants to give us all,
out of which comes great peace, comfort, and ever-growing
strength and energy.

- An additional corollary is the marvelous way in which
officers and staff picked up the slack and kept everything
going. Martha and the secretaries, the elders and deacons;
Rick and Gary and the parents who led confirmation;
Charles and Bill and the faithful members of First Light
(my intergenerational choir); Carol Sosa and her leadership
in Bethel; the guest preachers; the Rev. Bob Jacob (who, like
Martha, got more than he bargained for in coming here!);
Associate Doug Hoglund (who took one of the more than
a half-dozen weddings that were scheduled), to say nothing
of those who drove Amy (and later, me) around and pro-

vided food for the body. Fantastic! Words cannot begin to express our thanks.

- The faithfulness of our God (perhaps this should have been first), Who fulfilled His promise never to leave us or forsake us, whether in the ambulance, in ICU, the operating room, or during the time of recovery. Paul wrote from prison to the Philippians about *"the peace of God, which passes all understanding (which) will keep your hearts and your minds in Christ Jesus" (4:7)*. In that peace, one can understand how he could also write, *"For me to live is Christ, and to die is gain... My desire it to depart and be with Christ, for that is far better. But to remain in the flesh is more necessary on your account" (Philippians 1:21, 23b–24)*. Within that conviction, we are at peace, and we can in any situation give thanks!

Final Sermon at Roslyn Presbyterian Church

The End, or the Beginning?
June 11, 2017
Rev. Dan Reid

Old Testament Scripture: 2 Chronicles 32:27–30

New Testament Scripture: 2 Timothy 4:6–8

Text: "I have fought the good fight, I have finished the race, I have kept the faith." (2 Timothy 4:7)

Over the past weeks and months, I have spent a lot of time wrestling with the subject I was to address this morning: a summary of sixty years of ordained ministry. The text came rather readily: *"I have fought the good fight, I have finished the race, I have kept the faith."* But having stated that, what was I to do with it? Give examples of how I have fought a good fight, finished the race, and kept the faith? That seemed rather self-serving.

Besides, when the Apostle Paul, perhaps the greatest missionary of all time, wrote these words, he was in prison, anticipating his death. How could I possibly relate to that? Then my CPA-personality turned to my record book, and I set down sixty years of statistics: almost 4,000 preaching and speaking engagements; 402 weddings; 502 funerals, memorial services, and committals (and another one coming up on Friday); 735 infant, youth, and adult baptisms.

But here again, having stated these statistics, what would I do with them? Tell cute anecdotes of weddings, funerals, and baptisms? Somehow that wouldn't fit the occasion, either. Then I was reminded of the words of Paul frequently used (as this morning) after the prayer of confession: *"Therefore, if anyone is in Christ, he is a new creation…"* *(2 Corinthians 5:12a).* And I remembered what Paul also wrote, this time to the Philippians: *"Brothers, I do not consider myself yet to have taken hold of it.* (In other words: I have not yet arrived.) *But one thing I do: Forgetting what is behind and straining toward what lies ahead, I press on toward the goal to win the prize for which God has called me heavenward in Christ Jesus" (Philippians 3:13–14).*

That I can relate to because that's my story. It's a story of God's transforming power in a series of three significant interventions. But I need to start at the beginning. Many doubt this, but my basic personality is that of a shy introvert. I was one of the youngest and smallest in my class at Germantown Academy. High school was never really a fun time for me. From time to time I was picked on (though never bullied. There is a vast difference.). Then I went off to Franklin and Marshall College, and everything changed. It was a fresh start. I was recognized and respected. By my senior year, I had become president of the student council—which I think might have been the start of my colossal ego trip. My theory is that one masks the insecurities of being a shy introvert by pretending to be what he isn't; hence, the false ego.

Of course, along the way in those four years of college, I finally responded affirmatively to God's call to ministry; I met and dated Amy; and after graduation and our wedding, we were off to Princeton Seminary. In retrospect, I believe that in those first two years of seminary, I was more focused on the fruits of marriage than I was the fruits of the Spirit! However, I did have the good sense to elect as many Bible study courses as I could along the way. That was helpful down the road.

But then, in my senior year, it hit me that I needed to find a job after twenty years of education! Fortunately, I had stayed in touch with a man I had met in college, whose wife at that time was Christian Education director in Amy's church, First Presbyterian in Lancaster. Ernie was three years ahead of me, and when I entered seminary, he was already out in Southern Minnesota, serving the little congregation in Round Lake. He was also supplying a vacant congregation twelve miles up the road in Brewster. One thing led to another, so after graduation, ordination, and the birth of our son, we headed out the 1,200 miles to Brewster, in Southwestern Minnesota.

Looking back, I have to say I started out in the summer of 1957 dumber than dirt. I was so wet behind the ears that I should have worn a towel around my neck! I was constantly asking my friend Ernie down in Round Lake for advice and direction. (A few years ago, when we were invited back for an anniversary, I thanked the congregation for giving me a five-year graduate course in my seminary education. I have often said there must be a special place in heaven for congregations breaking in pastors right out of seminary!)

Well, the congregation and I both grew, as did my ego. In the summer of 1961, after four years in Brewster, while we were back East on vacation, I somehow got invited to preach both in my home church in Germantown and in Amy's church in Lancaster. There were rave reviews (although, in all honesty, I have to say I have never been invited back to either church!), and we returned to Brewster with my feeling that I was too big for that little church. I needed to move on to something more in keeping with my ability.

Well, God has an interesting way of answering a prayer like that. Two months later, there appeared at our house the Rev. Roger Kunkel, with whom I had been associated in Synod youth work. Roger was only two years out of Princeton and had started out as assistant pastor at Lakeside Presbyterian Church up in Duluth—at that time, the third largest Presbyterian congregation in the Synod of Minnesota (at least, on the books). Perhaps because he was available, after only those two years, Roger was elevated to be senior pastor, when the senior pastor had moved on (that was possible then) and drove all the way down to Brewster to invite me to be his copastor. Well, at last I was being recognized for *my* (note emphasis) talent and ability. I jumped at the chance, finished out the year in Brewster, and we moved to Duluth in June of 1962.

I spent a lot of time that summer preparing my vesper talks for the annual late-August senior high conference. I remember my theme was "Sermons from Sports." The young people really responded, and I remember returning to Lakeside, thinking, *Man, I'm good!* (I am reminded of the time Tony Campolo said, "I was good. In fact, I was so good I wanted to take notes on me!") What I didn't realize at the time was that my ego was writing checks on a balance marked "insufficient funds!"

After that, things seemed to go downhill. Believe it or not, I never had a job description, so I am sure I didn't do all I was supposed to do and did some things I shouldn't have done. Somewhere along the way, I felt what I would describe as a missionary call. What did that mean? Going to medical school and replacing Albert Schweitzer in Africa? I spent many afternoons walking around in the land of the sky blue waters, looking down on beautiful Lake Superior, wrestling with the meaning of God's rather vague call.

God chose to intervene and begin to interpret in the spring in a rather unique way. Out of all the pastors in Duluth, I was asked to give the invocation and benediction at the annual banquet of the Duluth chapter of Alcoholics Anonymous. I went and was convicted by the speaker. They played a tape of a recovered alcoholic, the real-life father of one of the actors playing doctor on TV (doctor shows were really big back in the spring of 1963). I heard him say that perfectionists make dandy alcoholics. It is an escape when they can't deal with the imperfect world around them. I heard myself being described. I realized that, had I ever begun to drink, with my personality, I'd have made a dandy alcoholic! *Pop!* went the balloon of my ego as I thought, *There, but for the grace of God go I.*

We finished out the year in Duluth and went back to the country: the congregations in Claremont and Kasson, in Southeast Minnesota, west of Rochester. This is where my missionary call became real. What does a missionary do? He learns the language of the natives and identifies with them. For seven and one-half good years, that's exactly what I did—even learned to drive a tractor! This was a dramatic change from my attitude in Brewster, where I somehow felt I was better than those simple farm folk, and that congregation was simply a stepping-stone to bigger and better things.

Then in November of 1968, my mother called to say my dad had suffered a massive stroke and was in a rehab facility. We came east that next summer on vacation, assessed the situation, and realized it was time to move back home. Presbyterian wheels grind slowly, and it took eighteen months, but God led us to the Lenape Valley Presbyterian Church beginning in February of 1971.

Folks look at our twenty-seven years there and believe it was great. It didn't start out that way. The first five years were rough. There were two challenges. One was the culture shock of moving from the slow pace of rural Minnesota to the frantic pace of a Philadelphia suburb. My teens in Claremont were great kids—would do anything I asked them to. The teens in Lenape Valley were still back in the '60s—and you know what that was like!

The other challenge was following a saint. Jack Heinsohn, the organizing pastor, was a gifted evangelist and dearly loved and respected. (I had built a career by following pastors who were either ineffectual or disliked!) Anyway, how do you compare stories of learning to fly on a trapeze (Jack grew up in the circus) with learning to plow on a tractor? No comparison whatsoever! Finally, in 1975, I conducted some really difficult funerals, and when the dust settled, I realized I had finally become the pastor.

The congregation and I grew until 1985 when I was asked to be the moderator of Philadelphia Presbytery. Now, a lot of men and women have been moderators of Philadelphia Presbytery; but for me it was a second incident of God's positive intervention. You see, with my basic personality defect of being a shy introvert, I was incapable of thinking on my feet. One classic example: there was a big town meeting out in Claremont, Minnesota, to discuss the possible merger of that little school (two dozen in a graduating class) with neighboring Dodge Center. With my fine educational background, I thought it was a good idea and stood up to speak. What happened was two or three minutes of eloquent gibberish! When I sat down, I'll bet no one knew whether I was for or against the plan. It was really embarrassing.

But when I became moderator, God fulfilled the promise of Jesus to the disciples when He sent them out: *"Do not worry about what to say or how to say it. At that time you will be given what to say, for it will not be you speaking, but the spirit of your Father speaking through you"* (Matthew 10:19–20). In the Book of the Acts, often it was said that the Holy Spirit gave the apostles power. With me, it was God's second gift: confidence.

However, there was a second challenge. In 1984, when Bob Boell was moderator, I was asked to substitute for him at a banquet. Now, at that time, every committee of Presbytery had at least fifteen minutes on the docket at each of the 8-10 stated meetings of Presbytery each year. I was stewardship chairman at that time but inevitably was preceded on the docket by Dick Foster, who was evangelism chairman. So I was introduced at the banquet with words something like this: "There are two men I always look forward to hearing at Presbytery because they are always funny: Dick Foster and Dan Reid!" Wow! What a challenge! Dick Foster was always funny; Dan Reid didn't always feel like being funny, but it seemed to be expected of me!

I was genuinely concerned because back in the attic of my mind were all those off-color jokes and comments from my pre-Christian days. I prayed mightily that year, in all the stated meetings, ordinations, installations, and banquets that none of them would slip out. God was gracious, and none did.

So there I was. The air in the balloon of my ego was pretty much out, and now I had the confidence to think on my feet. But God wasn't finished with me yet. Almost another decade later, in October of 1994, I was hauled off to Presbyterian Hospital, there to have triple bypass surgery. I have often spoken of the blessing of pain in connection with that. My main artery was almost 100 percent occluded, and my severe angina woke me up at five on a Monday morning. Do you remember that young Russian skater who had the same problem? But without the blessing of pain, he died. I'm still here.

Now, I'm sure you are aware that many who have recovered from heart attacks or strokes have different personalities. They become more mellow, more emotional. They cry and perhaps laugh more. That's what happened to me in God's third intervention.

You see—while my family might dispute this—my recollection is that I grew up in a home without feeling or emotion. Looking back, I can understand this. I've told you before that my mother was an adult child of an alcoholic, and ACOAs necessarily survive by suppressing their emotions. My dad, on the other hand, I don't think ever really got over being betrayed by his first wife. I can't ever recall either parent ever saying to me "I love you." I knew they did, but it was never expressed. No feelings or emotion.

What this meant in my makeup was that I was essentially without feelings as well. For example, in the summer of 1958, Amy's dad—against his doctor's advice—and her mother drove the 1,100 miles from Lancaster, PA, to Brewster, Minnesota. He wanted to see that year-old grandson. A severe diabetic, he died within forty-eight hours of a heart attack. I remember being sad but otherwise felt no emotion. The same was when my parents died. So God fixed that defect in my personality by clogging my arteries! What a difference. I now had no trouble getting choked up and crying. I have told you before that when my aortic valve replacement surgery six years ago was scheduled for over Christmas, I realized I would be missing out on our annual beautiful Christmas Eve candlelight communion service. A few evenings before the surgery, we were watching a Gaither Christmas video, which concluded with them singing "Silent Night." When I realized I would be missing out on that, I broke down and cried.

Last Sunday, a lady from my home church in Germantown (our mothers were good friends) asked me to stop by on Monday morning. She was a lonely lady, whose best friend was a cat of seventeen years, which she was going to have to put down on Monday morning. Would I come and pray with her?

Now, at one time I might well have said, "Joan, come on. You can always get another cat!" Instead, I went and we talked cats for forty-five minutes, and I prayed with her. You see? I don't believe God is finished with me yet, but what changes over these past sixty years: popping the balloon of my ego, giving me confidence to think on my feet, and making me into a more feeling and empathetic person.

I want to close with two things. First, a quote that I believe comes from the Southern black church: "O Lord, I ain't what I useta be. And O Lord, I ain't what I wanta be. But Lord, I ain't what I'm gonna be! Praise God. Amen."

Then I want to sing the second verse of a song associated with the late George Younce, with the Gaither Vocal Band. It's called "Saved by Grace."

> How could I boast of any thing I've ever
> been or done?
> How could I ever claim as mine the vic'tries
> God has won?

Where would I be had God not brought me gently to this place?

I'm here to say I'm nothing but an old sinner, saved by grace!

I'm just a sinner, saved by grace!

When I stood condemned to death, He took my place.

Now I live and breathe in freedom, with every breath I take.

Loved and forgiven, I'm back with the living,
Saved by grace!
And that's the truth.
Amen.

About the Author

The Rev. Daniel W. Reid was born February 26, 1933 in Germantown Hospital. He was confirmed and became a member of the First Presbyterian Church in Germantown, Philadelphia, on Maundy Thursday, 1943. He was educated in Germantown Academy (class of 1950), Franklin and Marshall College (history major, 1954), and Princeton Theological Seminary (1957). He was ordained by the Presbytery of Philadelphia in his home church, First Presbyterian Church in Germantown, Philadelphia, June 11, 1957. He and his family then traveled to Minnesota, where he served for over thirteen years:

First Presbyterian Church, Brewster, Minnesota, 1957–62
Lakeside Presbyterian Church, Duluth, Minnesota (as assistant), 1962–63
The Presbyterian Churches of Claremont and Kasson, Minnesota, 1963–71

The family then moved to the Lenape Valley Presbyterian Church, New Britain, Pennsylvania, 1971–98. He retired from Lenape Valley on Easter Sunday, 1998, and for the next six years did occasional supply work when requested. Then in March of 2004, he began thirteen years as part-time supply pastor of the Roslyn Presbyterian Church in suburban Philadelphia. His final retirement took place on the sixtieth anniversary of his ordination, June 11, 2017.

He married the former Amy Strayer of Lancaster on June 12, 1954. Together they have raised four adult children: Wayne, Deborah, Brenda, and Sally, who are married and have added five grandchildren: Peter, Bekah, Matt, Steffi, and Jake.

With the exception of three sermons, the messages "from the pastor's desk" were all originally published in newsletters in Brewster, Claremont, and Lenape Valley—a forty-year span.

May they be helpful to you as you read them.

CPSIA information can be obtained
at www.ICGtesting.com
Printed in the USA
LVHW091634080721
R16841500001B/R168415PG691954LVX00001B/1